ECONOMIC POLITICS IN THE UNITED STATES

Second Edition

This book uses macroeconomic performance to evaluate democratic institutions and processes in the United States. Originally published in 1995, this revised edition gives a more pessimistic assessment than the first did. Employing macroeconomic performance as a lens to evaluate democratic institutions, the author uses public choice and political economy models of political behavior that allow for opportunism on the part of public officials and shortsightedness on the part of voters to see if democratic institutions lead to inferior macroeconomic performance.

We have learned more about how and why democracy can work well or badly in the years since the first edition. It was not previously apparent how much the good economic performance of democracy in the United States was contingent on informal rules and institutions of restraint that are not part of the definition of democracy.

Since that first edition, the United States has experienced soaring government indebtedness, unintended adverse consequences of an effort to make housing more affordable, and massive problems in the financial system related to perverse incentives that were not restrained by public policies, informal institutions, or policy rules. Each of these was permitted or encouraged by the incentives of electoral politics and by limitations on government, the two essential features of democratic institutions.

William R. Keech is Research Professor of Political Economy in the Department of Political Science at Duke University. Keech is the author of numerous books, including the first edition of this book, *Economic Politics: The Costs of Democracy* (Cambridge University Press, 1995), and his articles have appeared in academic journals such as the *American Political Science Review*, *Public Choice*, and *American Economic Review*. Most of his academic career has been at the University of North Carolina at Chapel Hill and at Carnegie Mellon University. He has been president of the Southern Political Science Association and a member of the Council of the American Political Science Association. He received his PhD from the University of Wisconsin at Madison.

Economic Politics in the United States

The Costs and Risks of Democracy
Second Edition

WILLIAM R. KEECH

Duke University

CAMBRIDGE
UNIVERSITY PRESS

CAMBRIDGE
UNIVERSITY PRESS

32 Avenue of the Americas, New York, NY 10013-2473, USA

Cambridge University Press is part of the University of Cambridge.

It furthers the University's mission by disseminating knowledge in the pursuit of education, learning, and research at the highest international levels of excellence.

www.cambridge.org
Information on this title: www.cambridge.org/9780521178679

First published 1995
Second edition 2013

Printed in the United States of America

A catalog record for this publication is available from the British Library.

Library of Congress Cataloging in Publication Data
Keech, William R.
Economic politics in the United States : the costs of democracy / William R. Keech., Duke University. – Second edition.
pages cm
ISBN 978-1-107-00414-6
1. Democracy – Economic aspects – United States.   2. Representative government and representation – Economic aspects – United States.   I. Title.
JK271.K318   2013
338.973–dc23   2013015861

ISBN 978-1-107-00414-6 Hardback
ISBN 978-0-521-17867-9 Paperback

To Cody, Tommy, and KC, our grandchildren

Contents

Figures and Tables

FIGURES

TABLES

Preface to the Second Edition

This is a revised second edition of *Economic Politics: The Costs of Democracy* (Cambridge University Press, 1995). That book used macroeconomic performance since World War II in the United States to make general statements about democracy. The main conclusions were that democracy had basically benign influences on economic policy and performance. Political economy and public choice models of opportunistic behavior by politicians did not identify systematically inferior policy, as had been suggested or intimated by Nordhaus (1973), Tufte (1978), and others.

I am no longer so optimistic. In the intervening years, the United States has taken a wrong turn economically, and I believe that the wrong turn has much to do with the incentives of democratic politics. But these developments are not inevitable features of democracy. They are often avoided by other democratic nations and have been avoided in the past by the United States.

I have changed the title of the book to *Economic Politics in the United States: The Costs and Risks of Democracy*. Such a title might have been a more honest title of the original book, given its predominant focus on the United States, but the revised title highlights the fact that democratic politics have gone astray in that country. This book will consider democratic politics in the United States as just one example of how democracy can work constructively or otherwise in the context of economic policy making and performance.

Even if the consequences of democracy for economic performance had not changed in the years since 1995, some improvements are in order for the original book. Most obviously, the data in that book end in 1992 and need to be updated. I would also like to clarify the meaning of the title. Why and how is the United States a democracy? The original book begged the question of what makes the United States a democracy and implicitly used the United States as a representative and even a leading case of democracy. I have studied definitions and measures of democracy since then in the context of a project that extends the questions to Latin America and will be much clearer on what makes the United States a democracy. I will distinguish two main features of democracy: elections and limitations on government.

This much might make a case for a revised edition of a book with the same basic message of benign consequences of democracy for economic performance. But new developments have made it clear to me that democratic institutions and practices in the United States have not recently been so healthy and benign. As practiced in the United States, democracy has recently had undesirable consequences for economic performance. Opportunistic responses to the incentives of democratic politics have made it likely that the American standard of living will not be maintained indefinitely into the future. These practices are not inherent in democracy, but they are at least in part related to democratic incentives.

Two new, unfavorable basic manifestations of economic problems have arisen in the United States that are related to the incentives of democratic politics. The first is fiscal policy and the emergence of large annual federal deficits and increasing national debt. The second is the financial crisis of 2007–9 and its aftermath. The themes of contemporary U.S. fiscal policy have been to cut taxes or avoid raising them, to spend as needed or desired, and to postpone painful choices. Few politicians have cultivated a democratic constituency for fiscal responsibility. In several ways, both the onset and the aftermath of the financial crisis are related to the incentives of democratic politics. And, of course, the deep recession that resulted has made the fiscal situation even more dire than it would have been without the financial crisis. Both the fiscal and the financial crises will be linked to excessive present orientation in American politics.

THE FISCAL CRISIS

In the political climate of the past few decades, cutting taxes has been the favored solution to many economic problems. A rationale for this has been to encourage economic growth. There is something to this rationale, but a low tax burden is only one cause of growth. For example, an educated and healthy workforce provides human capital for growth, but education takes government revenues and, therefore, is not favored. Tax minimizing is sometimes at odds with growth maximizing, and the United States has chosen the former.

Each year the United States has postponed dealing with the rising costs of entitlement programs (in particular, Social Security, Medicare, and Medicaid), and it has gotten more difficult to do so. The war in Iraq added enormously to the fiscal pressures on the United States, as elaborated in Stiglitz and Bilmes (2008). This is the only time in American history when a war was associated with reductions in taxes.

THE FINANCIAL CRISIS OF 2007–9, AND THE ENSUING RECESSION

A case will be made that the crash was due at least in part to the incentives of democratic politics. Easy credit and the encouragement of home ownership were ways to please voters without direct, foreseen, or immediate budgetary consequences. The failures of regulation can be connected to incentives of democratic politics by way of the limitations on government feature of democracy. Lobbying Congress and administrative agencies is an important First Amendment right "to petition the Government for a redress of grievances," but it has been used to excess. A deep recession in a country that lacks fiscal discipline and is already deeply in debt is especially threatening to future prosperity.

Even though recent experience in the United States illustrates some dangers of democracy, a longer view of U.S. history shows that the dangers are not inherent in that form of government. What have been lost are informal institutions of prudence and restraint. These new themes are expressed in a new Chapter 5 on Unintended Consequences, Moral Hazard, and Time-Consistency, and at various places in the other chapters.

For their careful reading of the entire revised edition, I would like to thank Henry Chappell and Jim Granato. For readings of particular chapters, I would like to thank James Campbell, Neil deMarchi, Luis Dopico, Richard Froyen, Michael Munger, and John Seater. Douglas Hibbs deserves special thanks. I am also grateful to audiences in the History of Political Economy Seminar and the Triangle Dynamic Macro Seminar at Duke University, and the Political Economy Colloquium at the University of Wisconsin–Madison. Needless to say, I bear full responsibility for the final version. Rebecca Hatch and Tusi Undes Wen have been very effective and cooperative research assistants. Duke University has a remarkable group of people in its political science and economics departments who are interested in political economy, which makes it an exciting place for me to be. I gratefully acknowledge the help and support of the staff of the Duke Department of Political Science, especially Doric C. Cross, and of the Duke University Libraries, especially Maurice Parker.

Scott Parris has been an extremely patient and supportive editor through both editions of this book, and a few false starts on other projects. I am very lucky to have had the opportunity to work with him. My wife, Sharon, has been a patient and supportive partner, who has shared both editions of this project.

Preface to the First Edition

This book uses macroeconomic issues to address questions about how democracy works. It continues the kind of investigation I pursued in my first book, *The Impact of Negro Voting: The Role of the Vote in the Quest for Equality* (1968, 1981), which used racial issues to study the consequences of extending the franchise. It is a statement of applied democratic theory that uses economic issues to bring into focus questions about democratic institutions and practices. It brings together a body of research that has been written largely in the past fifteen years on the political dimensions of macroeconomic policy and performance. The book draws on work done by economists and by political scientists in roughly equal measure, and it is designed to present a variety of arguments fairly and neutrally.

I have taken aim at several audiences. First, the book is written to be accessible to a nontechnical audience of advanced undergraduates and thoughtful nonacademic citizens who might be interested in the relationship between politics and the macroeconomy, and in its implications for democratic theory. No special training in economics or political science is presumed. Although the book is meant to be readable by the nontechnical general public, it draws heavily on technical academic literature. As such, it makes the case that this literature is relevant to issues of broad public concern. Another audience is graduate students and faculty in political science and economics. For them, the book covers territory in the other discipline that may not be familiar, but more than this, it is an argument and an interpretation of known political and economic facts and ideas. In this way, it is also designed for the colleagues who have created the literature on which I draw.

The book was drafted with the support of the University of North Carolina at Chapel Hill, which provided a research leave for the fall of 1992, and the support of Harvard University and the Massachusetts

Institute of Technology, each of which provided me office space and an opportunity to extend my research leave to a full academic year by teaching a course on the topic of the book (to undergraduates at Harvard and to graduate students at MIT). An early draft was presented in May 1993 in a three-day "minicourse" sponsored by the Harvard Program in Political Economy, directed by James Alt and Kenneth Shepsle.

Of course, the gestation period is much longer than this. My interest in economics goes back to my employment by the Brookings Institution in the early 1970s, where I learned that economists have many interesting and important ideas and theories about politics that were not part of my political science graduate training in the early sixties. My understanding of economics owes much to a Professional Development Grant from the National Science Foundation (1977–8). I am grateful to the late Jack Walker for persuading me that the University of Michigan and its Institute for Public Policy Studies was the best place to use this grant. Many people there were important to my postdoctoral education, but Paul Courant and Edward Gramlich deserve special thanks for tutoring me in economics. I have also learned a lot from the excellent macroeconomics group at UNC Chapel Hill, among whom Richard Froyen deserves special thanks.

My understanding of the topic has profited enormously from what I learned from collaboration in research projects with Henry Chappell, an economist, and Carl Simon, a mathematician and economist. I thank the National Science Foundation Division of Social, Behavioral, and Economics Research for grants through the political science and the economics programs that supported my work with Chappell and with Simon. Parts of Chapters 2, 3, 4, 6, and 8 have been worked out in papers and articles co-written with Henry Chappell, Dean Lacy, Patrick Lynch, Irwin Morris, Kyoungsan Pak, Carl Simon, and Carol Swain. Several figures were adapted from those in Richard Froyen, *Macroeconomics: Theories and Policies*, 4th ed. (Macmillan, 1993). Hyeon-Woo Lee provided invaluable research assistance. Scott Parris has continued to make me glad to be working with Cambridge University Press.

An extraordinary number of colleagues have been willing to read and evaluate the entire manuscript, providing many penetrating observations. I have responded to their suggestions as well as I could, but many of their comments made it clear how far I am from saying final words on the subject. Several others helped in many different ways. I especially thank Alberto Alesina, James Alt, Robert Bates, Nathaniel Beck, Hakan Berument, Richard Broholm, Lawrence Broz, Henry Chappell, Robert Erikson, Ita Falk, Eduardo Feldman, Bruno Frey, Richard Froyen, James Granato, Thomas

Havrilesky, Sharon Keech, Margaret Levi, Peng Lian, Emily Loose, David Lowery, Patrick Lynch, Timothy McKeown, Michael Munger, Irwin Morris, Paul Peterson, George Rabinowitz, Andrew Rutten, Kenneth Shepsle, Beth Simmons, Carl Simon, Jurg Steiner, Motoshi Suzuki, John Tryneski, George Tsebelis, Peter Van Doren, Stephen Weatherford, Klaus Wellershoff, and students at Harvard, MIT, and UNC and the participants in the Harvard minicourse. The penultimate draft was test marketed at the University of California at San Diego by Nathaniel Beck, at Harvard University by Alberto Alesina and James Alt, and at the University of Texas by Brian Roberts.

Finally, the University of North Carolina at Chapel Hill and its Political Science Department have supported my work and intellectual growth in countless ways in the thirty years since I was first hired. Sharon Keech has done so as well. She has given this manuscript a penetrating nonacademic citizen's critique, and in many ways she has made it possible. The dedication is to our son and daughter.

PART ONE

INTRODUCTION

This book evaluates democracy in terms of its consequences and uses macroeconomic performance as the setting in which to assess these consequences. Chapter 1 introduces the question the book is designed to address. I will contrast realistic and opportunistic models of democratic politics with the assumption that government is benevolent, wise, and motivated to do the right thing.

Chapter 2 reviews what is known and not known about macroeconomics. There is a well-developed body of theory about the relationship between a government's policy choices and macroeconomic outcomes. I will draw on that theory, recognizing that there is much less consensus among economists about macroeconomics, the study of broad economic aggregates such as inflation, unemployment, and economic growth, than there is about microeconomics, the study of individual behavior, prices, and quantities in markets.

1

Macroeconomic Politics and the Costs
and Risks of Democracy

The United States, which sometimes thinks of itself as the world's leading democracy, is showing that democracy does not always work well. The American fiscal crisis is the clearest evidence of this. Federal deficits and federal debt are matters of political choice as well as of circumstance. Some good choices have been avoided and some poor choices have been made by the U.S. government. The links between democratic politics and the financial crisis of 2007–9 are more subtle and contestable, but this book will show how various decisions and practices leading up to the crisis and various responses to the crisis can be linked to democratic politics.

This is not to say that formal democratic institutions in the United States are flawed. It is to say that formal democracy works best when supplemented by informal institutions of prudence and caution. Such informal norms and practices have weakened in recent decades and the U.S. economy is showing the effects; it will probably continue to do so into the foreseeable future.

Nor is it to say that the message of democratic politics as benign in the first edition of this book was not correct for the time it was written. What has happened since to make for a more mixed message about the consequences of democratic politics has two sources. The first is the failure to act on problems that were foreseeable in 1995 or, worse yet, decisions that made the fiscal outlook worse. The second is that random events have made the economic world more dangerous, and American institutions were not prepared to deal with unforeseen random shocks to the financial system.

According to one conventional view of macroeconomic politics in contemporary democracy, governments are responsible for performance regarding inflation, unemployment, and income growth. Periodic elections give voters an opportunity to judge that performance and to approve or disapprove, choosing new leaders if performance has been unsatisfactory.

3

From that perspective, democratic institutions provide ways to ensure both the accountability of public officials and the adequacy of government performance. A persistent or unusual problem may lead to a reform that is designed to resolve the problem, such as the creation of a quasi-independent monetary authority in 1913 or the establishment of a new set of budgetary procedures in 1974.

According to another conventional view, the democratic process is not so benign. In that view, politicians are selfish and opportunistic, and voters are naïve. Incumbents manipulate their performance to appear misleadingly good at election time, and both challengers and incumbents make unrealistic and insincere promises. Voters are myopically oriented to the present, which makes them unprepared to hold incumbents accountable for their performance over entire electoral periods or to relate electoral choices to future well-being in a meaningful way. Economic performance deteriorates. Politicians exploiting popular discontent propose simplistic and superficial reforms that fail to solve the problems.

The truth is likely to be some mixture of these extreme alternatives, which I designate as the benign and the malign views. The truth is likely to vary over time and place. The purpose of this book is to address the validity of these alternative views and to map the territory in between. In the original 1995 edition of this project, my conclusions regarding the United States leaned toward the benign, but events since then have made me less sanguine and more pessimistic.

THE COSTS OF DEMOCRACY

This book addresses questions about the effects of democratic institutions on economic performance when such institutions are taken to mean generically the institutions of accountability and of government by consent of the governed. Do democracies produce efficient results, as Wittman (1989) contends? Or do they lead to the accumulation of special privilege and protections from market competition that reduce efficiency and growth, as Olson (1982) contends? Democratic institutions are, of course, designed to be meaningful bulwarks against tyranny and against the rulers' exploitation of the ruled. But periodic elections themselves might generate perverse incentives to manipulate the macroeconomy.

In American political institutions, the system of checks and balances and the Bill of Rights provide constraints on government and on popular majorities that may control the government. But there may be ways in which the short-term incentives inherent in a popularly based political process need further restraint.

What are the counterfactual alternatives to democracy as it exists in the United States? One is authoritarian governmental institutions. Very few authoritarian governments have a good record of economic performance. Among contemporary countries, China and Singapore stand out. South Korea, Taiwan, and Chile moved significantly toward being efficient, modern, wealthy economies under authoritarian government and have since become democratic. But authoritarian government is not an option for the United States.

A strategy of comparing real-world democracies with real-world dictatorships is not appropriate for a comparison that would include the United States, because there is no authoritarian system at a comparable level of economic development. Latin America provides a more appropriate setting for comparing democracies and dictatorships at comparable levels of development.

Human nature is reflected in both authoritarian and democratic governments. The aspects of human nature that are most threatening to good economic performance are selfishness and greed, on the one hand, and a present orientation on the other. Competitive markets can harness selfishness and greed on the part of individuals for the general welfare, as Adam Smith long ago pointed out. And the separation of powers can have a comparably constructive effect of setting ambition against ambition, as "Federalist #51" observed. As *The Federalist Papers* (Hamilton, Madison, and Jay 1961) make clear, American political institutions were designed to provide good government in spite of the foibles of human nature. But few formal institutions work against a self-defeating present orientation. The leading example in the American context is a bicameral legislature with a Senate elected for a six-year term in order to counteract the present orientation of a House of Representatives, which is never more than two years from the next election.

I follow the suggestion of Robert Dahl's *Democracy and Its Critics* (1989) and consider "anarchy," or the absence of government, and "guardianship," or government by the wise, as abstract and generic conceptions of desirable alternative procedures. Unlike government by the wise, anarchy has some negative connotations, but Dahl is emphasizing its lineage as a leading competitor to democracy and guardianship. Here the term "anarchy" should not be taken to imply chaos. The theory of competitive markets addresses how a spontaneous order with desirable properties emerges from minimal government. Of course, the desirable characteristics of competitive markets implicitly assume the protection of property rights, the enforcement of contracts, and a basic level of law and order, which are presumably provided by such a government.

For this analysis of the nature of democratic institutions and their consequences for macroeconomic policy, we focus on concrete, observable experience in the United States. Although the book has this focus, it is not just a book about American economic politics. The focus on a single country has several advantages. Much of the literature in the field of political macro-economics has been written about the United States and is therefore directly useful. Also, the focus on a single country will facilitate attention to the historical development of institutions, to the time dimension, and to the process of democratic politics in ways that would be less feasible if many countries were included. Both institutional choice and process will be substantively important in the analysis and conclusions.

There are also disadvantages to the focus on the United States: it is only a single country, and though it is an important one, it is far from typical or representative. Also, its macroeconomic experience covers only a limited range. Unlike some other democracies, it has never experienced hyper-inflation.[1] It has experienced sharply rising ratios of public debt to gross domestic product, but until the present, that experience has been tame compared to what Japan, Italy, Belgium, Ireland, and Greece have seen. Focus on a single country forgoes the advantages of systematic and explicit comparisons, but I hope by the end, the reader will agree that the advantages outweigh the disadvantages.

For alternatives to democratic procedures, we consider incremental changes within those procedures, either toward anarchy or toward guardianship. For example, a reform in the direction of less government intervention in private markets, such as the deregulation of the banking industry that has taken place since the 1980s, will be considered a move in the direction of anarchy. Similarly, a reform in the direction of insulating economic policy from popular influence, such as lengthened terms for members of the Federal Reserve Board, will be considered a move in the direction of guardianship. Thus, democratic institutions can include features of both anarchy and guardianship, and those institutions may perhaps be improved by trying different mixes of the two.

---

[1] There was very high inflation in the colonies between 1775 and 1783, as well as in the Confederacy, caused by the printing of paper money to finance war (Sachs and Larraín 1993, p. 728).

Dahl's (1989) study is a normative analysis of the theoretical arguments for democracy and other candidates vying for the title of the most desirable form of government. But real-world alternatives include several forms of dictatorship, many of which are not defended (or defensible) as desirable by any viable political theory. Ronald Wintrobe (1990) distinguishes "tin-pot" and totalitarian dictatorships on the basis of their guiding motivations. Totalitarians seek to maximize their power over the population under their control, whereas tin-pot dictators seek to minimize the costs of keeping themselves in power in order to enjoy the benefits of office. Totalitarian dictatorships include those (such as the former Soviet Union) based on Marxist ideologies that favor economic development and that pay lip service to the goal of maximizing the welfare of the people. Others (such as Nazi Germany) are based on racial or nationalistic ideologies. The tin-pot type of dictatorship, such as the Marcos regime in the Philippines, provides a more relevant comparison with democracy for the purposes of this book, because it was merely corrupt without grandiose aspirations.

Mancur Olson (1993) provides a direct theoretical comparison between opportunistic democracies and opportunistic, revenue-maximizing dictatorships. The latter are similar to Wintrobe's tin-pot dictators, in that both use their power to enhance their own private economic welfare. To make the comparison fair, Olson assumes that the dictator wants to maximize the revenue that can be extracted from the people being ruled, whereas a democratic majority wants to maximize revenue so that it can be redistributed among that majority. Both the dictator and the democratic majority wish to enhance the society's productivity for selfish reasons. Both are constrained in their selfishness by the possibility that beyond a certain point, further increases in tax rates will reduce the tax base and actually lose revenue that could be redistributed to themselves. Olson explains how the "encompassing interest" of a majority in increasing the income of the society at large is greater than that of a dictator, because it directly receives some of the income that is produced, as well as the redistribution that it votes for itself. So far, democracy does better by the people, even if a selfish majority wants to maximize the politically determined redistribution from the society at large to itself.

However, it does not follow that democracies will redistribute less than dictatorships, because democratic policies are often responsive to small minorities and special interests that have far less incentive than does a majority to consider "the social costs of the redistributions they obtain" (Olson 1993, p. 571). As Olson's rich analysis makes clear, comparison of the economic performances of democracy and dictatorship is a large and complex task.[2]

Instead of comparing democracy and other forms of government, this book will conceptualize the performance of democracy relative to objectively desirable policies, when such policies can be identified. Of course, there is little agreement about what policies are objectively desirable, and that fact is one of the themes of this book. However, it will be possible to characterize certain central features of democratic politics and to show how they relate to the quality of policy. When democratic policies deviate from optimal policies in a systematic way, this will be considered a cost of democracy, whether or not a real-world alternative set of institutions would do better.

The costs of democracy include the reasonable and unavoidable prices of things that are basically desirable. Costs are similar to prices and implicitly are to be compared to benefits. Costs are to be minimized, but some costs are likely to be the inevitable prices of things that are valuable, and they are to be understood and tolerated. Democracy is a system that operates under the logic of the relationship between a "principal" (the public) and an "agent" (the government). I argue that democratic procedures have modest and bearable costs, but that they are comparable to the "agency costs" that are incurred whenever a principal delegates authority to an agent. As William Bianco has said, "the problem is not representative government; rather representative government is an example of a generic and intractable problem" (1994, p. 167).[3]

This book will argue that democracy does not systematically lead to inferior macroeconomic policy. In some situations, however, democracy, like other systems, can produce inferior policy. Also, a democracy may face debilitating conditions that it did not create, and there are ways in which some kinds of democratic institutions may obstruct the cure or correction of such conditions. But democracy comes in many forms, and democratic performance may vary under different conditions and institutional arrangements. A common response to poor performance is to propose changes in formal institutions, such as term limits for legislators or constitutional amendments mandating a balanced budget.

---

[2] An additional important feature of the comparison that is included in Olson's article is the association among individual rights (including property rights), democracy, and prosperity.

[3] See Besley (2006) for a deep and insightful treatment of agency issues in representative government.

I argue that informal institutional changes are often sources of performance problems and that, when this is the case, formal changes are unlikely to be successful correctives. For example, changes in the norms and patterns of behavior were what led to our contemporary problem with federal budget deficits. Formal institutional correctives such as the Gramm-Rudman-Hollings law have not solved the problem because they have not confronted the incentives that created it. A constitutional amendment would be no more successful unless it were to be based on procedures that confront such incentives.

It is also possible that informal changes in behavior can be constructive. The most important decisions about the formal structure of the American central banking institutions were made in the Federal Reserve Act of 1913 and in revisions to that act in the 1930s. However, the institutional change that made the Federal Reserve one of the world's most independent central banks was an informal agreement called the "accord" that was implemented in 1951. The meaning of democracy in any particular context depends not only on the formal constitutional rules but also on informal institutions that define patterns of behavior.

MACROECONOMIC ISSUES PROVIDE A LENS

Macroeconomics will provide a lens through which we can focus on these questions of democratic theory. The performance issues of central concern are those regarding inflation, unemployment, and income growth. Income distribution will be peripheral, though occasionally relevant. The lens will filter out other important problems, such as the environment, racial justice, war and peace, and so on. This strategy is not meant to imply that those questions are less important than economic performance. I do mean to show that a focus on macroeconomic issues can be especially revealing about the nature of democratic processes, and not simply because they are matters of continuing concern.

Macroeconomic issues are often consensual, in that there is wide agreement on the desirability of the goals, specifically the desirability of income growth and the undesirability of inflation and unemployment. There is plenty of disagreement as well, particularly when it comes to strategy for achieving those goals, but compared with the bitter disagreements surrounding numerous other issues, such as abortion, for example, there is an underlying consensus on the nature of standards. This fact makes it easier to draw conclusions about the performance of democratic institutions on the basis of relatively objective benchmarks. For example, democracies (like dictatorships) may postpone hard decisions whose resolution might improve their future prospects, or they may make decisions that will provide benefits in the present at the expense of the future. Democracies (like dictatorships) may be vulnerable to moral hazard and to time-consistency problems. Macroeconomic issues facilitate systematic attention to the time dimension of political decision making in ways that help us make inferences about the costs of democracy. My concern is less how democracy performs relative to dictatorship than how democratic performance might be improved in areas in which improvement is possible.

Even though macroeconomic issues are relatively consensual and performance oriented, they are, at most, a short step away from conflict of interest. Good macroeconomic performance can make everyone better off, and poor performance can cause everyone to suffer, but the particular policy choices that are made often have distributional dimensions. Even when distributional issues do not arise, there are important differences in beliefs about the desirability and consequences of alternative policies.

Macroeconomic issues will not highlight some kinds of costs or problems of democracy. These include corruption and venality, which, of course, are not unique to democratic systems. Macroeconomic politics is public politics; the incentives for public officials are large-scale vote shifts and personal and partisan reputations. The most important decisions concern large-scale movements of fiscal and monetary instruments. Any possibilities that politicians have for personal enrichment are not likely to loom large in the politics of inflation, unemployment, and growth. And even though this claim must be qualified by the distributive character of many tax and expenditure decisions, this is a book about very general questions regarding how well democracy works, and how reforms of democratic institutions might make it work better.[4]

SOME ECONOMIC ISSUES

Because our focus is on economic performance, we must address several issues in order to do justice to the topic.

---

[4] These sentences were written before the financial crisis of 2007–9, which may qualify them. Certainly, many workers in financial institutions saw their incomes rise. Leaders of government-sponsored enterprises (GSEs), such as Fannie Mae got rich (Morgenson and Rosner 2011, ch. 1 and passim). Also, Igan, Mishra, and Tressel (2009) and Mian, Sufi, and Trebbi (2010a, 2010b) show that much money was spent lobbying Congress.

Are There Clear Goals and Optimal Choices for Policy?

There is considerable agreement about the basic goals of macroeconomic policy, but much less agreement about their relative importance and how to achieve them. Generally, inflation and unemployment are to be minimized, whereas income growth is to be maximized.[5] Although there may be debate about the appropriate targets and trade-offs necessary to attain such goals, there is no question that some extreme values are undesirable. Hyperinflation, such as annual rates of inflation of more than 1,000 percent experienced in some Latin American countries, is highly undesirable. Similarly, rates of unemployment and negative income growth such as those experienced in the United States during the Great Depression are also clearly undesirable. This book will argue that the relative importance of goals is defined and redefined within the democratic political process rather than outside of it.

Does the Economy Regulate Itself, or Does It Need Guidance?

We must be clear about our understanding of the way the economic world works. To what extent is macroeconomic performance dependent on or subject to control of guidance by public officials? I try to be agnostic on this issue and to recognize reasonable alternative points of view. As we will see, professional economists have differing viewpoints on this issue, and there is a continuing evolution of theory and method. The prevailing professional opinion on this issue tends to change over time.

Rules versus Discretion

An intuitive approach to public issues would suggest that public-spirited officeholders should make policy according to what seems appropriate at the time, that is, to use their discretion. But not all officeholders are public spirited, and discretion may yield to opportunism and inappropriate expediency. Discretion can even be inferior when officeholders are public spirited.

---

[5] More precisely, macroeconomists think that inflation should be at a low but positive rate; that unemployment is to be at its natural, or non-accelerating, rate; and that growth should not be at the expense of basic levels of consumption. But with the exception of unemployment, these subtleties are not important in the public politics of macroeconomic policy. (See Chapters 2 and 3.)

An alternative that is suggested from time to time in the literature on macroeconomic policy making is that there should be rules to guide and restrict the behavior of public officials to try to eliminate opportunism or systematic biases of the democratic political process. Examples include proposals for requirements that the federal budget be balanced and that monetary policy be defined in a systematic and predictable way. Such rules might be appended to the Constitution, as has been proposed for a balanced budget amendment, or they might simply be defined by legislation.

I oppose a balanced budget amendment, even though I think deficits are a serious problem, because I do not think the enforcement issues have been adequately addressed.[6] Simply putting a goal into the Constitution does not ensure that it will be achieved, or even taken seriously. The Fifteenth Amendment established the principle that the right to vote shall not be denied on grounds of race, color, or previous condition of servitude, but it took almost a century for it to be enforced. The Eighteenth Amendment, which prohibited intoxicating liquors, also failed to achieve its purpose.

I am sympathetic to arguments that rules and precommitment are likely to be superior to discretion, and that they might have saved the United States from a lot of the problems it now faces. But I argue that changes in formal rules without attention to incentives and to informal patterns of behavior are likely to be misguided.

Structure, Outcomes, and Instruments

It is important to be clear about some language and concepts. We conceive of a nation's economy as a *structure* of behavioral relationships regarding the demand and supply of goods and services. Measures of the performance of this structure include *outcomes* such as inflation, unemployment, and income growth, which may be viewed as satisfactory or otherwise. Policy *instruments*, such as tax rates and interest rates, may allow public officials some control over the outcomes, as mediated by the structure of the economy.

Different understandings of the nature of the structure and of the relationships between instruments and outcomes are at the heart of disagreements about the three issues mentioned earlier. That is, different macroeconomic theories have different answers to questions about the appropriate goals for public policy, about whether the economy regulates itself, and about whether public officials should use their discretion.

---

[6] See Primo (2007).

SOME POLITICAL ISSUES

We should also be explicit and clear about some political issues, if only to acknowledge their importance.

What Motivates Public Officials?

We usually do not know the answer to this question, but useful theories have been built on the basis of assuming some answer. Politicians are, from time to time, presumed to be motivated by pursuit of the public interest, or more narrowly defined policy goals, or votes, or the rewards of office, or some combination of these factors. This book will be agnostic about the motivations of politicians but will consider seriously the alternatives. It is possible to learn the implications of different motivations by modeling politicians as benevolent dictators and as vote-maximizers, for example, and then comparing the results.

The Values and Wisdom of Voters

Voters may be narrowly self-interested or altruistic. Voters may or may not always know what is good for them. The incentives involved in appealing to voters may or may not be constructive. Voters may or may not be able to take a long-term view of the alternatives. I try to be agnostic about these issues but critical of the argument that appealing for votes ipso facto implies fundamentally perverse incentives on the part of political candidates. However, I do think that public preferences are at the root of some of the deficit problems that the American public deplores, and that there can be a large gap between public preferences and public understanding of the consequences of those preferences.

Accountability and Independence

The accountability provided by periodic elections may increase the risk that politicians will take a short-term view at the expense of long-term welfare. Alternatively, independence of the requirement that officeholders appeal to voters may facilitate a focus on the long run, but it may lead to a lack of accountability. The requirement that politicians appeal to voters may lead to a focus on simpleminded and superficial solutions to problems, to the neglect of complex and realistic solutions that more independent institutions, such as the Federal Reserve System, might offer.[7] I defend the independence of central banks, as well as the need for periodic elections.

The Meaning of Politics and the Political

In ordinary usage, the term "politics" often has derogatory connotations, as if politics were inherently undesirable. Herbert Simon observed that "in our society, we have an unfortunate habit of labeling our political institutions in two different ways. On the days when we are happy with them, we call them democracy; on the days when we are unhappy, we call them politics" (1983, p. 99). This book is about "politics" in macroeconomic policy, and it is intended to rise above that "unfortunate habit."

In the chapters to come, we will be seeking out important ways in which the term "politics" is used to designate things we do not like. For example, Chapter 3 describes and analyzes a theory in which incumbents are said to manipulate the economy in self-serving and opportunistic ways when elections approach, fooling the voters at the expense of the public's interest, insofar as those interests can be objectively defined. When such behavior occurs, it is certainly politics in the undesirable sense.

We will also consider ways in which "politics" means differences of opinion and judgment among reasonable, sincere, and informed individuals, as opposed to differences in tastes and preferences. We will find such differences in beliefs to be unavoidable at just about every stage of policy making, from disagreements among voters about candidates and parties to disagreements among academic economists advising the government about fiscal or monetary policy. In this sense, politics is about the resolution of contestable issues. Democratic institutions provide ways in which such differences are at least provisionally resolved through rules for public discourse and policy making that are themselves contestable and subject to change. This is one of the reasons why process is important.

IMAGES OF THE DEMOCRATIC PROCESS

We will try to arrive at an understanding of the nature of the democratic process regarding macroeconomic issues in terms of three possibilities.

---

[7] By the end of this book, I will be emphasizing that there are two meanings of "accountable." The first is "to be subject to sanction," such as removal from office by way of periodic elections. The second is to "explain, report, or justify." The issue will become subtle when we consider the independence of the Federal Reserve, and whether or not it should be required to announce its targets (see Chapter 8).

The Democratic Process as Optimizing

We might consider that democratic processes inherently choose the best outcomes, but what would that mean? One might say that democratic processes define the best outcomes, but that would be begging the question. We occasionally hear it said that the cure for the ills of democracy is more democracy, implying that there are inherently desirable features in the democratic process. John Rawls's conception of "pure procedural justice" (1971) exemplifies this notion. Under pure procedural justice, the procedure is so perfect that any decision that comes out of it is rendered desirable by virtue of the fact that it emerged from the process.

An example might be May's demonstration that majority rule always makes appropriate decisions when there are two alternatives and when the preferences of all voters are equally valid (May 1952). Majority rule is, of course, fundamental to the democratic process, and more generally a metaphor for the process. However, May's proof under these limited circumstances cannot sustain the case that the democratic process optimizes, because the conditions do not hold. The argument breaks down, as Arrow (1963) has shown, when there are more than two alternatives.

This book will not argue that democratic processes systematically choose the best outcomes (i.e., that they optimize), for a variety of reasons. Too many varied procedures might be called democratic. Also, there is too much contestability about the value of the outcomes, and we know too little about the connection between the process and the outcomes.

Arguments that democratic processes choose optimal outcomes are likely to be tautological and nearly meaningless. Still, outcomes that are produced by a fair process in democratic institutions have a provisional legitimacy that can make them acceptable until the same institutions produce different outcomes, or until the institutions are changed to some other variant of democratic procedures.

The Democratic Process as Pathological

An opposite claim is that democratic processes may be pathological, that they lead systematically to undesirable or inferior outcomes. To make such a case, we would need to identify the standards for outcomes by which it could be made, and we would need to show the systematic connection between the procedure and the outcomes. If claims of pathological consequences are to be supportable, we would want to know if they are true in general or true only under certain conditions, regarding, for example, voter preferences or institutional processes.

One of the tasks of this book is to identify (macroeconomically oriented) arguments that there are systematic pathologies in democratic institutions and to identify the conditions under which they are likely to occur. In fact, few such arguments exist. This book will argue that the democratic process is not inherently pathological, although we identify some risks and pitfalls. If it were true that generic democratic processes systematically produced undesirable results, such a fact would have become more obvious by now. In fact, there are undesirable possibilities in democratic politics, and this book is designed to identify ways to avoid them. The general observation is that the world's most prosperous and free nations are overwhelmingly democratic.

The Liberal Interpretation of Voting

William Riker defended a very modest interpretation of voting in which

> we should never take the results of any method (of voting) always to be a fair and true amalgamation of voters' judgments. Doubtless the results often are fair and true; but, unfortunately, we almost never know whether they are or not. Consequently, we should not generally assume that the methods produce fair and true amalgamations. We should think of the method, I believe, simply as convenient ways of doing business, useful but flawed. (1982, p. 113)

More generally, "All elections do or have to do is to permit people to get rid of rulers ... The kind of democracy that thus survives is not, however, popular rule, but rather an intermittent, sometimes random, *even perverse* popular veto" (Riker 1982, p. 244, emphasis added).

Riker criticized as incoherent and unrealistic an alternative populist conception of democracy wherein voting is thought to be a true and meaningful expression of popular will. For Riker, "liberal democracy is simply the veto by which it is sometimes possible to restrain official tyranny" (1982, p. 244). Such a view occupies a broad middle ground between the views that the democratic process is either optimizing or pathological.

The reader will not be surprised to find this book taking the middle ground, for it is designed to map the vast territory between these extremes. How much more can we say about democratic processes than that it may be possible to restrain official tyranny by rejecting incumbent public officials? Because macroeconomic topics involve performance indicators that lend themselves to comparative evaluation, we have a better chance of mapping the territory than did Riker, who considered only popular preferences, which he took to be varied without limit, and all equally valid from a democratic perspective.

One advantage of the economic issues that we will consider is that they allow us to relate political choices to the performance of the economy, with the possibility that the performance may be disappointing. This interpretation of democracy is compatible with maximizing long-term growth and prosperity, and also with stagnation and decline. The experiences of several Western democracies and now the United States show that both things can happen in the context of periodic elections.

HOW AND WHY THE UNITED STATES IS A DEMOCRACY

The United States is generally considered a democracy, and that was the undefended presumption of the first edition of this book. In this edition, I argue that the United States is a democracy because it has two features that I consider essential: contested elections and limitations on government. By these standards, the United States has been a democracy throughout its history under its Constitution.

All three leading indexes that are commonly used as measures of democracy call the United States a democracy from the beginning of their measures in two cases, and for at least well over a century for the one that goes back to 1800. Specifically, the DD index (for Democracy and Dictatorship) assesses the United States as a democracy from 1946, the first year measured, through 2008, the last year of measurement.[8] Freedom House gives the United States a perfect score of one (out of seven) on both political rights and civil liberties for each year it measures from 1972 through 2012. The United States is given the designation of Free (as opposed to Partly Free or Not Free) for each of those years.[9] Polity IV gives the United States a perfect ten for democracy and a zero for autocracy from 1871 through 2010.[10]

My definition of democracy is minimalist, like the DD definition of Cheibub, Gandhi, and Vreeland (2010), but it adds a dimension. Like DD, it considers the presence of contested elections a necessary condition of

---

[8] Data accessed September 2, 2011, at https://sites.google.com/site/joseantoniocheibub/ datasets/democracy-and-dictatorship-revisited. See Cheibub et al. (2010) for an explanation of the index.

[9] Data accessed April 21, 2010, March 17, 2011, and December 2, 2012, at http:// www.freedomhouse.org/.

[10] Data accessed September 2, 2012, at http://www.systemicpeace.org/polity/polity4.htm. Polity IV gives the United States scores of eight and nine, with an occasional ten between 1809 and 1871. The lowest Polity IV score for the United States is seven, which is the measure for 1800 through 1808. In many uses of Polity IV, countries are called democracies if they score seven or eight or above.

democracy, and it accepts their four rules for identifying a democracy.[11] But my definition adds a second dimension – limitations on government.

Why would limitations be an essential feature of democracy? First of all, in the countries that developed the institutions of democracy most gradually, limitations on government preceded elections. In England, the Magna Carta (1215) established that a representative body could limit the powers of the king. The Glorious Revolution of 1688 further limited royal powers and enhanced the powers of Parliament. In the United States, the separation of powers, federalism, a limited list of federal government powers, and a Bill of Rights were all ways of limiting government. Such limits were initially much more central features of the American Constitution than were elections. Not until the nineteenth century did electoral features become major democratic concerns in either country.

Second, limitations make explicit the idea that the winners of elections must follow rules that protect individual and minority rights, and they assure that no election will be the last. What keeps the winners of elections from trampling on the rights of the losers? Constitutional limitations on government are the standard way to do this. But not all limitations on government will count as being relevant to democracy, as will be explained later.

Charles Lindblom explains the roots of democracy as follows: "The history of democracy is largely an account of the pursuit of liberty ... One way (man) has tried to insure his liberties ... is by instituting the more or less democratic regimes we call polyarchies, polyarchy being the means, liberty the end" (1977, pp. 162–3). Lindblom continues: "*Polyarchies are systems of rules for constraining rather than mobilizing authority. They grow out of the struggle to control authority rather than to create it or make it more effective*" (1977, p. 165, emphasis added).

Lindblom's observations put the finger on a key difference between democracy and authoritarianism. For my purposes of relating institutions to economic performance, authoritarian governments are those that may be designed to create and to mobilize authority, and this could well be an advantage for carrying out reforms designed to improve economic performance. Democracy, in contrast, has essential features that may work against each other: competitive elections can be used to mobilize authority, and

---

[11] These are (1) the chief executive must be chosen by popular election or by a body that was itself popularly elected, (2) the legislature must be popularly elected, (3) there must be more than one party competing in the elections, and (4) an alternation in power under electoral rules identical to the ones that brought the incumbent to office must have taken place (Cheibub et al. 2010, p. 69).

limits on government can be used to constrain authority. Thus, these two features of democracy could work in concert, but they may be in tension with each other.

Witold Henisz (2000) has developed a measure of political constraints based on the number and agreement among veto players that comes close to what I have in mind for limits on government. For this measure, which ranges between zero (no constraints) and one (most constrained), the United States has scored very close to 0.85 for the entire period from 1960 through 2012.[12]

Note that DD, Polity, and I do not use universal suffrage as a criterion of democracy. This means that the United States is not punished by Polity IV or by me as a democracy for lack of women's suffrage before the Nineteenth Amendment. Furthermore, for Polity IV, DD, and for this book, the United States is not punished for its ninety-five-year failure to implement the Fifteenth Amendment, which said in 1870 that the vote shall not be denied or abridged by race, color, or previous condition of servitude.

My own defense of this stance is that what is of enduring importance about democratic elections is contestation. Standards of participation vary with cultural values, which have steadily changed in the direction of greater inclusiveness. But to say that a country that denies major groups of its citizens the right to vote is to say that a country cannot be a democracy before women, for example, can vote. Such a decision would rule out more than half of American history as not democratic.

Why would this be inappropriate? Because I believe that contestation is more important for democracy than is participation. Having universal participation in uncontested elections is less meaningfully democratic than limited participation in contested elections. The political experience of the United States before 1920 or 1965 is meaningfully democratic in spite of the limitations on equal access to the ballot.[13]

Robert Dahl, who has been writing authoritative books on democracy for more than half a century, would not fully agree. For Dahl, political partic-ipation and political equality are central to democracy. In *Polyarchy* (1971),

---

[12] Data accessed April 15, 2013, at http://mgmt5.wharton.upenn.edu/henisz/POLCON/ ContactInfo.html. See also Beck et al. (2001) for an alternative measure, which is part of the World Bank Database of Political Institutions.

[13] Note that I avoid the concept of meaningful choices, which I consider too vague. Anthony Downs's model of two candidates having identical platforms is consistent with meaningful options (1957). On the other hand, the American party system before the Civil War was designed to keep slavery from becoming an electoral issue. But both involve contested elections in a way that is meaningfully democratic.

Dahl developed an index of democracy that multiplied an index of contestation with an index of participation.[14] In *How Democratic Is the American Constitution?* (2002), he considers political equality a central democratic value, and he judges that the United States is far from that standard. The most fundamental reason is the political inequality that is embedded in the Constitution because of the apportionment of two senators per state, regardless of population.

THE ARGUMENT OF THIS BOOK

There are costs of democracy in the sense that, even at best, inevitable inefficiencies are to be found in any system in which agents (such as presidents) act on behalf of principals (such as voters). There may also be ways in which the incentives of the electoral process lead systematically to outcomes that are demonstrably inferior. Such pathologies are possible, but they are not inevitable features of democratic politics.

However, arguments about the costs of democracy are slippery, because there are no uncontested fundamentals against which to make evaluations. No Archimedean points offer the intellectual leverage with which to judge the performance of democracies. The standards for evaluation of democratic performance are written in sand rather than set in stone. Consider these issues in terms of Charles Plott's (1991) "fundamental equation":

$$\text{preferences} \; (\times) \; \text{institutions} \rightarrow \text{outcomes}$$

This equation simply describes the fact that the preferences and values of voters and politicians interact in a political process taking place in electoral and policy-making institutions. The interaction produces policy outcomes.

Democracy may also have costs in the sense that the incentives of democratic politics may prompt incumbents to seek to produce outcomes that will appear better to voters at election time than they will later from a broader and more meaningful perspective. These are costs in the sense that they are compared to the inefficiencies associated with any principal-agent problem. These costs can occasionally be large and perhaps can be considered pathological, such as explosive growth of public debt or hyperinflation. But obviously, such outcomes are conditional rather than inevitable features of democratic politics.

---

[14] Although Dahl himself did not apply his index to a wide range of countries over a long period of time, Tatu Vanhanen (2000) did.

The desirability of any outcome could be defined in terms of the voters as the ultimate source of authority in a democracy. Or it could be defined in terms of the institutional processes that aggregate the preferences. Or it could be defined in terms of some objective standard for the outcome. My argument will be that none of these provides an unconditional basis for evaluation. Instead, there is a logical circularity among preferences, institutions, and outcomes. That is, there is feedback from outcomes to preferences and to institutions.

Any of the three elements might be taken as a standard for evaluation purposes. Taking preferences as a fixed basis for definitive standards, we can evaluate the way institutions process these preferences into outcomes, and then compare the results to the preferences. Or taking outcomes as the basis, we can compare the outcomes produced by the political process to the "best" outcomes. Or taking the institutional procedures as definitive, we might argue that the outcomes produced by processing the preferences are legitimized or rendered desirable by the very fact of having emerged from the desirable processes, as in pure procedural justice (Rawls, 1971).

This book will argue that none of these three alternatives is satisfactory, because none of the three elements provides definitive standards that are not subject to revision in terms of the other two. Institutional processes are accepted as definitive so long as they produce outcomes that are basically satisfactory in terms of existing preferences. But when the outcomes become unsatisfactory, we may try to improve them by changing the institutions. And the preferences themselves may change when experience shows that better performance is feasible or suggests that worse performance is inevitable.

These arguments will be developed through the remaining chapters in the following way. Chapter 2 describes what macroeconomic theories say about what is feasible and desirable for economic outcomes and for the choice of instruments. Professional macroeconomists are our main source of authoritative knowledge about how the economic world works, but here, too, there is uncertainty and disagreement, and not a single set of authoritative answers. The differences in beliefs might be described as political in a perfectly respectable and non-pejorative sense, because many of these features are inherently contestable.

Chapters 3 and 4 describe the most common models of routine politics in terms of macroeconomic issues. Chapter 3, on electoral cycles, abstracts some basic features of democratic elections in institutions of accountability for incumbents, as derived from the incentive to maximize votes. This chapter describes a theory that seems to illustrate economic politics at its worst, the self-serving manipulation of the timing of economic outcomes in order to win elections.

Chapter 4, on partisan differences, abstracts some basic features of democratic elections as institutions for choosing among candidates and among alternative future policies. Partisanship models describe how differences in interests or preferences among voters or differences in partisan choices translate into differences in outcomes. Both of these standard models capture important features of reality, but they leave much unexplained about how politics influences economic outcomes. The electoral cycle models and partisanship models also leave much unsaid about the costs of democracy.

Chapter 5 is a new chapter entitled "Unintended Consequences, Moral Hazard, and Time-Consistency." This addition addresses the financial crisis and links it to the incentives of democratic politics in a way that goes beyond the original 1995 edition of this book. The idea of unintended consequences is intuitive and will make concrete the possibility that good intentions can prevail under democratic institutions in ways that have undesirable and unintended consequences. Moral hazard is a familiar concept in modern social science, meaning that insuring against adverse consequences can make agents more careless in avoiding them than they would be if they bore the full cost. Time-consistency is an ancient concept given modern relevance by Kydland and Prescott (1977). Its central idea is that the best thing to do under all times and circumstances may not seem to be the best thing to do at any particular time or circumstance. These issues will be illustrated with the financial crisis of 2007–9.

Chapters 6 and 7 discuss sources of authority and the arguments regarding what macroeconomic policy ought to do. Chapter 6 describes and analyzes goals for economic policy outcomes as defined in public law and by economic analysis. Although it is easy to identify extreme values of, for example, inflation and unemployment that are clearly bad, I argue that the identification of specific targets as best or optimal values is inherently contestable. Provisional definitions of optimal values for growth, unemployment, and inflation rates are useful for analytical purposes, but ultimately those choices are political in a perfectly respectable and non-pejorative sense, because they are inherently contestable.

Voters constitute the ultimate source of authority in a democracy, but Chapter 7 argues that voter preferences are seldom clearly defined. They provide only relatively loose constraints on what public officials can do, and only imprecise guidance about what public officials should do. The electoral process sometimes seems to offer perverse incentives for politicians to follow irresponsible policies, but I argue that electoral incentives do not force politicians to be irresponsible in order to be successful.

Chapters 8 and 9 are about the institutions and procedures through which macroeconomic policy is made. Chapter 8 concerns monetary institutions and policies and Chapter 9 concerns fiscal institutions and policies. There are two basic risks of democratically influenced macroeconomic policy. One is that the economy may be stimulated beyond sustainable levels in order to make things seem better than they in fact are. Such a move might be carried out through monetary policy. Alternatively, monetary policy is these days the leading institution for stabilization policy.

The second risk is that popular desires for public programs will not be disciplined or restrained by direct experience of the costs of these programs through taxes. Irresponsible fiscal policy would occur when unsustainable policies regarding taxing and spending would be chosen or passively continued.

Yielding to the popular temptation to evade macroeconomic discipline will have both fiscal and monetary reflections. Fiscal policy might manifest a lack of discipline by producing inappropriate deficits and excessive borrowing. Monetary policy might yield to the same temptation by printing money to cover expenditures, as an alternative to borrowing. These two chapters will analyze the ways in which such risks are handled. The formal and informal institutions have been changed and may be changed in the future in order to improve policy making, perhaps because outcomes are deviating from the ranges of tolerable alternatives, or because a winning coalition believes that it can impose its policy preferences on the future through changes in institutions.

However, it is not clear that the people who brought about institutional changes (such as those created by the Federal Reserve Act of 1913 or by the Budget and Impoundment Control Act of 1974) always knew what they were doing. Sometimes new institutions have unanticipated consequences, and sometimes they are stopgap responses to public pressure to "do something."

Chapter 10 draws these various themes together into a conclusion that treats the interaction represented by Plott's fundamental equation as a fluid process that feeds back on itself. The interaction among these elements will involve actions and choices by human beings who express and implement preferences about which they often feel strongly. This is the kind of behavior that is best understood in the context of rational choice models, in the style of economics, and we will make use of such models. The interactions also involve speech, persuasion, and discourse, which can take place on a high plane of ideas or at the level of demagoguery. The political process will also be considered as a setting for argument and persuasion.

Some costs of democracy are inevitable and unavoidable in the best of political systems. However, the tone of public and even academic discourse can deteriorate to a level at which arguments are not posed and answered, to a level at which arguments are replaced by utterances designed to humiliate, to divide the opposition, and to rally the troops. Such tones and levels might be considered pathological. Even at such a low level of discourse, the fundamental democratic institution of regular elections provides an opportunity to throw the rascals out. This is a useful and meaningful minimum provided by Riker's liberal theory of democracy. Under other circumstances, discourse can be of much higher quality. It is likely, though not assured, that the quality of policy choices and outcomes will also be higher under such circumstances, but then again, that quality is likely to be defined and redefined in the discourse itself.

2

Macroeconomic Theories and Their Political Implications

The purpose of this chapter is to present to the reader the theories and the views of professional economists about how the macroeconomy works. Political choices regarding monetary and fiscal policy operate in an environment of real-world constraints; to understand the political choices and their consequences, we must understand the nature of these constraints.

As this chapter will show, macroeconomists have had divergent views about how the economy works, but there has been some convergence. For some, this convergence has survived the financial crisis of 2007–9. For others, macroeconomic training in recent decades has been "a costly waste of time" ("The Other-Worldly Philosophers," *Economist*, July 18, 2009, p. 65). The recent crisis is seen both as a criticism and a vindication of the efficient markets hypothesis, which holds that prices of securities fully reflect all available information.[1] And although there is some convergence as well as continued divergence in macroeconomic thinking, neither trend includes a prominent development in the discipline, behavioral economics, which has recently addressed macroeconomic issues.

Theoretical convergence or not, there is little agreement among macroeconomists on the causes of the recent financial crisis, what policies contributed to it, who is responsible, what to do to get out of the ensuing recession, and how to avoid future crises. Still, we must go to macroeconomic theory to understand the way the economic world works, to explain and predict, and to know what is possible and what is not. For better or worse, the message of this chapter is that no single, authoritative, uncontested theory explains the way the macroeconomic world works. This fact means that political disagreement about economic issues is likely to involve

---

[1] See Fox (2009) for an accessible and complete treatment.

differences of opinion and belief about what is realistic and feasible for the macroeconomy, as well as about what is desired.[2]

The chapter is organized as follows. Most of it will be a historical tracing of developments in macroeconomics from the classical system, to early Keynesianism, to monetarism, to rational expectations and real business cycles and a new Keynesian synthesis. Supply side economics and behavioral macroeconomics will be briefly discussed. This historical analysis will be organized by three questions about whether the economy is self-regulating, the role for policy, and the potential for political mismanagement.

POLITICAL ECONOMICS AND ECONOMIC THEORY: THREE QUESTIONS

Economic theory is the source of our most authoritative understanding of the way the macroeconomic world works, and there is an impressive body of such theory. As such, it seeks to identify what is possible, it seeks to identify the consequences of alternative sources of action, and it "defines the norms that determine when certain conditions are to be regarded as policy problems" (Majone, 1989, pp. 23–4). But macroeconomic theory does not speak with one voice. Competing theories are derived from competing systems of belief about the way the world works. We will review a sequence of these theories with an eye to their answers to the following three questions.

Does the Economy Regulate Itself?

The answer to this vague question is fundamentally important, because it has obvious implications for the roles of public officials and for the issue of whether government should take an active or a passive stance toward economic stabilization. The answers given to this question vary substantially across different schools of macroeconomic thought. However, the

---

[2] Milton Friedman has argued that "differences about economic policy among disinterested citizens derive predominantly from different predictions about the economic consequences of taking action – differences that in principle can be eliminated by the progress of positive economics – rather than from fundamental differences in basic values, differences about which men can ultimately only fight" (1953b, p. 5). This chapter argues that there has been considerable progress in positive (as distinguished from normative) macroeconomics since Friedman wrote, but that in fact major disagreements still remain among professional scholars.

different answers are usually based on assumptions that are starting points for further analysis, rather than on conclusions derived from careful investigations.

We will see that there is progress in macroeconomic theory, and that each new theory addresses a limitation of what occurred previously. There is a "neoclassical synthesis" (see Hoover 1988, pp. 9–10) and a "new neoclassical synthesis" (Goodfriend 2002). But even so, these theories can be grouped according to their initial and basic (though not always clearly articulated) assumptions about whether or not the economy has forces that lead it to desirable equilibrium paths. These assumptions are associated for the most part in predictable ways with conclusions about whether or not government should intervene in the economy.

What Role Does the Theory Imply for Public Officials?

Not surprisingly, the theories that assume that the economy regulates itself see less of an activist role for public officials in stabilization policy than do the theories that make alternative assumptions. In general, the theories that see the economy as a self-regulating system advocate that policy makers follow rules. The theories that see a role for discretionary choice in response to changing conditions are usually those that do not see the economy as regulating itself. Some theories have stressed the role of fiscal policy, the balance of taxing and spending, and others have stressed the importance of the control of the money supply or interest rates.

What Are the Risks of Mismanagement due to Political Incentives?

If discretionary action is expected of public officials by a macroeconomic theory, there may be risks that such discretion will be misused, perhaps because of the incentives of the electoral process. Buchanan and Wagner (1977) have argued that this is the case with Keynesian economics. Other theories suggest that officials should follow rules for fiscal and monetary policy to avoid the risks of mismanagement. Usually, scholars other than those responsible for the theory identify the risks of mismanagement for a given theory.

In this book, I try to be agnostic about the alternative theories, and to present them fairly in their own terms. In spite of the risk of making the book sound as if it is more about macroeconomics than about politics, I present the leading alternatives early for the following reasons. Many of the models of politics that follow assume a macroeconomic theory, and it is desirable that the reader be aware of the theoretical underpinnings of a given argument and that there are alternatives. Also, many of the dynamics will be more understandable if the reader has some grasp of the theory in which given models are set.

A secondary consequence for some readers may be the impression that macroeconomics is in "crisis" or "disarray," terms that have been used even before the recent financial crisis by some of its own practitioners.[3] There is surely a sharp contrast between the scientific agreement that exists in the field of microeconomics (the study of individuals and firms interacting in markets) and the scientific disagreement that exists in macroeconomics (the study of the overall performance of economies). As a sympathetic outside observer, I would urge tolerance and an open mind on the part of the reader. The central point of this chapter is that regardless of how contestable they are, views of how the macroeconomy works color and influence a variety of viewpoints on politics. What follows is not meant to be a comprehensive review, but rather a sketch of the alternatives that are most consequential for understanding political models.

THE CLASSICAL SYSTEM

Macroeconomics as a subfield of economics did not exist, as we know it, before the 1930s, but at that time the prevailing view in economics regarding the issues that were to become known as macroeconomics was known as the classical system.[4] The economy was seen as a self-regulating system, even though there was, of course, a recognition that business cycles existed.[5] A key feature was that aggregate supply, or the productive capacity of the economy, was a function of capital, labor, and technology that was fixed in the short run. The amount of output the economy would produce and the numbers of people employed were determined entirely by factors on the supply rather than the demand side of the economy.

The classical system explained how government manipulation of demand-side variables would fail to increase output. A fundamental reason was that output, or aggregate supply, was fixed in the short term. That is, the

---

[3] Blinder has referred to "utter disarray" (1987, p. 67). Blanchard and Fischer have referred to a theoretical crisis (1989, p. 27). Ironically, as the profession is attacked in the press (*The Economist*, July 18, 2009, pp. 65–9), Blanchard has pronounced that "the state of macro is good" (2009).

[4] The sketches of alternative theories that appear in this chapter draw heavily on Froyen (2009).

[5] See Keynes, "The Postulates of Classical Economics" (1936, ch. 2).

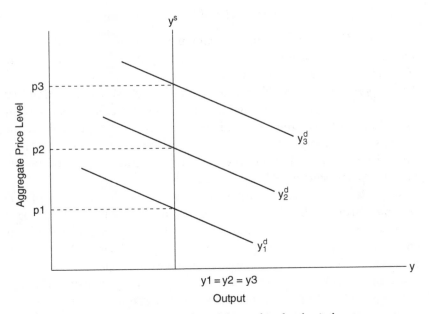

Figure 2.1. Aggregate supply and demand in the classical system

aggregate supply curve was vertical. Manipulation of aggregate demand by increasing the money supply would merely change the price level without changing output (Figure 2.1). A government budget deficit would change the balance of savings and investment in the composition of output, but not the total amount.[6]

In a world described by the classical system, there was no role for discretionary government stabilization of economic fluctuations in the form of active fiscal or monetary policy. The main role of public officials was to maintain a favorable climate for business by protecting property rights, enforcing contracts, maintaining a sound and stable currency, and balancing the government's budget. Because there was no role for a systematic, active fiscal or monetary policy, no systematic risk of mismanagement was identified. However, rigid adherence to the gold standard has been identified by some authors as a part of the causes of the Great Depression and as an obstruction to policies that would have ended it.[7]

---

[6] Fiscal policy might affect output in the long run in the classical system through the effect of marginal tax rates on economic activity or through the effect of government borrowing on real interest rates.

[7] See Temin (1989) and Eichengreen (1992a). See also Friedman and Schwartz (1963).

EARLY KEYNESIANISM

During the Great Depression, unemployment rose to 25 percent in 1933, and real gross national product output dropped 30 percent from 1929 to 1933. The gross national product did not regain its 1929 level until 1939.[8] That experience made it difficult to maintain the classical assumption that the economy regulates itself. Recent scholarship has argued that government interventions prolonged rather than shortened or cushioned the Depression.[9] Roosevelt's New Deal programs were both popular and controversial at the time, but the whole experience of the Depression undermined popular belief in self-regulating markets.

Keynesian economics, launched with the publication in 1936 of *The General Theory of Employment, Interest, and Money* by John Maynard Keynes, provided an explanation for why labor markets might not clear and why massive "involuntary" unemployment could persist. Keynes contended that the "postulates of the classical theory are applicable to a special case only and not to the general case, the situation which it assumes being a limiting point of the possible positions of equilibrium" (1936, p. 3).

Keynes called his theory the "general theory" because it applied to a variety of situations, not just to that described in "the classical economics." Thus, Keynesian economics began with the presumption that they economy does not always regulate itself. That hardly seemed controversial in 1936.[10]

Keynesian economics explained the Depression in terms of inadequate aggregate demand for goods and services, and it proposed a way for government to use its taxing and spending powers to stimulate that demand. Although the *General Theory* said little about fiscal and monetary policy, Keynes did show how a multiplier could make public expenditures "pay for themselves over and over again at a time of severe unemployment," but he points out that this becomes "a more doubtful proposition as a state of full employment is approached" (Keynes 1936, p. 127).[11] Keynes's followers developed more focused theories by which intentional government deficits could stimulate aggregate demand.[12]

The political implications of Keynesian economics are several, depending on the situation. Under the conditions of inadequate aggregate demand and

---

[8] See Froyen 2009, p. 63.

[9] See Cole and Ohanian 2004. See also Fishback 2010.

[10] See Keynes (1936, p. 15) on involuntary unemployment, and Hoover (1988, sec. 3.4) on the "persistence of the Keynesian problem."

[11] Keynes draws on an article by R. F. Kahn (1931) for the concept of the multiplier. I am indebted to Neil deMarchi for pointing this out to me.

[12] See Stein (1969, 1994, 1996). See Meltzer (1988) on Keynes's own views.

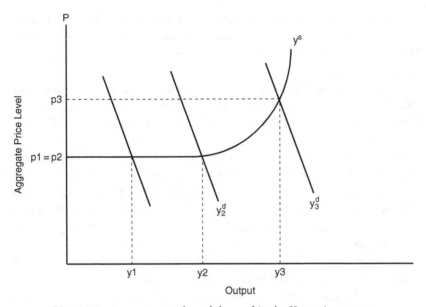

Figure 2.2. Aggregate supply and demand in the Keynesian system

large amounts of unused capacity for production, an outward shift in the demand curve could be an unambiguous welfare improvement. Figure 2.2 illustrates this possibility with an aggregate supply curve that is partially horizontal, as was implicit in early Keynesian models that assumed the price level to be fixed. If the economy is in a region where the supply curve is flat, then an outward shift in aggregate demand can increase output without increasing prices. As far as this argument goes,[13] everybody's economic welfare is improved, while no one is hurt. Such a change is known as a "Pareto improvement."

Under these assumptions, the political problem for the Keynesians was the need to persuade policy makers of the wisdom of that course. Once recognized, the issue seemed to its proponents to be without costs and trade-offs. Politics, in that case, involved the introduction of new ideas into public debate, and the argument that those ideas could help solve public problems.[14]

---

[13] This does not consider the tax burden of the shift in aggregate demand.
[14] See Buchanan and Wagner (1977, ch. 6).

This argument was not an easy sell in the United States. President Roosevelt had met with Keynes and had not been favorably impressed. The similarity between Keynesian recommendations and the programs of the New Deal was more coincidental than intentional. Two decades later, Cary Brown summed up a careful quantitative analysis by saying that "fiscal policy, then, seems to have been an unsuccessful recovery device in the thirties – not because it did not work, but because it was not tried" (1956, pp. 863–6).

The originally proposed full employment bill of 1945 was of Keynesian inspiration (Bailey, 1950, ch. 2), but the process of amendment into the Employment Act of 1946 involved removal of the portions of the original proposal that had been most explicitly Keynesian, such as using the federal budget as an instrument to achieve full employment. Congress passed the bill but, in doing so, rejected Keynesian recommendations.

A weakness of Keynesian theory had been the lack of attention to the risks of inflation, which had not been a problem amid the falling prices of the Depression.[15] That issue was addressed in an article by A. W. Phillips (1958), who identified an inverse relationship between unemployment and wage growth across a long historical period in Britain. By extension, that relationship implied a similarly inverse relationship between unemployment and inflation, which became popularly known as a "Phillips curve," such as that pictured in Figure 2.3.[16]

The trade-off between inflation and unemployment became widely understood as offering policy choices. Two leading economists cautiously described it as a "menu," and they anticipated that positions on the issue would be determined by "the tug of war of politics" (Samuelson and Solow 1960, p. 193).

"Politics" here implies a conflict of interests, or at least a divergence of preferences about the choices involved in the trade-off leading to desired points on the Phillips curve. A world characterized by such an exploitable trade-off needed politics to make the choices about where to be on the curve. The economics of the Phillips curve made no judgment about what choices should be made. With no objective economic basis for choice, politics became a basis for choosing among alternatives that were considered

---

[15] Keynes was not unaware of this danger: "When full employment has been reached, any attempt to increase investment still further will set up a tendency in money-prices to rise without limit" (1936, p. 118).

[16] For a fascinating treatment of the history of this article, its publication, and its author, see Sleeman 2011.

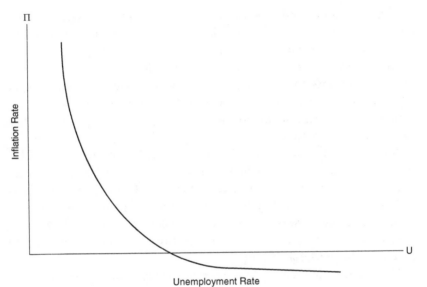

Figure 2.3. A simple Phillips curve

normatively neutral in economics. The political process is used to make a choice among alternatives that depend on values, rather than on any authoritative or objective analysis of what is desirable. This kind of politics is benign, as opposed to malign, in the terms identified in Chapter 1.

James Buchanan and Richard Wagner identified another, more malign kind of politics associated with Keynesian economics. In their book *Democracy in Deficit* (1977), they did not challenge the economics of Keynes. Rather, they identified some secondary political incentives for irresponsible use of Keynesian prescriptions. They identified a kind of politics that has, in their view, adverse consequences. In the Keynesian view, the primary goal of macroeconomic stabilization policy is to stabilize output by manipulating aggregate demand, typically shifting it outward to eliminate involuntary unemployment and increase national income. Originally, that was to be done with fiscal policy, such as increasing expenditures or cutting taxes. Those actions amounted to creating intentional deficits to achieve the higher goals of stabilizing employment and output.

Once the belief in the goal of balanced budgets was relaxed, because of the identification of certain circumstances (such as a recession) in which balance was undesirable, there were secondary political incentives to find opportunities to defend deficits. Politicians could please voters by cutting their taxes without cutting expenditures, or by increasing expenditures without increasing taxes, all in the name of stimulating the economy. Keynesian prescriptions for economic stabilization allowed a public justification for deficits that had not existed before. Buchanan and Wagner suggested that these prescriptions provided a pretext for yielding to a natural political temptation to do something that had previously been considered irresponsible.

Once the Keynesian economists had persuaded the relevant political community that reductions in unemployment and increases in output were more important than adhering to the goal of annual budget balance, that goal never again had quite the same moral or political importance.[17] Furthermore, once it was acknowledged that deficits were sometimes desirable, it became much more difficult to identify circumstances in which the deficit was inappropriately large.[18]

The problem identified by Buchanan and Wagner was that in the absence of a norm of balancing the budget, the public preferred lower taxes and higher public expenditures, other things being equal. Those natural incentives to tax less or to spend more would reinforce the case for intentional deficits when they were genuinely needed to stimulate aggregate demand. However, the same incentives would create pressures to tolerate deficits for macroeconomic conditions under which deficits were not appropriate. The natural incentives to opt for low taxes and high expenditures would not change when there was not a macroeconomic case for intentional deficits.

Stabilization goals that would demand balancing the budget or even creating a surplus would not have the political advantage of compatible secondary incentives. Such goals would have to fight the normal incentives not to raise taxes and not to cut expenditures. Insofar as secondary incentives are operative, one would expect that budgets would be disproportionately unbalanced. That is exactly what has happened. In the five decades since the first actively Keynesian administration took office in 1961, nominal surpluses have occurred in just five years: fiscal 1969, which overlapped the Johnson and Nixon administrations, but was defined by President

---

[17] The idea seems never to have lost its resilience with the public, but the attitudes of the "political community" seem to have changed. See Bratton (1994), Blinder and Holtz-Eakin (1984), Modigliani and Modigliani (1987), and Peterson (1985).

[18] Chapter 6 will review some efforts to define appropriate standards.

Johnson's final budget, and fiscal years 1998 through 2001, in the second Clinton administration. See Table 6.2.

Even though the values held by the public did not shift, the informal institutions of budgeting changed when that norm for public officials was broken. After the case for intentional deficits was embraced to stimulate the economy in the 1960s, it became difficult to identify precisely when intentional deficits were no longer appropriate, and when efforts to balance the budget might be harmful to economic performance. Judgments about when those points are reached can easily be clouded by the secondary incentives. To increase taxes or to cut expenditures when that might be appropriate for stabilization purposes runs against the secondary incentives to keep taxes low and expenditures high, and it becomes difficult to agree that such politically painful actions are necessary.

This problem of incentives identifies a potential problem for democratic politics. If deficits are harmful (and professional economists disagree on this point), the incentives of the electoral process may not be constructive and may even be perverse. But that is a potential rather than an inevitable perversity in democratic institutions. If deficits were politically inevitable, we would have observed them throughout the entire democratic experience, but we have not. Budgets had been balanced as often as unbalanced over American history, until 1960. Except for wartime periods, there have not been long periods in which there have been no surpluses and in which public debt as a fraction of total output has been steadily rising, as is now the case.

Why should national budget deficits be a political problem now, when they were not a problem before? The answer, I think, does not hinge on the presence or absence of formal rules against deficits, such as those that exist in forty-nine of the states, or such as the balanced budget amendments to the Constitution that have been proposed on the national level. There was no such rule in the period before deficits became a problem. The answer has two components. One has to do with political norms, which were broken with the victory in national politics of Keynesian ideas in the 1960s. The other has to do with the difficulty of balancing the budget when the imbalance has grown to such a large fraction of national output. We will return to these issues in Chapter 9, when we consider fiscal policy.[19]

---

[19] This perspective on deficits is not highly compatible with rational choice perspectives. See Alesina and Tabellini (1990) and Tabellini and Alesina (1990) for explanations that are.

The Theory of Economic Policy

One of the achievements of Keynesian economics was the theory of economic policy, or traditional policy analysis.[20] That is a mathematical expression of the idea that policy instruments under the control of the government might be manipulated systematically to achieve given target values for outcomes such as inflation and unemployment.

The basic idea is that the complex interrelationships of a nation's economy can be represented by a structural model, that is, a system of equations that the uninitiated reader might think of as a "black box." A complete version of such a model would represent markets for labor, for goods, and for financial services and the connections among them. The relationship between a fiscal or monetary policy choice and a desired change in the economy would be defined by the equations that constituted the model of the economy. The model could be estimated to identify the policy instrument choices that would achieve the outcomes that would maximize the welfare function.

This framework would seem to approach the ultimate achievement in making the public policy process scientific. Goals could be set in the political process, and the theory of economic policy would provide an objective technology to achieve them. There is no doubt that the theory of economic policy represents a substantial intellectual achievement. However, it has been subjected to at least two themes of major attack, to be described more fully in the later section of this chapter on the new classical economics and real business cycles. The new classical theory attacked the premise that economic agents would respond to Keynesian manipulation (the "Lucas critique"). The real business cycle theory attacked the "systems of equations" methodological approach.

Keynesian economics has received more attention here than do the other alternatives. The reason is that Keynesian economics is the main source of macroeconomic rationales for government intervention in the economy. Because it advocates active intervention, it is especially subject to the dynamics of political choice.

MONETARISM

Not all economists were swept away by Keynesian economics, but the objections to it were not immediately crystallized into a coherent alternative

---

[20] According to Meltzer (1988), Keynes himself had little enthusiasm for this work. See Tinbergen (1952) for the landmark statement of the theory of economic policy.

theory. Milton Friedman, the main creator of monetarism, offered a coherent alternative that for decades provided a basis for a continuing debate within economics about what could and should be done in regulating the economy. Monetarism returned to the presumption that the macroeconomy was a self-regulating system, and that presumption by itself implied that the appropriate role for government would be less than that implied by Keynesian theory. Monetarism asserted the importance of money and monetary policy but did not advocate activist policy choices. One of its key assertions was that monetary policy could have significant effects on real economic outcomes, but that it did so with "long and variable lags" (Friedman 1953a, p. 144). Because these lags were long and variable, one could not be sure that the stimulative effect of an increase in the money supply would be felt prior to the time the economy had already begun to recover. One could not be sure that it would not have an undesired, inflationary effect.

The general implication of such observations was that discretionary policy was as likely to destabilize the economy as to stabilize it, and it should be avoided. Friedman is famous for his consistent recommendation that monetary policy be guided by rules, rather than by discretion. The rule he suggested is a rate of money growth fixed at a level designed to allow the money stock to grow at a pace that would be consistent with the overall trend for the rate of growth of the economy.

If political risks are associated with monetarism, one such risk might be that adherence to a rule might become too rigid at a time when it was inappropriate, such as Eichengreen (1992a) and Temin (1989) have argued concerning the gold standard during the Depression. There seems to be a trade-off between the need for flexibility and the need for discipline.[21] We will return in Chapters 8 and 9 to a discussion of rules or commitment versus discretion in monetary and fiscal policies.

Monetarism provided a basis for understanding the perverse consequences of one of the more widely discussed kinds of political manipulation. The Nordhaus (1975) model of the political business cycle, to be described in Chapter 3, showed how the effort to create prosperity before an election might be unsustainable and might lead to lasting adverse consequences. Although Nordhaus was not known as a monetarist, the expectational Phillips curve model of the economy he used was quite similar to the model articulated in 1968 in Friedman's presidential address to the American Economic Association. That address showed that the theoretical

---

[21] See Lohmann (1992).

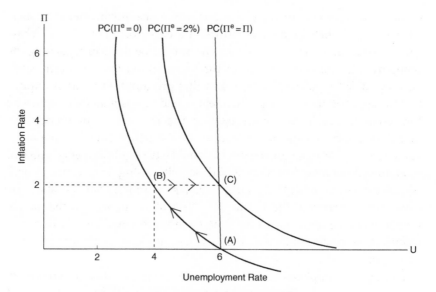

Figure 2.4. Long-run and short-run Phillips curves

basis for the stable Phillips curve trade-off was weak and inadequate. Friedman introduced a distinction between short-run Phillips curves, in which there was a trade-off or inverse relationship between inflation and unemployment, and long-run Phillips curves, in which there was none.

The long-run Phillips curve is a vertical line in a Phillips curve space, reflecting the combinations of inflation and unemployment that are sustainable. The curve shows that the natural rate of unemployment is compatible with any rate of inflation. A policy-induced increase in the money supply could lead firms to confuse a general increase in prices with a relative increase in the prices of their own products. They could respond by increasing nominal wages and hiring more workers. That would constitute a movement to the left on a short-run Phillips curve, as illustrated in Figure 2.4. As soon as workers realized that the general level of prices had risen, they would see that their real wages had declined, and employment would return to its previous level, at the natural rate of unemployment, but at the new, higher level of inflation. For Friedman, such a sequence would reinforce his earlier argument for a rule to guide a stable rate of money growth, as well as prohibition of such manipulation. His work laid the groundwork for identifying some of the risks of discretionary, politically motivated macroeconomic stabilization policy in the form of the political business cycle (Nordhaus 1975).

Keynesian and monetarist theories had divergent implications for the behavior of public officials, but neither had a theory of political motivation. Like much of macroeconomic theory, each was addressed to disinterested, public-spirited policy makers. However, the two theories led to very different observations about the risks of political mismanagement. Keynesian theory involved some prescriptions for activist discretionary fiscal policy that Buchanan and Wagner (1977) argued were subject to risks of mismanagement because the incentives of the political process might interfere with appropriate policy.

Monetarist theory involved no such prescriptions and recommended the avoidance of discretionary policy. Monetarist theory provided a model that Nordhaus (1975) used to show the adverse consequences of political manipulation. Thus, early Keynesian theory proposed discretionary action that would add to the risks of politically motivated mismanagement, whereas monetarist theory recommended the avoidance of discretion but was nonetheless the basis for an argument about the adverse consequences of politically motivated discretion.

NEW CLASSICAL ECONOMICS

The new classical economics, which includes the rational expectations school of macroeconomics, was as emphatic as monetarism in asserting the self-regulating character of the economy, and it was even more emphatic in arguing that discretionary stabilization policy was futile.[22] Friedman's work had shown that attention to the microeconomic processes involved in the inflation-unemployment relationship could generate new insights and improved understanding. The new classical school went even further than monetarism in the search for microfoundations, and it looked for them in the basic premises of microeconomics. These premises hinged on a fundamental assumption that human beings were rational, utility-maximizing actors. New classical theory was also explicitly based on the assumption that all markets, including labor markets, would clear; that is, excess supply would be mopped up by reductions in prices. For example, involuntary

---

[22] The Great Depression poses a major problem for the view that the economy regulates itself. See the discussions by Lucas and by Sargent in Klamer (1984, pp. 41, 69). Conservative economists such as Robert Barro and Milton Friedman blame government policy. See Cole and Ohanian (2004) and Kehoe and Prescott (2007).

unemployment represents excess supply in the labor market, which will be cleared by reductions in wages to the market-clearing level. In Robert Lucas's words, "there is an involuntary element in *all* unemployment, in the sense that no one chooses bad luck over good; there is also a voluntary element in all unemployment, in the sense that however miserable one's current work options, one can always choose to accept them" (Lucas 1981, p. 242, emphasis in original).

In the new classical view, there is no role for activist or discretionary *monetary* stabilization policy, and the general policy recommendation was similar to that of the monetarists: that fixed rules be followed. *Fiscal* stabilization by way of deficit spending would also not make a difference insofar as economic agents think that they will have to pay back the deficit with future taxes.[23] In general, new classical theory generated a rationale for a startling claim called the "policy ineffectiveness proposition," which asserted that systematic stabilization policy was impossible. This was an attack on the Keynesian theory of economic policy described earlier.

Lucas argued that the kinds of models used in that theory "provide *no* useful information as to the actual consequences of alternative economic policies" (1981, p. 105, emphasis in original). The reason was that the equations in these models were not truly fundamental. They did not capture invariant properties of behavior, and their parameters were likely to change in response to policy changes. For example, when a new fiscal or monetary policy is announced, economic agents may change their behavior in response to the policy, with the result that the goals of the new policy will be frustrated.

According to the new classical view, economic agents, including the public, form their expectations rationally. That is, they are forward looking, use all available information optimally, and do not make repeated mistakes. From a position of economic equilibrium, businesses will respond to a monetary policy stimulus only because they confuse a general increase in prices with a relative increase in the demand for their products. Once they figure out that the stimulus came from monetary policy rather than from a real increase in demand, they will readjust back to their previous levels of employment and output.

---

[23] This is a very old idea, known as Ricardian equivalence. In a thorough review of the literature John Seater (1993) argues that although Ricardian equivalence surely does not hold exactly as a theoretical proposition, there is considerable reason to believe that it holds as an approximation. That is, the debt/tax mix does not have much effect on other economic variables.

By extension, monetary policy can affect real behavior only by surprising people, and, therefore, it cannot be systematic. Policies that are not surprises will be expected by rational agents and will be neutralized. The only way for policy to be effective is for policy makers to "trick economic agents into behaving in socially preferable ways even though their behavior is not in their own interest" (R. G. Hall, quoted by Sargent and Wallace 1976, p. 176). In effect, Lucas pointed out that macroeconomic policy making is not decision theory in the sense of a game against inanimate nature; rather, it is a game involving other actors, who may respond strategically rather than passively to policy initiatives.

Even a public-spirited policy maker may try to create a monetary surprise that will increase output, for reasons that will be elaborated in Part Two of this book. But the people will expect the inflation but not respond with the output. A credible set of rules might be designed to keep the policy maker from yielding to that temptation. We will return to such rules in Chapters 8 and 9. Lucas did not shrink from the implication that his views imply a lesser role for economic policy advisors: "As an advice-giving profession, we are in way over our heads" (1981, p. 259). The policy recommendation of the new classical theory is similar to that of the monetarists: that rules should guide policy making. Discretionary monetary policy can only destabilize the economy by confusing people about what conditions to expect. Stable, predictable rules for monetary policy provide an environment in which markets can work more effectively than they can under the destabilizing influences of discretionary policy.

The risk of political mismanagement that is prominent in this theory is the time-consistency problem. In new classical macroeconomics, this problem offers a basis from which one can make a case for rules, but dynamic consistency is a subtle and important issue that goes beyond this variant of theory, and it deserves attention in its own right.

Introducing the Time-Consistency Problem

The time-consistency problem is an important general issue of public policy in which there is an inconsistency between the best general plan and the best thing to do at any given time. Two of the most intuitive formulations of the problem concern policy toward hostages and toward patent law. In the former case, a good general policy for all times is never to negotiate for hostages, because if that policy is believed, there will be no incentive for terrorists to take hostages. However, once hostages are taken, the incentives are strong to negotiate. Similarly, a good general policy is to encourage the development of new products by giving patents that will protect the innovators from economic competition that would drain away their incentives to innovate. However, once a new product exists, such as a cure for AIDS, there may be a powerful incentive to remove the patent protection and let the public enjoy the benefits of competition. Each of these cases reveals an inconsistency between what is best at a particular time and what is best for all times – the difference between a best policy ex ante (for all conditions) and the best policy ex post (after conditions have been realized).

The problem is that conditions will deteriorate if it is expected that the ex post best policy will be followed. Even though a government announces its intention to follow the ex ante best policy, its determination to do so may be questioned by those who understand its incentives to deviate ex post. For example, a government may announce that it will never negotiate for hostages, but if its policy is not believed, the expectation that it will negotiate will encourage the taking of hostages. Similarly, if a government policy to protect inventions with patents is not believed, the expectation that the government will not enforce patents will lead to fewer inventions. Bailing out banks that are considered to be "too big to fail" is an application of this principle that will be taken up in Chapter 5.

The modern proponents of this venerable idea are Finn Kydland and Edward Prescott (1977), who are also contributors to an extension of new classical economics called real business cycle theory, to be discussed later in this chapter. Kydland and Prescott presented several examples, including one macroeconomic case, and Barro and Gordon (1983) developed the macroeconomic implications.[24] The models assume rational behavior on the part of all parties. The basic idea is that unemployment is too high or national income growth is too low, even in a rational expectations equilibrium, because of distortionary features of tax policy or labor markets. For example, individuals may respond to taxes by altering their behavior from its most efficient pattern to reduce their tax liability. Or collective bargaining agreements, minimum wage laws, or unemployment compensation policies may restrict labor supply, keep unemployment too high, or output too low. Both patterns of behavior may reduce economic efficiency, and the policy maker may deal with that problem by instituting a surprise

---

[24] One of Kydland and Prescott's examples involved government aid to people who built on floodplains, and the 1993 Mississippi Valley floods illustrated the relevance of this example. See Albert R. Karr, "False Sense of Security and Cost Concerns Keep Many on Flood Plains from Buying Insurance," *Wall Street Journal*, August 31, 1993.

burst in the money supply, designed to reduce unemployment or increase output.[25]

The increase in the money supply will cause an unexpected increase in prices. Economic agents have trouble distinguishing between a general increase in prices (i.e., inflation) and an increase in the demand for their services or products. If they think it is the latter, they will respond with increased economic activity, thus fulfilling the desire of the public officials to increase output or reduce unemployment. But if, in fact, the increase in prices was a general increase, or inflation induced by the government, the effects will be short lived. If the tactic is tried repeatedly, over time the public will learn to expect inflation and will cease to respond. The result is that there will be no change in unemployment or output, but only increased inflation, to the detriment of everyone.

This application of the dynamic consistency problem is central to much of the contemporary study of political macroeconomics. The public and the policy makers are both considered to be rational, in that both seek to maximize their utility and are assumed to be capable of learning when they need to change their behavior to do so. In other words, both parties understand everything they need to know about their own interests and how to maximize them. But the problem still exists because the wage-setters act first, and they act on their expectations of a money growth rate set by the government. The monetary authority needs to fulfill that expectation just to achieve the natural rate.

Because most of the models of dynamic consistency problems do not directly imply a conflict of interest between the public and the government, we might expect that the whole problem could be avoided by eliminating the distortionary taxes or labor market policies. However, Alex Cukierman has argued that "the underlying source of dynamic inconsistency can be traced in all cases to some basic conflict between policymakers and some groups within the private sector" (1992, p. 21). These could be unions that preferred wages above market-clearing levels, or groups that preferred distortionary taxes that would be borne by other groups. Although Cukierman's assertion that a conflict of interest is behind the time-consistency problem may be too strong to do justice to general examples such as the hostage and patent issues, the conflict-of-interest view makes the existence of the distortions more understandable.[26]

---

[25] See Drazen (2000, chs. 4–6) for a general treatment of the time-consistency problem and solutions to it.

[26] Another economic example involves the temptation for popularly elected governments to tax away the capital stock. See Persson and Tabellini (1990, pt. 2).

In general, the time-consistency problem generates some insights that deserve to be introduced now, and to which we will later return. Kydland and Prescott and Barro and Gordon have argued that the time-consistency problem can be solved by having a rule for the appropriate behavior, thus avoiding the discretion that creates the problem. (Discretion in this case is the *ex post* best thing to do.) But how can rules be enforced? Would not the enforcer also be subject to the same time-consistency problem? Elections might be proposed as an appropriate institution of accountability, but voters themselves might be a source of the temptation to yield. Anticipating problems such as these, Barro and Gordon (1983) developed an argument suggesting that a reputation for following a rule may be an effective constraint on the temptation to yield to the time-consistency problem. This suggests that elections are not the only institutions of accountability for macroeconomic policy.[27]

In an enlightening review of new macroeconomics and political science, Iversen and Soskice (2006) "see time inconsistency as a relatively minor issue in the explanation of the pattern of macroeconomic policies and outcomes" (2006, p. 448; see also p. 430). Several prominent economists agree with them.[28] But Chappell, McGregor, and Vermilyea use records of Federal Reserve meetings to make a compelling case that decisions in the Federal Open Market Committee in the Arthur Burns era fit the time-consistency problem and help explain the great inflation of the 1970s (2005, ch.10).

In a larger sense, I find the time-consistency problem to be at the heart of the financial crisis and its consequences. For a bank or insurance company to be too big to fail is an example of the time-consistency problem. At least since the bailout of the Continental Illinois bank in 1984, major financial institutions have been protected from the downside of the market.[29] Properly working capitalism means that firms work for economic gains and profits, but also that they absorb the losses themselves. The United States has arrived at a system in which gains are private and losses are socialized. This is a time-consistency problem writ large, as will be explained in Chapter 5.

---

[27] Note Cukierman's comparison of trigger strategy versus learning models of rule enforcement (1992, ch. 11).

[28] See Chappell, McGregor, and Vermilyea (2005, p. 162).

[29] Gelinas (2009) dates the change to the early 1980s. McKinley (2011) dates it back to the 1920s.

REAL BUSINESS CYCLES AND NEW KEYNESIAN ECONOMICS

Real business cycle (RBC) theory is in the new classical tradition but, if anything, is even more radical. In Blanchard's words,

> Soon, however, the Mencheviks gave way to the Bolcheviks, and the research agenda became even more extreme. Under Prescott's leadership, nominal rigidities, imperfect information, money, and the Phillips curve, all disappeared from the basic model, and researchers focused on the stochastic properties of . . . a representative agent Arrow-Debreu economy . . . Three principles guided the research: Explicit micro foundations, defined as utility and profit maximization; general equilibrium; and the exploration of how far one could go with no or few imperfections. (2009, p. 211)

Real business cycle theory assumes (at least initially) that markets clear and that markets are efficient in achieving desirable outcomes. Its political implications grow out of the time-consistency issue presented earlier. Indeed, the 1977 Kydland and Prescott article that defined the time-consistency problem is one of the two articles that were the basis for the 2004 Nobel Prize that the two shared "for their contributions to dynamic macroeconomics: the time consistency of economic policy and the driving forces behind business cycles."[30]

A central understanding of RBC theory is that business cycles are caused by technology shocks. Other short-term fluctuations in the macroeconomy are attributed to changes in the costs of raw materials and in consumer preferences. Because the fluctuations are presumed to be the desirable result of rational decisions made by individuals, there is no reason for the government to try to smooth out the fluctuations, even if it could.

RBC theory has made several constructive contributions to macroeconomic theory. One is to insist that the study of economic growth and the study of economic fluctuations or business cycles be integrated. Another is to the methods by which macroeconomics is studied. RBC theorists have been at the forefront of critiques of the systems of equations approach, and have been major contributors to dynamic stochastic general equilibrium (DSGE) models, which dominate the study of graduate-level macroeconomics.

The main policy recommendation of RBC is to follow rules, rather than use event-contingent discretion. Prescott addresses the topic of this book in the final paragraph of his Nobel lecture (2006). He compares himself to

---

[30] http://nobelprize.org/nobel_prizes/economics/laureates/2004/index.html (accessed March 1, 2010). The other article was Kydland and Prescott (1982). See Prescott's Nobel Prize Lecture (2006)

Ragnar Frisch, who, along with Jan Tinbergen, won the first Nobel Prize in Economic Science in 1969:[31]

> Like Frisch, I am a fervent believer in the democratic process. The dimension on which I disagree is how economics and policy makers should interact. His view is that the democratic process should determine the objective, and economists should then determine the best policy given this objective. My view is that economists should educate the people so that they can evaluate the macroeconomic policy rules and that the people, through their elective representatives, should pick the policy rule. I emphasize that Finn and my "Rules Rather than Discretion" paper finds that public debate should be over rules and that rules should be changed only infrequently, with a lag to mitigate the time consistency problem. (2006, p. 232)

So RBC theory does assert that the economy regulates itself, though recent versions recognize nominal rigidities, such as sticky wages and prices. An appropriate rule for monetary policy would be to transparently aim at a low, steady rate of inflation, so that economic agents could coordinate their response to shocks with such a policy rule. Fiscal policy should minimize the distortionary effects of raising revenues to pay for government expenditure. The role for public officials in general is to respond to public preferences for particular policy rules. The main risk of political mismanagement is to deviate from rules and misguidedly to try to do the best thing for the current condition. Bailouts of firms that would otherwise fail would seem to be a good example.

Just as real business cycle theory is an extension of new classical macroeconomics, new Keynesian economics is an extension of traditional Keynesianism. New Keynesian macroeconomics fully accepts the new classical goal of incorporating solid microfoundations of rational individual behavior into the structure of macroeconomic models, while retaining the belief that some unemployment is involuntary. Another important innovation is to view the economy through the lens of imperfect competition.

The new Keynesians explain involuntary unemployment in three important ways. The first models the menu costs of changing prices, which explains why prices do not adjust to clear markets. The second models efficiency wages, by which labor is paid more than the market-clearing price to build loyalty, encourage efficiency, and avoid the costs of retraining workers. The last is insider-outsider models that distinguish workers with extra bargaining power, perhaps from labor unions, from those without.

---

[31] The 1969 prize was won for "for having developed and applied dynamic models for the analysis of economic processes" http://nobelprize.org/nobel_prizes/economics/laureates/1969/index.html (accessed March 1, 2010). This exact citation might well have been used thirty-five years later for Kydland and Prescott.

Real business cycle and new-Keynesian models share a commitment to solid microfoundations of macroeconomic analysis by way of careful modeling of individual-level behavior. This commitment has led to substantial convergence between the two schools.[32]

SUPPLY SIDE ECONOMICS

Supply side economics has a grand intellectual heritage. The very sensible idea that tax rates can be high enough to reduce revenue goes back to Ibn Khaldun, the fourteenth-century Muslim philosopher, and to such notables as Jonathan Swift, David Hume, Adam Smith, and Alexander Hamilton, among others. All recognized that high tax rates can reduce tax revenues by reducing economic activity.[33]

Supply side economics received a great deal of attention in the 1980s when it became known as a guide for the Reagan administration's economic policies. Some of the excessive claims associated with it are highly controversial and not supported by evidence, such as the idea that all reductions in taxes will lead to an increase in revenues.[34] Of course, at some high level of tax rates, a reduction in rates will lead to an increase in revenues, because people will work and produce more when they can keep more of their earnings. It has not been established that rates have been that high in the United States in the period of prominence of supply side arguments.[35] But there is considerable evidence that cuts in income tax rates do not cut revenues as much as the product of the rate difference times the previous tax base.[36]

In terms of filling the role of a major alternative macroeconomic theory to compete with Keynesian, monetarist, and new classical theories, supply side economics is not a serious contender. However, in an important sense, supply side economics reflects a once needed recognition that aggregate supply is an important macroeconomic issue deserving more attention than it had received for decades. In this regard, all economists are now supply-siders, in that they recognize that institutions and policies affect the

---

[32] See Froyen (2009, ch. 12) and Mankiw (1990).

[33] See Bartlett (2009, pp. 124–8) for a discussion of the intellectual origins of supply side economics.

[34] See Bartlett (2009, p. 124).

[35] But the top marginal rate in the U.S. income tax was 94 percent in 1944 and 1945. It was 91 percent from 1954 through 1963, and no lower than 70 percent between 1965 and 1980. See http://www.truthandpolitics.org/top-rates.php, accessed June 3, 2010.

[36] See Bartlett (2009, pp. 109–22).

incentives to produce and thereby influence the efficiency of the economy and the amounts of goods and services supplied.

The most prominent political manifestation of supply side economics is presumed intellectual support for a general aversion to taxes. This is reflected in the continuing vigorous opposition to almost any tax increases. This opposition has become a mantra for Republicans, whereas Democrats do not contest the principle, but respond by proposing tax increases only on "the rich." In spite of this legitimate concern for incentives on the supply side of the economy, supply side thinking has had an enormous and in my view not very constructive impact on politics. It has led to many politicians viewing tax cuts as the primary solution to many problems, whether or not an appropriate one, and to tax increases being politically deadly, whether or not appropriate.

In my view, this popularization of supply side economics has contributed to the fiscal crisis that will be discussed in Chapters 5 and 9. In conjunction with rising inequality in the United States, it has contributed to a class warfare that is corrosive of political life. The American income tax is now very progressive, and nearly half of the public pays no income taxes. There is much misunderstanding about who bears the income tax burden in the United States, and neither proponents nor the critics of tax cuts are enlightening about that subject. Popularized supply side economics has not contributed a theory of optimal taxation or to sensible discussion of budget policy. Its implicit target for tax levels seems to be zero. There is little apparent concern for fairness or efficiency on either side of the partisan political divide in the United States.

ANIMAL SPIRITS AND BEHAVIORAL ECONOMICS

Much of modern economics is based explicitly on the premise that individual economic agents are rational, selfish utility maximizers. Until the rational expectations revolution of the 1970s, this presumption was most central to microeconomics. Macroeconomics had dealt with aggregates without much attention to individual behavior.

As just noted, the rational expectations revolution had insisted that macroeconomic models be built with microfoundations of individual behavior that were totally rational and without animal spirits, which were defined by Keynes as spontaneous optimism as distinguished from mathematical expectation (1936, p. 161). I find this a constructive development and believe that macroeconomics has become much deeper by making it consistent with microeconomic models of individual behavior. This much can be seen as an effort to make consistent two respected bodies of knowledge.

The field of behavioral economics has flourished in recent years, building on compelling evidence that economic agents sometimes do not make rational decisions, that they make repeated and systematic mistakes, and that they operate with biases and heuristics.[37] Behavioral economics can be seen as an effort to make psychology and microeconomics consistent, and I also approve of that. Behavioral economics has been mainly about individual behavior and has not for the most part been applied to the study of macroeconomics.[38] An exception to this observation is the work of George Akerlof and Robert Shiller, and their book *Animal Spirits: How Human Psychology Drives the Economy and Why It Matters for Global Capitalism* (2009).

Let me say that the effort to make psychology and economics consistent makes sense to me. I find it as admirable as the new classical effort to make macroeconomics consistent with microeconomic models of individual behavior, and for the same reasons. Both are respected bodies of knowledge, and the payoffs of integrating psychology with economics have been high.

The Akerlof and Shiller book is structured into two parts. Part one contains five chapters under the heading of Animal Spirits, dealing with subjects such as confidence, fairness, corruption, money illusion, and stories. The basic premise is that economic agents are influenced by these phenomena, which are at least orthogonal to, if not at odds with, rational utility maximization. Part two deals with eight questions and their answers. These include the following: "Why do economies fall into depression?" "Why are there people who cannot find a job?" "Why do real estate markets go through cycles?" Their answers to these and other questions are compelling ad hoc combinations of the five variables of the first part of the book, such as confidence and money illusion.

As far as I can tell, this work has not made much of an impact on macroeconomic theory, although Shiller is regularly quoted in connection with his widely used index of housing prices.[39] But the Akerlof and Shiller book has been reviewed by Roger Farmer, who is an authority on animal

---

[37] See Ariely (2008), Thaler and Sunstein (2009), and Kahneman (2011).

[38] Ironically, behavioral economics has in my view been more central to the study of finance than to macroeconomics. See Fox (2009, chs. 10, 11, 16).

[39] See the S&P/Case-Shiller Home Price Indices: http://www.standardandpoors.com/indices/sp-case-shiller-home-price-indices/en/us/?indexId=spusa-cashpidff-p-us——.

spirits.[40] Farmer's (2009) review of Akerlof and Shiller makes three points: their definition of animal spirits is too broad, a 25-year research program has been focused on a much narrower definition, and the authors do not offer a credible alternative theory in the sense that it takes a model to beat a model.

The first two points need to be discussed together. Farmer refers to a research program that stays within the new classical paradigm of individual rationality. Farmer's (2008) *New Palgrave* article outlines this program, which revolves around self-fulfilling prophesies and multiple equilibria.[41] The program deviates from most new classical theories in that it does not assume that the economy regulates itself. A key point is that equilibria are based on rational but self-fulfilling expectations, could be desirable or undesirable, and have low or high unemployment. Farmer objects to giving up on the rationality premise in part because he does not need to do so to get to multiple equilibria, and he is able to derive interesting and useful results from his work (Farmer 2010a, 2010b). Fair enough.

The other point is less well taken. He says that behavioral economists

assert that what makes individuals truly happy is different from what they in fact choose to do. In Akerlof and Shiller's words, "capitalism . . . does not automatically produce what people really need; it produces what they *think* they need" (p. 26). To a classical liberal like me, this is a scary proposition since it gives a license to someone else, someone who *knows my true preferences*, to act on my behalf. Is this the government or the church? Both institutions have claimed that right in the past, with disturbing outcomes. (Farmer 2009, p. 357, emphasis in original)

This inference is not fair to Akerlof and Shiller. They do not go from behavioral economics to authoritarianism, either political or clerical. They do go from the quoted sentence to consumer protection agencies, limited liability corporations, and the accounting profession (2009, pp. 26–8). Richard Thaler and Cass Sunstein (2009) suggest using behavioral economics to frame choices to encourage better decisions. They call this "libertarian paternalism." One example of this is the status quo from which choices are made, such as allowing employees the choice of opting in or out of self-funded retirement system (2009, ch. 6).

Farmer's most telling critique of Akerlof and Shiller's *Animal Spirits* is that it "does not connect the five meanings of animal spirits into a coherent theory that explains why they make sense" (Farmer 2009, p. 358). Akerlof

---

[40] See Farmer (2008) his entry for animal spirits in the second edition of the *New Palgrave Dictionary of Economics*.

[41] See Farmer's own contributions to this program in Farmer (2010a, 2010b).

and Shiller do not build their argument on a systematic analysis of the strengths and weaknesses of previous macroeconomic research. Nor do they present a theory that is coherent and rigorous by the standards of contemporary macroeconomics. In my opinion, much is to be gained by making macroeconomics with its rationality assumptions compatible with what is known about psychology as elaborated in the growing field of behavioral economics.

THE STATE OF MACRO

At this writing in 2013, there are at least two themes in the study of macroeconomic stabilization.[42] On one side are arguments that there has been some convergence on something called "modern macro," and a prestigious macroeconomist has pronounced recently that "the state of macro is good" (Blanchard 2009). Blanchard notes convergence into a "largely shared vision both of fluctuations and of methodology." Michael Woodford, another leading macroeconomist, has found that "there are fewer fundamental disagreements among macroeconomists now than in past decades" (2009, p. 267).[43]

Outsiders might be forgiven for thinking that this consensus had missed something, as so few macroeconomists foresaw the recent financial crisis. Readers of *The Economist*[44] and of the *New York Times Magazine*[45] have seen trenchant criticisms of the field. Of course, successful prediction is not necessarily the hallmark of a science. Geology and evolutionary biology have good credentials as scientific disciplines even though they are strongest in helping us understand the past. Nouriel Roubini, Robert Shiller, and Raghuram Rajan used their economic expertise to alert us to a crisis, but many distinguished macroeconomists failed to do so. Nobel Prize–winning macroeconomist Robert Lucas observed that the efficient markets hypothesis (EMH) denies the possibility of predicting crashes: "The main lesson we should take away from the EMH for policymaking purposes is the futility of trying to deal with crises and recessions by finding central bankers and regulators who can identify and puncture bubbles. If these people exist, we will not be able to afford them" (2009, p. 67).

---

[42] This review has focused largely on the stabilization part and, for the most part, ignored the growth part of macroeconomics. This is because most of the literature linking political behavior to macroeconomic policy and performance is about stabilization.

[43] There is a symposium on "Macroeconomics after the Financial Crisis" in the fall 2010 *Journal of Economic Perspectives*.

[44] July 18, 2009, pp. 11–12, 65–9.

[45] Krugman (2009).

Olivier Blanchard has written an article for first *Annual Review of Economics* on "The State of Macro," in which he described "enormous progress and substantial convergence [into] a largely shared vision both of fluctuations and of methodology" (2009). This shared vision includes acknowledgment that aggregate demand fluctuates and that nominal rigidities matter, crediting Keynesian theories. The shared vision also includes an acknowledgment of the role of technological progress in fluctuations, crediting new classical theories.

Using a "toy model" that he designates as new-Keynesian, even though it builds on new classical assumptions, Blanchard concludes that the policy implications are that "Strict inflation targeting is good, both for inflation and for output" (2009). At this writing, with an anemic recovery, with unemployment more than 7 percent, and with the Dodd-Frank Wall Street Reform and Consumer Protection Act still being implemented, it is appropriate for Blanchard to list unemployment and credit and financial markets as needing further work in the advancement of macroeconomics.[46]

THE POLITICS OF MACROECONOMIC THEORY

This chapter has reviewed the main strands in contemporary macroeconomic theory as if they were branches of political theory. That is, I have focused on the political issues in these theories: what they contend that public officials should do, and what they identify as the risks of political mismanagement. Each of the theories consists of a relatively coherent body of knowledge. Each new theory seems to have grown out of some important limitations of its predecessor, and there has been intellectual progress. Proponents of the older theories have made revisions in response to the challenges of the newer theories, and there has been an evolutionary advance of knowledge, as well as some convergence. For example, it is possible to see Keynesian and monetarist theories as having converged in terms of structure, but disagreeing on rather narrow issues such as the sizes of various parameters in the equations on which they agree.[47]

What remains is a body of scientific thought whose diverging theories remain matters of dispute among the people who have the best professional credentials for evaluating such theories. This, I contend respectfully, is a

---

[46] If the convergence in theory is fragile and contestable, the convergence in method is not. Blanchard recounts the replacement of the systems of equations methods by dynamic stochastic general equilibrium (DSGE) methods.

[47] See Hoover (1988, ch.1).

political dispute, because it is about public issues, and because there are contending alternative viewpoints that cannot always be objectively resolved. Macroeconomic theory is contestable theory.

There has been progress in macroeconomic theory, and new developments build on the weakness of previous theory. The debate usually takes place on a high level, and it involves a dialogue under the conventional rules of fair and objective discourse. In that regard, it is often a model for what public and electoral politics should be. A distinction might be drawn between what economists study and how they study it. Typically, economic models are models of rational choice behavior in which individual actors seek to maximize their utility. Game-theoretic models of strategic interaction characterize how these rational economic persons may interact with each other in market and nonmarket settings. But rational actor models of strategic interaction are poor characterizations of what economists do. What they do is more like what Jürgen Habermas called communicative action, which "operates in the medium of language and is oriented toward reaching understanding" (Johnson 1993, p. 75).

Macroeconomists remain divided on the fundamental questions of whether or not the economy regulates itself and whether the proper role for public officials should be active or passive. However, as the theories have become more sophisticated about economic issues, they have moved steadily away from the presumption that good theory will be implemented directly without regard for the incentives of the political process. The remainder of this book addresses these incentives.

PART TWO

MODELS OF MACROECONOMIC POLITICS
IN A DEMOCRACY

This section reviews contemporary political economy models of political behavior. The first two chapters address models of routine electoral politics. Chapter 3, Models of Accountability and Opportunism, deals with the timing of elections and how opportunistic politicians might try to manipulate the economy for their own benefit. Chapter 4, Models of Choice, deals with how different parties might structure the choices available to voters. Both are models of regular politics revolving around elections, the most visible of the defining characteristics of democracy.

Both the electoral cycle and the partisan models have advanced in the past decades. One major source of this progress is the recognition of the wider implications of the uncertainty introduced by elections. Elections as institutions of accountability and choice also inevitably introduce the possibility that the identity of governments will change, and this uncertainty can have economic consequences that may or may not be constructive. Almost all models of routine politics assume that incumbents or parties are motivated by policy goals, office goals, or a combination of the two.

Chapter 5 is a new chapter in this edition about irregular or non-routine politics in the United States. It identifies some of the ways that political choices have had unintended adverse consequences. This chapter also deals with irregular events such as financial crises and shows the importance of time-consistency and moral hazard. It raises questions about the benign message of the previous edition of this book. Chapter 5 also addresses the second essential feature of democracy – limitations on government. In the United States, this includes separation of powers and the freedom to petition the government for redress of grievances (i.e., to lobby).

Models of Accountability and Opportunism: The Electoral Cycle

This is the first of two chapters that review the two most prominent models or theories of politics in macroeconomic policy making: the electoral cycle theory and the partisan theory. Each of these theories captures special features of democratic politics and helps us understand democratic dynamics. In doing so, they abstract from the institutional details through which economic policy is made. Each leaves a great deal about macroeconomic politics unexamined and unexplained. The electoral cycle model focuses on periodic elections as the democratic institution of interest, and the partisan model focuses on dual alternatives in these elections. Both types of models connect these features of focal interest to macroeconomic outcomes: unemployment, income growth, and sometimes inflation and income distribution.

In the real world, the impacts of elections and party differences are mediated through the complex institutional structure of fiscal and monetary policy making. For example, most of the contemporary models to be considered in these two chapters presume that governments influence macroeconomic performance through monetary policy, that is, through government control of the money supply and interest rates. Monetary policy is controlled by central banks, such as the U.S. Federal Reserve System ("the Fed"). Electoral cycle and partisanship models often assume that the Fed obediently follows the preferences of politically motivated public officials. In fact, the Fed is considered to be one of the most politically independent of the central banks in the industrialized nations. Therefore, the idea that it is merely a transmission mechanism for politically motivated policy is problematic. Similarly, fiscal policy, that is, taxing and spending policy, has been seen as a channel for political manipulation of the economy. In the United States, these policies are the products of complex interactions among the two houses of Congress and the president. No observer of the contemporary scene would claim that that there is reliable and predictable cooperation among these actors, whether or not they are controlled by the same party.

The institutions of monetary and fiscal policies are themselves (in principle) matters of choice. Their features will be the subject of Chapters 8 and 9, respectively. Some readers may wish to look ahead to familiarize themselves with institutional details. But such details are not necessary to understand the models presented in this chapter and the next, which intentionally ignore such issues. This chapter reviews a class of models that suggest ways in which elections themselves, the main institution for ensuring accountability in a democracy, may have undesirable consequences. We begin with a simple and intuitive version.

PASSIVE VOTERS AND CASUALLY OPPORTUNISTIC POLITICIANS

Edward Tufte has offered an intuitive account of how elections may lead to cyclical policy making. He first presents a rationale in terms of the beliefs of politicians. According to his distillation of the "politicians' theory" (Tufte 1978, p. 9), economic movements just before an election can be decisive: voters reward incumbents for prosperity and punish them for recession, and spurts in growth before an election will benefit incumbents. These beliefs provide an even greater incentive to try to show better economic performance near elections than at other times, or a "motive," in Tufte's words.

Tufte provided evidence of cycles in macroeconomic outcomes. As of 1978, he found two-year cycles in disposable income, with peaks just before congressional and presidential elections, and four-year cycles in unemployment, with troughs just before presidential elections. He also found two-year cycles in transfer payments, such as veterans' benefits and Social Security. Two-year cycles were found in areas that can be relatively easily controlled by government, such as the mailing of checks and, by extension, disposable income. It is less easy for government to manipulate unemployment, which was said to follow a four-year rather than a two-year cycle, rising through the first half of an administration and falling through the second half (Tufte, 1978, ch. 2).

The hypothesized motive for manipulation of such cycles is to enhance the incumbents' prospects for reelection. In fact, the incumbent party has lost eight of the sixteen American presidential elections since 1952; in three cases, the incumbent president himself lost. These facts suggest that there are limits to the electoral cycle hypothesis as a theory that integrates incumbent policy making and electoral outcomes. If incumbents were able to manipulate economic performance to win elections, we might expect them to have won more often than they have. In a case such as the 1980 election, incumbent defeat can be compatible with the electoral cycle hypothesis. It has been said with tongue in cheek that in the Carter administration, the cycle was run backward (i.e., with the best economic performance at the beginning instead of at the end of the term), and President Carter's defeat could be said to confirm a theory that manipulation pays, or at least that failure to manipulate is punished.

Tufte acknowledges that the Eisenhower administrations did not manipulate the economy according to an electoral cycle, but he argues that this case was exceptional, and he treats it as irrelevant rather than as a counter-example. In fact, Eisenhower's electoral success demonstrated that it is not necessary to manipulate the business cycle to succeed in politics. Still, the fact that the incumbent party lost eight of the past sixteen presidential elections does not say that incumbents do not try to induce electoral cycles or that they never succeed. But this record of defeat for the incumbent party clearly indicates that other things are also important.[1] Cyclical manipulation of the economy is not the key to understanding either election outcomes or the performance of the economy.

Regardless of the strength of the empirical evidence, Tufte provides a commentary that helps us conceptualize the costs of democracy. He argues that the "electoral-economic cycle breeds a lurching stop-and-go economy the world over [and] a bias toward policies with immediate, highly visible benefits and deferred, hidden costs – myopic policies for myopic voters" (1978, p. 143). This sounds pretty bad, but the resulting instability and inefficiency are "the price we pay for having elections," (1978, p. 149) according to Tufte, and should be compared with the kinds of policies that might result from having no elections at all. The implicit suggestion is that policies unconstrained by elections would be arbitrary and capricious, if not exploitative and tyrannical. But of course, there is no single prediction of economic performance for nondemocratic systems, any more than a single cyclical pattern characterizes economic performance under elections.

---

[1] See Weatherford (1987) for an analysis of how a president's economic ideology and the organization of an administration's economic advising can create a variety of circumstances that can undermine the power of any single hypothesis. Golden and Poterba (1980) argued that the amount of stimulus that would bring meaningful political gains would be more than that observed in empirical models of the manipulation of fiscal and monetary policies.

Tufte suggests that democratic control over economic policy is inevitably political, but that such manipulation may be no more serious than the resulting inefficiency (1978, p. 149).[2] Here, then, is a preliminary statement of the costs of democracy: inefficiency that is the reasonable price for something desirable, where the undefined alternative is implied to be much worse. This view is sensible, but not completely satisfying. I will try to define these costs more precisely and consider whether or not there are ways of minimizing them.

THE STRATEGY OF MODELING

To get more informative answers to such questions, we will use simplified abstractions of important features of political processes (i.e., models). Models strip away inessential details that distract from our focus on the question of interest. The strategy of modeling is central to economics and is increasingly common in political science. Much of the analysis in this book draws on what might be called the application of the methodology of economics to political questions.

For a model of the electoral cycle hypothesis, I will present an initial simplification by considering the electorate as if all voters had the same preferences for economic performance, and as if economic performance was their only concern. Thus, we ignore other issues and suppress possible conflicts of interest among voters. We consider the government as another single person, ignoring issues of collective decisions within government. We assume further that the government is motivated purely by the desire to win reelection, ignoring other reasonable possibilities. If the government fails to win reelection, it is replaced with another government that is just like it.[3] For now, we do not recognize differences among politicians, either in their policy goals or in their competence to achieve goals.

This view suggests a model in which the key interaction is across a horizontal divide:

government
<hr>
voters

---

[2] Note that Olson (1993) provides a basis for a hypothesis that some democracies may be more inefficient than some dictatorships.

[3] For some pure theory on such an interaction, see Barro (1973), Ferejohn (1986), and Fearon (1999).

Modeled in this way, the electoral cycle hypothesis is a pure principal-agent problem between voters as the principal and government as their agent.[4] This interaction depends on the following factors:

1. The motivation of politicians, modeled as the single goal of winning elections or of maximizing votes. For example, George H. W. Bush once said that "I will do whatever I have to do to be re-elected" (interview with David Frost, January 23, 1991). Note that this statement may have different interpretations. Elections are the main institution through which the people express their preferences, and the statement could mean that "I will do everything I have to do to give the people what they want." Of course, the statement lends itself to a more cynical interpretation, such as that "I will do whatever it takes to win, regardless of principle, and regardless of whether or not it fulfills the wishes and needs of the voters in a broad sense." The models we consider will help us sort out such interpretations.[5]

2. The behavior of voters, modeled as voters' decisions made on the basis of past economic performance. For example, voters are often thought to ask, "What have you done for me lately?" The models we consider will help us assess the consequences of such a standard for voting. In Chapter 7, we will consider directly the evidence on how voters behave.

3. The capacity of the government to manipulate the economic outcomes to which voters respond, presumably through fiscal or monetary policy. The models to be considered will vary somewhat according to their dependence on alternatives among the macroeconomic theories reviewed in Chapter 2.

Other models with other features will be seen throughout the book. But this initial formulation of an electoral cycle model characterizes that used by William Nordhaus in a seminal article to be described next.

PASSIVE VOTERS AND MAXIMIZING OPPORTUNISTIC POLITICIANS

William Nordhaus (1975) presents an account of how elections might lead to cyclical policy making, an account that differs from Tufte's. Nordhaus

---

[4] For an accessible introduction to agency theory in a political context, see Kiewiet and McCubbins (1991, ch. 2). See also Kreps (1990, ch. 16) for a more theoretical introduction.

[5] See Canes-Wrone (2006) for a subtle interpretation of "pandering" versus "leadership."

presents a formal mathematical model of how elections might systematically lead to demonstrably inferior policy outcomes. The formal model allows him to draw stronger conclusions than could Tufte, but these conclusions are contingent on the realism or verisimilitude of the model. To facilitate exposition, I substantially simplify what Nordhaus presents, without violating the spirit or the content of his work.

Nordhaus models goals with *objective functions*, which are mathematical equations that allow us to quantify the degree to which goals are achieved. An example of an objective function would be the well-known "misery index," which is simply the sum of the rates of inflation and unemployment. A mathematical way of stating this is to say that "misery" is an unweighted additive function of the unemployment and inflation rates: $M = U + \pi$. For example, the misery index in the election year 2008 was 9.7, given the unemployment rate of 5.9 and the inflation rate of 3.8.[6]

Nordhaus uses two versions of the misery index as objective functions, where the only difference between the two is the weighting of time. One, called the "vote function," is designed to show what a vote-maximizing politician will do. It is a misery index that is averaged over the period between elections, but weighted so that the part just before the election at issue counts most heavily, and the part just after the preceding election counts least. This is a way of presenting the idea that voters may forget or ignore the past and ask, mainly, "What have you done for me lately?"

The other objective function that Nordhaus uses is called a "welfare function," and it is designed to measure general social welfare, or wellbeing (not public assistance). This is also a misery index that is averaged over electoral periods, but it is weighted differently with respect to time. To simplify, we will treat it as not weighted at all, that is, counting the same weight for each time period, whether early or late in the electoral period. The idea is that citizens' well-being matters at all times, not just before elections.

These two objective functions allow Nordhaus to analyze alternative kinds of behavior by the government. They will permit us to infer what a government would do if it maximized votes, and to contrast that with what it would do if it maximized social welfare. Put differently, this allows a comparison between a generic politician, who is assumed to maximize votes, and a generic benevolent dictator, or guardian, who is assumed to maximize social welfare.

---

[6]   To infer misery indices for any other year from 1949 through 2011, see Table 4.3.

For example, consider the following misery indices for the Nixon administrations:

	Unemployment	+	Inflation	=	Misery
1969	3.5		5.5		9.0
1970	4.9		5.7		10.6
1971	5.9		4.4		10.3
1972	5.6		3.2		8.8
1973	4.9		6.2		11.1
1974	5.6		11.0		16.6

The average misery index for the first administration was 9.7, but the best figure was for the election year 1972, and conditions got much worse after the election. Many observers have argued that President Nixon manipulated the timing of economic events so as to maximize his chances for reelection in 1972, at the expense of well-being after the election.[7] Indeed, that experience may well have inspired the Nordhaus and Tufte scholarship, which appeared subsequently.

A politician who seeks to maximize votes might try to concentrate good times in periods before elections. That would make sense, given that goal, if voters were thought to forget or discount what had happened early in the electoral period, and if voters were not thought to be able to relate events near the election to conditions afterward.

But what would a politician who seeks to maximize the public welfare do? Such a politician would not concentrate the good times into periods in which the voters were paying more attention. He or she presumably would want to keep the misery index as low as possible all of the time, and he or she surely would not make things unsustainably good near elections at the expense of being worse later on.

Neither kind of public official can simply set the misery index as low as he or she wants, say at zero, because real-world limitations affect what can be done. So next we need a model of the possibilities and the limitations on the achievement of either goal. This is called a *constraint*, and it is a way of representing the way the economy works. The economics of the model of the constraint that Nordhaus used are those of the natural rate of unemployment, as explained in Chapter 2. Certain features of this model are no longer widely accepted in economics, but I present it for illustrative purposes.

---

[7]　See Sanford Rose, "The Agony of the Federal Reserve," *Fortune*, July 1974, p. 90. See also Abrams and Butkiewicz (2012) for evidence from the Nixon tapes.

The essential features of the model of the economy that Nordhaus uses are that inflation and unemployment are inversely related in the short run, but not over the long run. A "natural rate" of unemployment is determined by features of the labor market and the laws regarding it. This natural rate is consistent with any rate of inflation, including zero. Efforts to drive the unemployment rate below the natural rate will create inflation; moreover, unemployment rates below the natural rate cannot be sustained without accelerating inflation.

This is a model of intertemporal choice; it does not deal with distributional issues at all. A central feature is the way policy outcomes are dependent on what has happened before. The model explains how it might be possible for politicians to create unsustainably low combinations of inflation and unemployment before elections, at the expense of higher combinations afterward. In other words, Nordhaus presents a theory of how politicians might take advantage of voter naïveté by making things look good at election time, while their actions are such that they will cause things to be bad after the election. The way this works is illustrated in Table 3.1. Note again that this pattern hinges on a theory of the way the economy works, which may or may not be correct, as well as on other premises regarding political behavior.

Nordhaus's tightly constructed model allows him to derive powerful normative implications: "Under conditions where voting is an appropriate mechanism for social choice, democratic systems will choose a policy on the long-run trade-off that has lower unemployment and higher inflation than is optimal" (Nordhaus 1975, p. 178). It took radical simplification to get that answer, and the answer depends on the veracity of that simplification. Whatever its veracity, the result helps us think about the costs of democracy.

Nordhaus's model provides an explicit comparison between what happens in his stylized democracy and the "best possible policy." The best policy is defined by Nordhaus, and it is defined outside of the model, that is, exogenously. For Nordhaus, a superior policy is economically (technically) feasible. As he characterizes democracy, with passive voters who have no capacity to learn, superior policy is politically feasible only outside of democracy. Superior policy is feasible if a benevolent dictator or guardian is feasible, but we are not shown a system in which such a policy maker is a practical alternative.

This cost of democracy as conceptualized by Nordhaus seems a little more pathological than the one described by Tufte. The difference is that policy in the Nordhaus version is distinctly inferior to a feasible and clearly identifiable alternative. Also, it depends on behavior by voters that would indicate that they are not very smart, if not actually irrational. If Nordhaus were correct on all counts, we might say that the economically feasible and

Table 3.1. *Illustrating the Nordhaus model*

Π is inflation; U is unemployment; M is the misery index. U^n is the natural rate of unemployment, and Π^e, the expected inflation, is modeled as inflation in the preceding period.

Modeling goals with objective functions:

Misery index at time $t = M_t = U_t + \Pi_t$

Modeling the way the economy works, the constraint. What follows is a model of an expectations-augmented Phillips curve, with a natural rate of unemployment:

$$\Pi = \Pi^e - 0.5(U - U^n)$$

Assume that the natural rate of unemployment is 6 percent and that the policy maker can manipulate the actual unemployment rate at will. The resulting inflation is defined by the preceding equation.

Consider the following scenario as a possible result of an effort to maximize votes:

	Π	Π^e	U	Misery index
Period 3	0.0	0.0	6	6.0
Period 4	0.5	0.0	5	5.5
Period 1	0.5	0.5	6	6.5
Period 2	0.0	0.5	7	7.0
Period 3	0.0	0.0	6	6.0
Period 4	0.5	0.0	5	5.5

In period 3, inflation is zero, and unemployment is at the natural rate. At 6.0, the misery index is at its lowest sustainable rate. By reducing unemployment to 5 percent in the election year, the gain from lowering unemployment outweighs the cost due to inflation, and the misery index drops to 5.5, which is not sustainable. However, the misery index rises in the year after the election. To repeat the cycle for the next election, unemployment is raised to 7 percent in the second year. The average misery index is 6.25 under such manipulation, whereas it is possible to maintain the misery index at 6.0.

---

preferable outcomes are not politically feasible. But even that would be true only so long as voters are not able to learn to avoid self-defeating behavior. Nordhaus's voters are modeled as passive; however, active, strategic voters might defeat the manipulative behavior in this model. The rational expectations view gives voters much more credit, and an article by Brender and Drazen (2005) provides some supportive evidence.

SOPHISTICATED CITIZENS AS ECONOMIC AGENTS AND AS VOTERS

The Nordhaus model puts together three kinds of behavior: that of politicians, that of citizens as economic agents, and that of citizens as voters.

Nordhaus's assumptions about politicians and his view of citizens as voters are both still widely accepted. Contemporary studies offer richer assumptions about politicians and acknowledge that they may be motivated by policy goals and by the rewards of office as well as by the desire for votes, but the vote motive is still widely acknowledged. Also, Nordhaus's assumption that voters vote in response to retrospective evaluations of recent economic performance is also widely accepted.[8]

The weakest link in Nordhaus's model from the point of view of contemporary scholarship is that between the politician's decisions and the performance of the economy. Few informed observers believe that policy makers can manipulate the performance of unemployment or income growth with anything like the kind of precision that is assumed in the Nordhaus model of electoral cycles, if at all. The reason that politicians in his model can manipulate the unemployment and inflation rates depends on a contested, if not discredited, theory about individual-level economic behavior, specifically, an "adaptive expectations" model of the formation of inflationary expectations. Many economists think that citizens (as economic agents) are too rational to be manipulated in that way. According to "rational expectations" theory (which was originally associated with the new classical view but is now much more widespread), citizens would see that the government was trying to expand the economy from an equilibrium, and once they realized that, they would cease to respond.

Some readers may be appropriately puzzled by the different understandings of human behavior in the disciplines of economics and political science. Patterns of behavior that most economists assume to exist and call rational are considerably more sophisticated than the patterns that most political scientists believe to exist. Furthermore, most political scientists put far less weight on the assumption that human behavior is rational as a basic premise for their scholarly discipline.[9]

For example, according to a widely accepted contemporary understanding in economics, citizens would defeat most government manipulation of the economy in their capacity as economic agents. They would be able to learn that the government was trying to stimulate the economy beyond its

---

[8]   But see Erikson, MacKuen, and Stimson (2000).

[9]   Since the first edition of this book, a field of behavioral economics has emerged and gotten the attention of the economics profession, with articles in leading journals and Nobel Prizes in economic science. We saw in Chapter 2 on macroeconomic theories that it applies psychology to economic decision making. It has not to my knowledge been applied to the study of political business cycles as yet. See Ariely (2008), Thaler and Sunstein (2009), and Kahneman (2011).

natural capacities, and they would defeat that effort by not responding as employers, employees, investors, and consumers. That is, according to rational expectations views of the economy, the manipulation that Nordhaus models could not even occur, because the economy would not respond, because citizens are assumed to be rational economic agents who could not be manipulated in that way. In Chapter 7, we will encounter more observations about voter rationality.

According to widely accepted understandings in political science, however, citizens as voters might well reward politicians for such manipulation if it were to take place, because voters are seen as responding to recent past performance. Because each discipline has its own specialized audience, inconsistencies between them are not always confronted. We will return to this issue in Chapter 7 when we consider voting behavior. At this point, we can say that Nordhaus's model of electoral cycles in inflation and unemployment is of historical and theoretical interest. It is no longer taken seriously in economics, though other models of electoral cycles are.

Rational Expectations Models of Political Manipulation: Raising the Question of Competence

There have been several theoretical analyses of the interactions between the politicians who determine macroeconomic policy and citizens who are assumed to be rational in the demanding sense assumed by most economists. Such studies continue the assumption that politicians are alike in their goals and motivations. There are no divergent policy preferences, but they introduce the idea that politicians may differ in terms of their "competence."

This is an important innovation. Even in a simplified modeling world with no differences in political preferences, politicians may differ in their abilities to achieve agreed-upon goals. And elections are important institutions to allow voters to remove incumbents who fail to accomplish such goals. In the models that introduce competence, citizens are assumed to be rational utility maximizers and therefore to be able to interact strategically with government if necessary, rather than being passive, as they were in Tufte's and Nordhaus's studies. This, by itself, is an important advance. If government repeatedly manipulates the economy to fool voters, should we not expect that it is possible for voters to learn how to respond in their own interest?

When citizens are modeled as capable of strategic behavior, the interaction between citizens and government may become a game of asymmetric information, in which the government may use superior information to achieve its goals. For example, Rogoff and Sibert (1988) and Rogoff (1990) assume that the public can monitor the government's competence perfectly after a lag. This lag introduces a temporary information asymmetry that allows a government to deceive the voters about its competence. Even if voters understand perfectly the motivations of politicians and the constraints under which they operate, the government still might try to signal its competence by manipulating taxes, spending levels, deficits, money growth, or the balance of government consumption and investment before elections.

It is ironic that the effort to demonstrate the appearance of competence to democratic electorates would have destabilizing consequences. Rogoff and Sibert do not draw precise conclusions about the welfare consequences of such efforts, though they do say that "elections are not necessarily a bad thing, just because they result in excessive inflation or a suboptimal distribution of tax distortions over time. By holding elections, the public gets a more competent government, on average" (1988, p. 12).

Rogoff (1990, p. 31) shows that institutional reforms may restrain manipulation, but at the expense of useful information. In these very abstract and mathematical models, incumbents are modeled as caring about both reelection and social welfare, and the relative weights of the two concerns are permitted to vary. As such, their models leave us with new insights regarding possible costs of democracy, but without clearly identified pathologies.

We might expect that sophisticated voters could in time learn to act strategically against predictable kinds of manipulation if they understood the constraints as well as economists often assume they do. But the more enduring insight of these studies of rational electorates is that even at the most demanding levels of strategic interaction between voters and politicians, the government is likely to have and to exploit an informational advantage in what game theorists call an asymmetric information game.

A general formulation of the asymmetric information insight is found in the work of Cukierman and Meltzer (1986). This paper is not oriented to specific policy instruments, as the Rogoff papers are, but it is grounded in the realistic presumption that the performance of the economy is not perfectly predictable but is affected by chance. That is, it is stochastic, and its performance is affected by random shocks. Cukierman and Meltzer point out that the government will have better information than the public about the nature of such shocks and will use it in such a way as to make economic performance appear better than it actually is. They suggest that the difference between what the government does with its information advantage and what the voters would do if they shared the advantage is a cost of democracy. This cost is not measurable or systematic. It is, in fact, characteristic of any principal-agent relationship. It is the most generic accountability problem. In their words,

> Our model implies that any government with private information that maximizes its probability of reelection will choose not to maximize social welfare. The public expects the government to increase its welfare before an election at the expense of a greater loss of future welfare, and it judges the government's *competence* by its performance in advance of the election. A failure of the government to act in its own interest before the election gives an incorrect inference to the public about the government's *competence*. (Cukierman and Meltzer, 1986, p. 386, emphasis added)

The cost of democracy implied is not a systematically identifiable feature, such as an inflationary bias. Rather, it is an unpredictable product determined by how random shocks affect what government can achieve. This argument offers a general model of the costs of democracy, and it does not depend on a macroeconomic context to be meaningful. It does seem to presume a finely honed and discriminating monitoring of government behavior by the public. Ironically, a less attentive public might generate fewer "costs." We will return to this point in later chapters, especially Chapter 7 on voting behavior.

The systematic attention to the competence of governments is an important innovation in these studies. Competence is modeled in terms of random shocks and asymmetric information. One would think that competence would be related somehow to the training and experience of public officials, and to the similarity between their beliefs about the economy and its true structure. However, these possibilities have not been developed.

The Possibility That Cycles Might Be Induced by Private Behavior

All of the action in virtually all existing electoral cycle theories is due to the government manipulating policy to enhance electoral prospects. Brandice Canes-Wrone and Jee-Kwang Park (2012) suggest that there is a private sector source of cyclical economic activity due to elections. Citizens as investors are important economic actors, controlling about a fifth of the economy, and elections introduce uncertainty about who will be in office. This uncertainty leads investors to reduce the amount of private fixed investment in the quarter before elections. Canes-Wrone and Park find that the evidence supports their hypothesis, and that once this election-related reduction in private investment activity is controlled for, evidence shows that governments spend more just before elections. This suggests that the basically unimpressive results from empirical studies of electoral economic cycles may be due to the fact that they do not address the broader uncertainty-inducing effects of elections and do not include private investment. This contribution is a notable theoretical and empirical advance in the study of electoral business cycles.

A BRIEF LOOK AT SOME EMPIRICAL EVIDENCE

Empirical support for the electoral cycle idea is not, in general, strong. Studies rejecting the idea have been appearing at least since 1978.[10] More than a quarter century ago, two leading scholars concluded that "no one could read the political business cycle literature without being struck by the lack of supporting evidence" (Alt and Crystal 1983, p. 125). Recent reviews for the most part fail to find evidence of cycles on electoral periods. Yet the idea remains resilient in spite of largely negative findings.

A casual look suggests that the evidence for the electoral cycle hypothesis is not overwhelming. Table 3.2 aggregates data on unemployment, real national income growth, and inflation by year of the electoral cycle for the United States in the period from 1949 through 2008, or Truman through George W. Bush. Unemployment did rise and fall, on average, according to the hypothesized pattern, although the lowest average rate of unemployment occurred in the first year, rather than in the presidential election year. National income growth (the annualized rate of change in the gross domestic product [GDP]) did not show the predicted two-year cyclical pattern,

Table 3.2. *Average annual rates for unemployment, growth of gross domestic product, and inflation, by year of presidential term, 1949–2008*

Year	Unemployment	GDP growth	Inflation
1	5.4	3.3	3.4
2	5.8	2.8	4.2
3	5.7	3.6	3.6
4	5.5	3.7	3.8

Source: Bureau of Economic Analysis, Bureau of Labor Statistics, Economic Report of the President.

[10] See, for example, McCallum (1978).

though it was higher in the second half than in the first half of the "average" administration. The best value for inflation was in the year following elections, and the worst was the second year.[11] Ironically, the lowest values for both inflation and unemployment occurred in the year most distant from the next election, rather than in the election year. The average differences are quite small for all three variables. A detailed look at each administration shows considerable variation in the patterns, and the averages do not predict well for any given administration. Chapter 4 will show that partisan differences can help identify some patterns hidden within the variation.[12]

More careful statistical studies might show evidence of electoral cycles after controlling for other complicating variables. For example, in their article "Political Models of the Business Cycle Should Be Revived," Haynes and Stone (1989a) reported a sophisticated estimation of a sine wave pattern of macroeconomic outcomes following electoral periods. Their electoral cycle variable was significant in equations explaining income growth, unemployment, and inflation. Their results will be considered again in the next chapter because they identified an important interaction between the electoral cycle variable and partisanship. Without that interaction, the cycle variable predicted a difference of almost one percentage point in the growth of gross national product (GNP), almost one percentage point for unemployment, and a little more than half a percentage point for inflation.[13]

Of course, it is possible that such electoral cycles exist from time to time, but that they disappear. Keech and Pak (1989) found that an apparent electoral cycle existed for U.S. veterans' benefits between 1961 and 1978, but that it subsequently disappeared. The reason for the change is easy to identify. Instead of being adjusted by Congress, benefits have been indexed to fluctuate automatically with the consumer price index since 1979. Similar results will be found for Social Security, which has also been indexed.[14]

The most extensive and authoritative empirical study (Alesina, Cohen, and Roubini, 1992 a, 1992b) analyzed the possibility of electoral cycles for

---

[11] In none of these cases is the difference between adjacent pairs of numbers statistically significant at the 0.10 level according to a *t*-test for difference of means.

[12] Bartels (2008) shows a startling difference in income growth between the parties in the fourth year, very much to the Republicans' favor.

[13] Kevin Grier (1989, 1993) has found supportive evidence in careful econometric studies. See also Williams (1990).

[14] See Weaver (1988) for a complete discussion and analysis of the indexing of government programs.

economic variables in eighteen Western industrial democracies in the Organization for Economic Cooperation and Development (OECD) between 1960 and 1987.[15] Those findings were largely negative, but it is instructive to report them in terms of the distinction between policy instruments and outcomes, and between real and nominal quantities. We would expect that it would be most difficult to control real outcomes, but possible to affect nominal outcomes such as inflation, and most feasible to manipulate policy instruments.

These authors found no convincing support for electoral cycles in either unemployment or GDP, the real economic output. They did find some evidence that inflation, the nominal economic outcome, followed an electoral cycle, with inflationary spurts coming after elections. Some evidence showed that money growth was greater before elections in the OECD countries in general, but the supportive evidence varied by country (and was not strong for the United States). There was also evidence that budget deficits were greater before elections.

All of these findings are consistent with the idea that incumbent politicians may try, at least occasionally, to manipulate the policy instruments under their control to enhance their prospects for reelection. The consequences for economic outcomes seem to be felt only adversely, after elections, in the form of inflation. The real outcomes (unemployment and national income growth) are not responsive to political manipulation, as would be predicted by modern rational expectations models of the macroeconomy.

Even the most positive assertion that there are cycles based on electoral periods leaves much unexplained about the behavior of economic aggregates. Moreover, there is reason to believe that some of the evidence for apparent electoral cycles is really a reflection of the consequence of the defeat and replacement of one party by another.[16]

IN TRANSITION

The electoral cycle models we have discussed are models in which political manipulation regards the timing of economic events, and in which the institution for accountability of the agents to the principals is the possibility of sanction through electoral defeat. The models reviewed thus far show that

---

[15] See also Nordhaus (1989) and Schneider and Frey (1988).
[16] See Frey and Schneider (1978), Haynes and Stone (1989a), Campbell (2011) and the next chapter.

the very institution of democratic control, periodic elections, may provide some perverse incentives. In each case, whether voters were modeled as passive or as sophisticated, the behavior prompted by such incentives involved an effort to make things look misleadingly good before an election, though the reality might be worse afterward.

In general, the theories of electoral cycles have generated many interesting ideas, and they have helped us refine our thinking about the nature and risks of the electoral process. They have helped us think more clearly about the costs of democracy. As it stands, however, there is little empirical evidence that electoral cycles for economic variables are important, and there is not a well-formulated case that there are pathologies of democracy reflected in such cycles.[17] The models do help demonstrate that the most fundamental institution of public accountability, in which officeholders faced the possibility of removal in periodic elections, may be subject to perverse incentives.[18]

In an effort to explore the relationship between elections and macroeconomic performance in Latin American democracies, Karen Remmer found virtually no support for the hypothesis that incumbents might manipulate economic variables to make things look misleadingly good before elections. Instead, she found that competitive elections "have enhanced, not undermined, political leaders' capacity to address major problems of macroeconomic management" and that they "should perhaps be seen less as threats to economic stability than as catalysts for policy reform and responsible economic management" (Remmer, 1993, pp. 393, 403).

Democratic elections are more than opportunities to evaluate the performance of incumbents. They are also vehicles for popular choice between alternatives. This is the feature that is analyzed in the models of Chapter 4.

---

[17] In a mathematical argument based on the Nordhaus model, Keech and Simon (1985) found that adverse welfare consequences from political manipulation of the economy depended on the parameters of the model. Keech and Pak (1989) found no evidence that an electoral cycle in veterans' benefits contributed to the growth of expenditures beyond what could be expected otherwise.

[18] Berdejó and Chen (2010) show that the decisions of unelected judges follow electoral cycles.

4

Models of Choice: Partisanship

Partisanship models have received considerably more attention and empirical support than electoral cycle models. Leading scholars, such as Alberto Alesina and Douglas Hibbs, have argued that partisanship is the most fundamental basis for political influence over macroeconomic policy and outcomes. There are, indeed, systematic partisan differences, but economic movements are so fluid that party differences are often overwhelmed by larger tides of change. A limitation in most of the existing studies of macroeconomic partisanship is that they have assumed that party differences regarding goals have remained fixed or constant. That assumption has rarely been documented or tested, and I will argue that partisan goals are, in fact, variable. Even fixed goals may be relaxed under certain circumstances that make them unusually costly, but I contend that partisan goals are themselves variable, subject to conditions that are still only poorly understood.

Also, the institutional framework in which American parties operate is not constant. Changes in the institutions in which fiscal and monetary policies are made are likely to affect the implementation of alternative partisan goals, even if those goals were to remain constant (see Chapters 8 and 9). Most of the empirical demonstrations of partisan differences have focused on presumably fixed differences between the Democratic and Republican Parties regarding control of the presidency. But a growing literature has argued that other patterns of variations in the control of office are also consequential. Most prominently, divided partisan control of the presidency and Congress can affect policy outcomes. Outside the United States, partisan competition is made more complicated in many democratic countries by the continuing presence of more than two parties. A two-party system that offers only dual alternatives is, by comparison, a radical simplification of the actual possibilities.

This chapter traces the development of models of dual partisan competition from the simple to the complex. For the most part, the later, more complex models are superior representations of the world, but all of them involve substantial simplifications that are designed to enhance understanding. The sequence of models traces two kinds of intellectual development. One is grounded in politics and involves the development of a better understanding of partisanship. The other is grounded in economics and involves a changing understanding of the nature of the choices available to policy makers. Some of the latter developments involve widely acknowledged improvements in economic understanding, whereas others involve enduring theoretical disputes in economics.

FROM ELECTORAL CYCLE TO PARTISANSHIP

Recall that the electoral cycle models of routine politics involved an interaction between an undifferentiated public and a generic elected official. A second set of models of routine politics deals with alternative parties competing for control of government. Models of partisanship deemphasize or suppress any general conflict of interest or strategic interaction between politicians and voters, as was implied by the electoral cycle models, and instead emphasize conflicts of interests or ideology between sets or "teams" of voters and politicians. Instead of a principal-agent problem between voters and elected public officials, the partisanship model emphasizes the nature of the choices between the alternatives presented in majority rule elections. Instead of the horizontally divided interaction that defined the models in Chapter 3, the partisanship model is based on competition over a vertical divide:

Blue Team (Politicians and Voters) | Red Team (Politicians and Voters)

From a normative perspective, these models speak less directly to the questions of the costs or pathologies of democracy than did the electoral cycle models discussed earlier. First, the basic macroeconomic differences between the parties are usually presented as normatively neutral, that is, as matters of taste. Second, there are few cases in which a dynamic process of competitive interaction between parties over macroeconomic policy is modeled so that the results are related to a general social welfare function. In fact, when partisan goals are modeled with objective functions, partisan variation is typically presented simply as different sizes of the parameters that define the relative weights that parties place on basic targets, such as unemployment or inflation. The parties are typically placed on the same normative plateau, and no superior welfare function is defined.

This is not to say that partisan competition is necessarily neutral or even constructive. Conventional wisdom suggests (as did the electoral cycle models discussed earlier) that competitive pressures may lead incumbents to seek short-run political advantage at the expense of serious attention to long-run problems. The presence of a challenging party may add to the incentives for the incumbent to choose irresponsible policies with short-term benefits at the expense of sustainable plans.[1] The partisan models to be reviewed here are derived mostly from narrowly defined studies of routine and repetitive political patterns, and they do not, for the most part, capture this undesirable feature of partisan competition.

However, one of the issues that emerges from these models is the possibility that the options available to newly elected parties may be restricted, intentionally or otherwise, because of the actions taken by previous incumbents.[2] And other studies have shown how partisan polarization and divided partisan control of the branches of government may have adverse consequences.[3] The reader should note that the limitation to dual alternatives considered here rules out a whole class of collective choice problems that emerge when there are more than two alternatives, as in European parliamentary systems. Those problems, which raise questions about the meaning and coherence of a popular will, as expressed in elections, will not be addressed in this book.[4]

SOURCES OF PARTISAN DIFFERENCES

Parties can differ about anything, from the relationship between church and state to foreign policy, but this book will concentrate on party differences related to macroeconomic issues such as inflation, unemployment, and income growth. In Chapter 3, we saw that some studies have recognized

[1] See Gerber and Lupia (1995) for a demonstration that more electoral competition does not necessarily lead to better outcomes.

[2] See, for example, Persson and Svensson (1989).

[3] See, for example McCubbins (1991).

[4] For a compelling argument that the popular will is incoherent and undefinable, see Riker (1982). Riker also suggests that majority rule works better when the electoral alternatives are narrowed to two. See also Hirschman (1991, p. x), who argues that "curiously, the very stability and proper functioning of a well-ordered democratic society depends on its citizens arraying themselves in a few major (ideally two) clearly defined groups holding different opinions on basic policy issues." The rationale for this statement is not provided, though one can be found in Riker (1982).

that governments may differ in competence even when there are no differences in their economic goals. Conventional wisdom and popular opinion
often hold that one party is better than the other at maintaining prosperity.
In the language of political science, this pattern is called "issue ownership."[5]

Economic issues themselves have many dimensions. Prosperity is a consensual issue, but many economic issues are divisive. The general strategy by
which prosperity is to be maintained is often a basis for partisan conflict. In
most countries, one party will defend the free market as the way to ensure
prosperity, whereas another will advocate government intervention into the
economy to do the same thing. Different preferences regarding the size of
the public sector are related to those differing views on the free market in
obvious ways. Parties with a high demand for public services are usually
parties that advocate public intervention, whereas those with lower demand
typically defend the free market. Basic predispositions such as these are
often at the heart of differences between Republicans and Democrats.

Social class differences over the distribution of income and wealth are
often matters of political conflict and are almost always potentially so.
Distributional issues may underlie partisan differences in macroeconomics.
In fact, that is the basis for Douglas Hibbs's explanation for why the
Democrats have been more averse to unemployment than Republicans
and vice versa for inflation. He documented that lower-income, blue-collar,
wage-earning workers are more vulnerable to unemployment than are
higher-income, white-collar, salary-earning workers. Even after unemployment compensation, lower-income workers have the most to lose from
unemployment (Hibbs 1987, ch. 2). The distributional consequences of
inflation are not so clear, but Hibbs argues that higher-income people
have more to lose from inflation than do those in lower-income strata. In
general, he argues that inflation is not nearly so costly as unemployment,
but that insofar as it has distributional consequences, they are worse for
upper-income groups (Hibbs 1987, ch. 3).

This distributional basis for relative aversion to inflation and unemployment fits well with conventional wisdom and the reputations of the parties.
Hibbs documents that the different class groupings do in fact have these
objective interests, and that the interests are related straightforwardly to
their subjective preferences regarding relative aversion to inflation and
unemployment (1987, ch. 4). That is, the "downscale" groups are more
concerned about unemployment than inflation, and the reverse holds for
"upscale" groups. The downscale groups vote disproportionately for

[5] See Petrocik (1996); Lewis-Beck and Nadeau (2011); and Wright (2012).

Democrats as the party with the greater concern for and best record on unemployment, whereas the upscale groups tend to support Republicans as having comparable credentials regarding inflation.

Even though Hibbs shows that there is an objective basis for the differences between the parties concerning relative aversion to unemployment and inflation, his book also presents another theme. He argues that unemployment is a worse evil than inflation, and he suggests that a reasonable concern for the general welfare would emphasize the evils of unemployment far more than the evils of inflation. In other words, the objective basis for party differences can be questioned and is contestable. Hibbs suggests that those who would emphasize the fight against inflation at the expense of rising unemployment may be misguided and that a stance more in keeping with the general welfare would concentrate on reducing unemployment. Whether he is right or wrong, Hibbs gives an interpretation of the general welfare, but without using something so explicit as a welfare function. As we will see in Chapter 6, there are other reasonable interpretations of the general welfare.

Parties differ in their beliefs and ideologies about macroeconomic issues, and such beliefs may be grounded in the objective self-interests of their clienteles or may be more purely matters of judgment. As matters of judgment, they are subject to evaluation and persuasion in public discourse (Johnson 1993). Matters of judgment may be grounded in objective circumstances and are not always purely intellectual. Both American parties are now vigorous advocates of economic growth and compete for support on that basis. They differ less in their commitment to that goal than in their strategies for achieving it. Quinn and Shapiro (1991) point out that there may be important differences in the strategies that parties use to achieve such growth. They characterize Democrats as following a "consumption-led" strategy for growth, in which government policies are designed to put money into the hands of consumers. Republicans are characterized as following an "investment-led" strategy, in which policies are designed to encourage capital formation. Those and other ideological differences may be rooted, in obvious ways, in the interests of the clienteles of the parties.

There is no particular reason to think that any of these bases for partisan differences in goals would be fixed. The clienteles of parties may change, and partisan issue stands may also change. A clear noneconomic example of this is seen in the changing stances of the Republican and Democratic Parties with respect to equal rights for African Americans and in the shifting partisan allegiances of American blacks. If the Democratic Party was able to change from the party most identified with white supremacy to the party most identified with the aspirations of blacks over the course of a few decades, why should we not expect similar changes in economic policies and clienteles? In fact, in the nineteenth century, the Democratic Party was the party of free trade and limited government, whereas the Republicans advocated trade protectionism and public spending programs. Now all of those positions have been substantially reversed. In a world as fluid as this, partisan goals with respect to inflation and unemployment are unlikely to be as enduringly invariant as is implied in some of the models to be discussed later. Changes can come about because of the addition of new clienteles, as in the case of the Democrats and blacks, or because of changes in the preferences of enduring clienteles, as in the attitude of the business community toward public spending.

Changes in the manifestations of partisanship can occur because of conditions that change in the short term or over the long term. For example, James Alt (1985) has shown that partisan differences regarding unemployment are partly dependent on whether or not a party promised to do something about it in the preceding election campaign. Garrett and Lange (1991) have shown that increasing international interdependence has affected the strategies for intervention in the economy for governments on both the left and the right in industrial democracies, without eliminating partisan differences.

A BASIC MODEL: PARTY DIFFERENCES ON A STABLE MENU OF CHOICES

The foregoing review has recounted some of the familiar facets of conventional wisdom about American politics. Hibbs (1987) documented them empirically, but the most important part of his research was his systematic statistical study of the differences in unemployment and income growth rates between the parties.

The fundamental empirical results reported by Hibbs were that unemployment rates have been lower and rates of national income growth have been higher under Democrats than under Republicans. In fact, the two phenomena are widely acknowledged to be related through "Okun's law," which defines an inverse relationship between unemployment and income growth.[6] Empirically, in the period since World War II, recessions, as officially defined by the National Bureau of Economic Research, have in

---

[6] See Hibbs (1987), pp. 50–1.

Table 4.1. *Recessions in the United States since World War II, by party of presidential administration in which it started*

Period	Party
November 1948–October 1949	Democrat
July 1953–May 1954	Republican
August 1957–April 1958	Republican
April 1960–February 1961	Republican
December 1969–November 1970	Republican
November 1973–March 1975	Republican
January 1980–July 1980	Democrat
July 1981–November 1982	Republican
July 1990–March 1991	Republican
March 2001–November 2001	Republican
December 2007–June 2009	Republican

Source: National Bureau of Economic Research, http://www.nber.org/cycles.html

fact been somewhat more likely to occur under Republican than under Democratic administrations, as Table 4.1 shows.[7]

There were eleven recessions in the sixty-six years between 1946 and the end of 2011, or about one every six years. The Republicans were in office for nineteen more years than the Democrats, so were more at risk. Counting crudely by attributing a recession to the party in office when it started, two recessions began in the nineteen Democratic years, or one every eight plus years, and nine that began in the twenty-eight Republican years, or one every three plus years, on average.

It would be quite premature to see any causality in that difference. Business cycles are not well understood, and it is clear that recessions occur irregularly. Clearly more is going on than partisan change. A recession did occur at the beginning of each new Republican administration elected to replace a Democratic administration: 1953, 1969, 1981, and 2001. That could have been because of the autonomous policy choices of Republicans, if they preferred lower growth rates, or it might have been because of the circumstances under which the Republicans took over from the Democrats, perhaps after a period of high inflation, as will be explained later. Or if, as is widely assumed, new presidents are not fully responsible for the economy until they have been in office for about a year, it could be that

---

[7] See http://www.nber.org/cycles.html.

responsibility for these recessions should be shared with the Democrats who had been in office before the election. This possibility will be addressed later.

Several scholars have investigated whether or not there are systematic differences between Democrats and Republicans in macroeconomic performance. Douglas Hibbs was the first to do this with statistical rigor (1977, 1987). He found that Democrats performed better than Republicans on unemployment and income growth in the period from 1953 to 1983. Even more dramatic findings that Democrats had consistently superior economic performance to Republicans were presented by Larry Bartels in a book called *Unequal Democracy: The Political Economy of the New Gilded Age* (2008), which was the subject of a laudatory symposium in *Perspectives on Politics*, an official publication of the American Political Science Association (March 2009). Bartels's findings span the period from 1948 through 2005.

James Campbell (2011) replicates and updates Bartels's study. Campbell finds that Bartels did not properly take into account the economic conditions at the time of transitions from Democratic to Republican administrations, and that Bartels's results may be a result of specification error (2011, p. 2). Bartels includes as one of his independent variables a one-year lag of real per capita GNP growth, and he finds that with such a lag, party differences are statistically significant in the direction of Democratic administrations having higher economic growth and lower unemployment. Although Campbell replicates this, he points out that the one-year lag does not have a significant impact on economic growth, which would be a remarkable and implausible finding, given widely acknowledged inertia in the economy: "The lack of a lagged effect in the economy is, frankly, unbelievable. The lack of a lagged effect of the economy on subsequent economic conditions is equivalent to claiming that the economy begins anew on New Year's Day" (2011, p. 10).

Campbell provides an alternative specification, in which the lag is specified as the last quarter or the last two quarters of the previous year for a dependent variable defined annually. These lags are all significant at the $p < 0.01$ level, but when the lag is specified in this way, the party difference becomes statistically insignificant. This means that Bartels's findings of superior Democratic performance are not robust to the specification of the lag function.

This much simply challenges Bartels's findings of Democratic superiority. But Campbell goes further and argues that the recessions that occurred in the first year of each new Republican administration were the responsibility of the Democrats who preceded them. This may well be so, and the grounds for the conclusion might be of (at least) two kinds. First, it could be by the assumption, which in fact is shared by Bartels and Campbell, that the performance of the economy changes slowly, and that it is reasonable to attribute the first year of a new administration to the previous administration. Of course, one year is an arbitrary but not unreasonable assumption for actual causal patterns that could be shorter and longer and surely not the same for all transitions.

Or, second, the grounds might be empirical. Campbell also addresses the causal issue with his statistical model, which shows statistically significant positive lags for third- and fourth-quarter growth in real GNP per capita on the following year of such growth. To illustrate that the outgoing Democrat was responsible for the recession that happened in the first year of each new postwar Republican administration (1953, 1969, 1981, and 2001), the growth rates for the last two quarters should be negative. But the average of the third- and fourth-quarter growth rates of the outgoing administration (Campbell 2011, table 6, p. 17) is positive. So the argument that Democrats are responsible for the recessions in the first year of the four transitions to Republicans is more by assumption than causal demonstration. Comiskey and Marsh (2012) respond to Campbell's challenge with a reanalysis that controls for the business cycle in three ways (differences of means, time since the peaks and troughs of the cycle, and spline regression).[8] Democratic superiority reemerges for most of their investigations.

The Issue of Compatibility with Economic Theory

None of the previously mentioned authors is nearly as self-consciously careful as Nordhaus (1975) in presenting his assumptions about how the economy works and how that issue bears on the political model being presented. Hibbs often seems implicitly to assume that parties are operating on a stable menu of choices represented by a naïve Phillips curve. That idea represents an understanding of the way the economic world works that is no longer accepted by economists, though it was widely accepted by them in the 1960s.

That idea worked its way into conventional political discourse in the following manner: an inverse relationship was thought to exist between inflation and unemployment, as represented by the curve in Figure 4.1. Governments were thought to be able to choose positions on that curve and to stay in those positions. It was natural to think that a partisan government

---

[8] Unlike most previous scholars, Comiskey and Marsh also consider monetary and fiscal policy in their discussion.

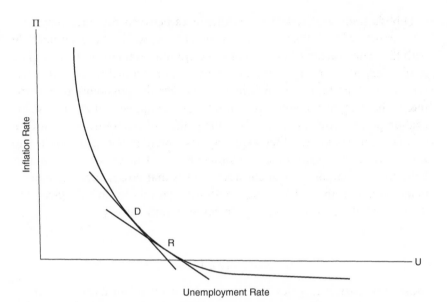

Figure 4.1 Partisan differences on a simple Phillips curve

that was more inflation averse than unemployment averse might choose a position low on the curve, such as R, and that a party with the opposite priority would choose a position higher on the curve, such as D.

As a "menu of choices" available to a government (Samuelson and Solow 1960; Hibbs 1977, p. 1474), this Phillips curve is the counterpart to the constraint explained earlier in the Nordhaus model of electoral cycles. It defines the real-world possibilities, and the theory behind it can help explain why a goal of zero inflation and zero unemployment would not be feasible. Virtually no economists still view this static, naïve Phillips curve as realistic, though it did seem to represent options during the 1950s and 1960s.

Note that this theory implies that when a new party takes over, the initial conditions of inflation and unemployment will be those chosen by the outgoing party, and the new government can move directly to its own preferred point. That may take time, and one of the strengths of Hibbs's analysis is his empirical estimation of those time paths. However, nothing in this theory implies that there is any restriction on the newly elected party's freedom of movement other than that the choices be on the Phillips curve and that it will take time to move to the new choice. Later in this chapter, we will consider models (by Hibbs and by others) that have other implications.

Hibbs's finding of steady-state differences between the unemployment rates associated with the Republicans and Democratic Parties is compatible with this dated theory of the economic constraint on political choice. As he acknowledged, it is less compatible with more contemporary theories (Hibbs 1987, p. 227), none of which recognizes the possibility of governments choosing sustainably different rates of unemployment through stabilization policy. Obviously, models of the politics of economic policy will be stronger and sounder if they explicitly acknowledge and incorporate the ways in which the possibilities are limited by the structure of the economy. Later in this chapter, we will consider models that do so, but as Chapter 2 made apparent, there is no single authoritative way to do this, given the diversity of views in contemporary macroeconomic theory.

Normative Issues

Most partisanship theories do not have an explicit normative model for comparing the results of politically motivated behavior with the best feasible values for social welfare functions, as Nordhaus's model of the electoral cycle does. (Recall Nordhaus's statement that democratic systems will choose "lower unemployment and higher inflation than is optimal" [1975, 178].) Hibbs's theory of partisan choice is also without a similarly explicit normative model, though he does argue explicitly that unemployment is a greater evil than inflation, and implicitly that Democrats are preferable to Republicans because they produce lower rates of unemployment.

I lay the groundwork for a more systematic normative model by linking a welfare function to the naïve Phillips curve, treating it for now as if it were a realistic representation of real-world possibilities, even though it no longer is. Consider again the misery index as a possible welfare function:

$$M = U + \Pi$$

This welfare function can easily be turned into an "indifference curve," that is, a line that reflects a set of points that are equally valued in terms of the welfare function. Such a line drawn in the Phillips curve space of Figure 4.1 would have a slope of -1, much like the line that is tangent at point D.

Because the social welfare function and the derived indifference curve represent what is valued, and because the Phillips curve once represented what was thought to be possible, a point of tangency between the two would provide a solution to the problem of identifying the best possible outcome. However, the fact that the misery index is an unweighted sum of the rates of unemployment and inflation is an arbitrary simplification. Suppose someone, perhaps a Democrat, argued that a single percentage point of unemployment is twice as undesirable as a single percentage point of inflation, writing this misery index as $M_D = 2U + \Pi$. Someone else, perhaps a Republican, who argued the opposite, would write the index as $M_R = U + 2\Pi$. A little calculation will show that the slope of M_D is -2, and the slope of M_R is -0.5.

The argument can be generalized by writing the misery index as

$$M = \alpha U + \Pi,$$

where α is a weighting parameter that equals 2 for M_D and 0.5 for M_R. The partisan preferences expressed by Hibbs can easily be represented by such indifference curves with different slopes. Given a stable menu of choices, parties could move from point to point on the curve representing the menu, and stay at any one of the points. This, of course, assumes that the curve represents the actual options.

In such a world, each party would have its own candidate for a social welfare function, and voters could choose between parties according to whose formulation they preferred. If there were no other issues in elections to choose between such parties, the winning party under majority rule could be considered to have the better definition of social welfare or the public interest, according to Rawls's considerations of pure procedural justice. By this criterion, "there is no independent criterion for the right result," but given a fair procedure, such as a democratic election between two parties, the outcome or result is fair, "whatever it is, provided that the procedure has been properly followed" (Rawls 1971, p. 86).

Strategic Considerations and the Need for a Theory of Change

But where did the positions of the parties come from, and why should they be fixed and immovable? It is a strength of Hibbs's analysis that he explains the sources of partisan positions in a description of the objective interests of their class clienteles. But there is no recognition in Hibbs's work of the strategic considerations that will surely emerge. Suppose a party found that its most preferred positions consigned it to repeated defeats. A party that was interested in putting its positions into practice might well decide to adjust its positions in order to enhance its prospects for election. Even if a party's true or deep preference were fixed, it might choose its publicly stated policy position, or platform, for electoral purposes according to strategic considerations.

For example, it might choose to minimize the distance of the winning policy position from its ideal policy and adjust its platform just enough to maximize the probability of defeating the other party.[9] If parties were to do that and were to stick to their electoral platforms once in office, that behavior would imply that party differences would not be fixed. Both causal observations and systematic study (Beck 1982) seem to support the idea that administrations will differ even if they represent a single party: Reagan was not like Eisenhower or like George W. Bush. Carter was not like Johnson or like Obama, and so on. If that is the case, there will be a less solid basis for expecting that in a dual system the differences between the parties will be predictably fixed, as Hibbs (1987) and other scholars in this area have assumed.

An early theory of strategic party competition that is explicitly grounded in macroeconomic issues questions the possibility of such strategic movement on credibility grounds. Alesina (1987, 1988a) assumed that the "true" preferences of the parties were publicly known and that strategic movement toward a vote-maximizing position would be discounted as insincere. Under most circumstances, the winning party would revert to its true preference after the election. Assuming that the true preferences were known, strategically defined platforms would not be credible.

In Alesina's model, moderating changes in partisan positions are possible, but they come from the interaction between the parties rather than from an effort to adapt positions to appeal more effectively to a majority of voters. Because parties in this model are assumed to prefer to stay at a position between the two parties' ideal points, rather than alternate back and forth between those points, they may converge if their time horizon is long enough. A major disadvantage of Alesina's model is that the probabilities of the parties winning is not affected by what they do in office, but it is one of very few models of strategic competition between parties on macroeconomic issues.[10]

In the electoral cycle model, governments were motivated solely by the desire to win elections. We saw that the empirical evidence for the idea that economic cycles follow electoral periods was not compelling, and even if it were stronger, that theory would be hard-pressed to account for the fact that incumbent parties have lost eight of the past sixteen elections. If the main

[9] See Alesina, Londregan, and Rosenthal (1993); Alesina and Rosenthal (1994); Chappell and Keech (1986b); and Wittman (1983) for models of electoral competition between parties with policy goals.

[10] See Alesina and Cukierman (1990) for a model that shows how parties can gain mobility by a "politics of ambiguity" regarding their goals.

objective of incumbent governments is to win votes, why do they lose? Clearly something else is going on. The partisanship theory has a similar problem: Hibbs argues that the parties represent the interests of different clienteles, but he does not explain how they adjust or might adjust their strategies in order to win elections. Presumably, parties can better please their clienteles when in office than when out, and it might pay them to adjust their policies in order to win election, but it is possible that they would not care about office so long as their goals were implemented. It would be sensible to model partisan goals as a combination of policy goals and the goal of holding office for its own sake. Such a model could take the following form:

$$\text{Partisan goal} = \beta(\text{policy goal}) + (1 - \beta)(\text{officeholding goal})$$

where $0 < \beta < 1$. A goal function such as this might help explain why parties lose elections as often as they do, by suggesting that they maximize their policy goals at the expense of officeholding.[11] Of course, it is possible that incumbents lose because of noneconomic issues, and it is not difficult to find noneconomic reasons that would help explain the outcomes of the eight presidential elections since World War II in which the incumbent party lost. For example, the defeats of the Democrats in 1952 and 1968 were related to unpopular wars. The defeat of the Republicans in 1976 was related to the Watergate affair and defeat in war. The defeats of the Republicans in 1960, 1992, and 2008 seem to have been more purely related to economic performance.[12]

Still, most of those defeats were also associated with economic performance that reflected the risk of fulfilling the incumbent party's goals too well. They were political reflections of the following much quoted observation: "For a generation, every major mistake in economic policy under a Democratic president has taken the form of overstimulating the economy and every major mistake under a Republican of overrestraining it" (Okun 1973, p. 175).[13]

Party differences in unemployment and growth rate, such as those Hibbs finds, could simply reflect shifts in targets on a stable menu of choices. If moves that go too far are mistakes, this implies that some middle ground on the Phillips curve will maximize votes, and a party that deviates too far from

---

[11] Alesina (1987) suggests that under some circumstances parties may even prefer to lose in order to better achieve their goals.

[12] See Chapter 7 and Figure 7.1.

[13] See also the comments by Charles Schultze reported in Nordhaus (1989).

that middle ground in the direction of its supporters makes the mistakes that are characteristic of a party with its particular goals. These character-istic mistakes may lead to defeat that will bring the other party into office. Sharp movements in unemployment or income growth under a new party may, in part, be predictable reactions to the conditions that led to the defeat of the incumbent. Hibbs anticipated these points in the concluding obser-vation of his chapter on electoral cycles: "Democratic administrations have been more likely than Republican administrations to get into difficulty with the electorate by pursuing overly ambitious employment goals that yield extra inflation. The Republicans, on the other hand, have more frequently suffered electoral setbacks because of their enthusiasm for disinflationary bouts of economic slack" (1987, p. 278).

Specifically, the Republican wins in 1968 and 1980 followed Democratic problems with inflation after having pursued ambitious employment goals. (Of course, the 1979 oil shock was another source of the Carter adminis-tration's problems with inflation.) The newly elected Nixon and Reagan administrations deliberately restrained the economy. Their decisions to do so might be explained by their having different targets (i.e., lower targets for growth and higher targets for unemployment). However, a decision to restrain the economy might also be explained by a goal of reducing inflation as the most important problem. Similarly, Democratic wins in 1960, 1976, and 1992, if not 2008, followed Republican problems with slack in the economy. The expansions that ensued after several of these elections were consistent with the higher growth targets espoused by the Democrats and with a desire to deal with the most important problem at hand. So long as the outcomes of elections are not independent of the economic performance of incumbent administrations, efforts to explain partisan differences in economic performance without taking into account economic circumstan-ces will not be fully satisfactory. Partisan strategies are likely to be con-tingent on economic conditions.[14]

The traditional naïve Phillips curve defines a stable menu of choices. If that view of the options were accurate, there would be perfect mobility from point to point. If a party were defeated for going too far in one direction, its successor could simply move along the curve to another point that was more preferred. If mistakes were made, as Okun suggests, they could be easily and painlessly corrected in a world characterized by that stable trade-off. That is

---

[14] Subsequent work by Hibbs (1992 and 1994) has developed a systematic model of this phenomenon.

not necessarily true for the next models we will consider, in which mistakes may be more costly.

PARTY DIFFERENCES IN A WORLD WITHOUT A STABLE PHILLIPS CURVE

In the following model, which assumes a natural rate of unemployment, mistakes are costly, though correctable. However, it is more painful to correct some mistakes than to correct others. The mistake that Okun attributed to Republicans is not difficult to correct. Overrestraint of the economy can be painlessly corrected in this model by stimulating the economy. Keynesian remedies for unemployment and poor growth are compatible with natural desires to increase spending or reduce taxes. However, the mistake one expects from Democrats is difficult to correct. Overstimulation of the economy can lead to inflation, and elimination of inflation is a costly undertaking. If the Democrats are defeated by the Republicans for making such a mistake, the Republicans may find that they must induce a painful recession. The political incentives of Keynesian stabilization policies are asymmetrical, as was suggested in Chapter 2.

These arguments may help explain a few episodes of what looks like the electoral cycle, and it provides an example of a way in which newly elected parties do not necessarily start with a clean slate. They may take office with problems left by their predecessors for them to correct, and different parties may leave different problems.

The Idea of a Natural Rate of Unemployment

Although the idea of a stable inverse relationship between inflation and unemployment lived on in the politics of economic policy and in public discourse for some time, it came under attack in the late 1960s in Milton Friedman's presidential address to the American Economic Association. Friedman argued that public authorities could not succeed in meeting specific targets for unemployment rates because of "the difference between the immediate and delayed consequences of such a policy" (1968, p. 7).

Friedman suggested that at any given time, there is a single natural rate of unemployment, a level that is consistent with equilibrium between the supply of labor and the demand for labor. This natural rate will vary with the size and qualifications of the labor force and with public policies that affect the incentives to take jobs. For example, the natural rate might rise with an influx of untrained teenagers into the labor force or with an increase in the legal minimum wage. It may drop with a decrease in the generosity of unemployment benefits. But it is not subject to any lasting change that could be brought about by monetary or fiscal stabilization policy. Parties that understand and accept the idea of a natural rate of unemployment might choose to lower unemployment by labor market policies such as minimum wage laws or unemployment compensation levels, but they could not expect to achieve lasting reductions with demand management policies.[15]

Friedman argued that monetary policy might lead to a temporary reduction in the unemployment rate, by virtue of confusion in labor markets between real and nominal wages. However, he argued that such a reduction could be sustained only by inflation, and indeed by accelerating inflation (Friedman 1968, p. 10):

> To state this conclusion differently, there is always a temporary trade-off between inflation and unemployment; there is no permanent trade-off. The temporary trade-off comes not from inflation per se, but from unanticipated inflation, which generally means a rising rate of inflation. The widespread belief that there is a permanent trade-off is a sophisticated version of the confusion between "high" and "rising" that we all recognize in simpler forms. A rising rate of inflation may reduce unemployment, a high rate will not. (1968, p. 11)

These observations were elaborated into the idea that a very steep, even vertical, "long-run Phillips curve" represents the sustainable combinations of inflation and unemployment. This would imply that any rate of inflation, including zero, would be sustainably compatible with the natural rate of unemployment. Lower rates of unemployment could be sustained only with accelerating inflation, according to this "adaptive expectations" theory. The Nordhaus model of the electoral business cycle elaborated in Chapter 3 is a theory of cynical political manipulation based on Friedman's ideas about the difference between long-run and short-run Phillips curves. Figure 2.3 is an example.

In a world characterized by a natural rate of unemployment and a long-run Phillips curve, there is not an obvious basis for party differences regarding targeted unemployment rates. Recall that with the naïve, static Phillips curve, different combinations of inflation and unemployment that were on the curve were thought to be infinitely sustainable. Under the natural rate theory, there is no sustainable unemployment rate other than

---

[15] Ironically, some of the policies that economic theory says would be likely to lower natural rates of unemployment would reduce the value of minimum wages and of unemployment compensation (Aluise 1991).

the natural rate. An effort to maintain unemployment below that rate would not simply lead to a higher, but stable rate of inflation. Such an effort would generate steadily rising inflation, that is, accelerating inflation, according to the adaptive expectations theory of inflation used in the Friedman argument described here, and used by Nordhaus in the electoral cycle model presented in Chapter 3.

One might expect governments of either party to target the natural rate in order to preclude or minimize inflation, but as Friedman pointed out, the government "cannot know what the 'natural' rate is" (1968, p. 10). As we will see in Chapter 8, which deals with monetary policy, that view led Friedman to advocate that government not even try to manipulate unemployment rates, but rather that it follow a rule for a fixed rate of monetary growth. (That advice has been largely ignored.)

A Welfare Function for a Natural Rate World

Recognizing that the exact location of a natural rate of unemployment is not known, we might still think of governments as hoping to keep unemployment at that natural rate, and to minimize inflation. Because the natural rate is thought to be compatible with zero inflation, an appropriate welfare function of the misery index might look like this:

$$M = \alpha|U - U^n| + \Pi$$

where M is misery, U is unemployment, U^n is the natural rate of unemployment, and Π is the rate of inflation. In this case, a misery index target of zero would be sustainable when unemployment was at the natural rate and inflation was zero.

Both parties might favor a target of zero if they agreed on the nature of the limitations on the possible policies. That is, if the parties had the same understanding of the way the economic world works, they might agree on a target of zero for the modified welfare function, even if they did not agree on the weighting parameter α, which defines the relative costs of deviations of unemployment from the natural rate and inflation. As will be explained later, some of the most interesting models of policy use a natural rate but involve target values for output growth (or unemployment) above (below) the natural rate. In this way, the time-consistency problem (see Chapter 2) is introduced into partisanship models.

Partisan Differences in a Natural Rate World

Nevertheless, even if parties agreed on the existence of a natural rate, they might not agree on what it is. Also, they might not agree on how important it is to reduce inflation from an initial condition other than zero inflation. Consider the actual figures regarding unemployment and inflation in the 1980s (Table 4.2). Assume that the natural rate was about 6 percent in the 1980s, which approximates considerable consensus. The table shows two unweighted versions of the misery index, one of the form just presented, M_n, with 6 as the natural rate, and an ordinary misery index, M_O, using unemployment and inflation figures for both Reagan administrations. According to both misery indices, economic performance steadily improved throughout the Reagan years, even during what was then the deepest recession in postwar history.

Because unemployment got worse before it got better, the change may not have been worth it to people who in 1981 had short time horizons and who cared more about unemployment than inflation. For example, if the weighting parameter α had the value of 2 for some people, say Democrats, the misery index would have gotten worse in 1982 before it got better. For some people, the human costs of unemployment and lost output are so great relative to inflation that performance such as that of the Reagan administration is not acceptable. Hibbs, for example, argued that inflation was lowered only through "enormous costs in terms of lost output, lower incomes, and higher unemployment" (1987, p. 288). He argued that the associated gap between actual GNP and its sustainable level translated into "about 825 billion dollars' worth of 1984:4 goods and services, or close to $10,000 per household" (1987, p. 292).[16]

Table 4.2. *Some misery indices for the Reagan administrations*

Year	U	$U - 6$	Π	M_n	M_o
1981	7.6	1.6	10.3	11.9	17.9
1982	9.7	3.7	6.2	9.9	15.9
1983	9.6	3.6	3.2	6.8	12.8
1984	7.5	1.5	4.3	5.8	11.8
1985	7.2	1.2	3.6	4.8	10.8
1986	7.0	1.0	1.9	2.9	8.9
1987	6.2	0.2	3.6	3.8	9.8
1988	5.5	−0.5	4.1	3.6	9.6

[16] The costs of disinflation can be measured with a Mundell-Sachs "sacrifice ratio," which relates the cost in unemployment or lost output to the amount of improvement in inflation. See Sachs and Larraín (1993).

Note the similarity between the experience of the first Reagan term and the pattern of the Nordhaus-type electoral cycle. Things got steadily better, so that the recession of 1981–2 was well in the past by the 1984 election. But the misery index achieved by 1984 was not unsustainable, unlike those implied in a Nordhaus-style electoral cycle, as explained in Table 3.1. In fact, it continued to drop through the next electoral period. Even though that experience may look like an electoral cycle, it can be understood as a corrective to the inflationary performance of the previous administration.

It can also be seen as the beginning of the Great Moderation, a period of reduced volatility in macroeconomic aggregates, most notably for our purposes, in inflation, unemployment, and GDP growth. Chapter 8 addresses the Great Moderation

Uncertainty and "Characteristic Mistakes"

Of course, a partisan government may not accept the idea of a natural rate of unemployment. Even if it does, it may estimate that the rate is lower or higher than the other party thinks. This idea can help provide an economic explanation for why incumbent parties lose. Suppose that the actual natural rate was 6 percent, but that Democrats, believing that unemployment is especially costly, were willing to take a risk by assuming that it was 5 percent. Similarly, Republicans, believing that inflation is especially costly, might choose to assume that it was 7 percent. These numbers, in fact, approximate Hibbs's estimates of target values for Democrats and Republicans. If we acknowledge the difficulty of precisely controlling the economy, the message is simply that Democrats tend to undershoot and Republicans tend to overshoot the natural rate in a world of uncertainty.

The Democratic losses of the presidency in 1968 and 1980 followed inflationary episodes that came after unemployment had been driven too low, which might be considered a characteristic mistake of the Democrats.[17] Republican losses in 1960 and 1976 came after the opposite kind of problem: unemployment had been allowed to drift too high, given Republican

---

[17] At 7.1, unemployment was not too low in 1980, but it had fallen from 7.1 to 5.8 in the first three years of the Carter administration. Clearly, Carter's macroeconomic policies were complicated by the inflationary consequences of the 1979 oil price shock.

aversion to inflation. This might be considered a characteristic mistake of the Republicans. Both parties were defeated after different kinds of poor economic performance that were characteristic of the risks inherent in their respective values and preferences.[18]

The Electoral Cycle as an Artifact of Republicans Following Democratic "Mistakes"

The best examples of the kind of electoral cycle Nordhaus identified are provided in the first terms of the Nixon and Reagan administrations. That is, each administration inherited inflation, and each induced a recession early in the term, a recession that was ending by the time of the next election. Nordhaus's nonpartisan model suggests that such a pattern is simply a result of cynical vote manipulation. Another interpretation is possible, given the fact that each of those administrations began with inflationary problems inherited from a defeated Democratic administration. One way to reduce inflation is to induce a recession, which reduces demand and the expectation of inflation. If that is done immediately, early in the term, the recession may well be over by the next election, at which time prosperity can be returning, with lower inflation. That may be what happened in these two cases, which have been presumed to be leading cases of the electoral cycle.[19]

Campbell (2011) makes much of the widely shared assumption that a new president is not responsible for the performance of the macroeconomy in his first year, but as pointed out earlier, one year is an arbitrary, if convenient, assumption. Moreover, actual responsibility does not turn on and off like a light at the end of the first year any more than it does at inauguration. The previous discussion shows how, for example, the first several years of the Reagan administration might have had objectively poor economic performance that could be attributed to a constructive effort to rid the economy of inflationary pressures that were the result of Democratic mistakes. The effort to evaluate the economic performance of different partisan administrations is challenging indeed.

---

[18] Note that these examples all come before 1984. Chapter 8 proposes an explanation in terms of the "Great Moderation."

[19] See the comments by Charles Schultze reported in Nordhaus (1989, pp. 56–63).

STUDIES OF PARTISANSHIP EMBEDDED IN MODELS OF THE ECONOMY

An implicit theme of this chapter has been that party differences can mean different things given different understandings of the way the economic world works, that is, of the ways in which economic reality constrains political choices. Several studies, using models built around several explicit conceptions of the macroeconomy, have shown that government partisanship influences unemployment and income growth in the United States.[20] Thus far in this chapter, we have considered party differences in a world with a static, naïve Phillips curve, and we have considered them in a world with a natural rate of unemployment. But the natural rate theory we have considered is not the only one. As drawn from Milton Friedman's 1968 address, as used by Nordhaus in his electoral cycle model, and as used thus far in this chapter, this has been a natural rate world in which expectations regarding inflation have been formed adaptively, that is, as a function of past values of inflation. This view has been seriously challenged by "rational expectations." In rational expectations theory, the mistakes of overstimulation are, in principle, easier to correct than in the previous natural rate model. If expectations are rational and policy makers are credible in telling the public that they mean to eliminate inflation, a painful recession should not be necessary.

There is even less room for sustainable party differences in a rational expectations world than there is in the adaptive expectations world. As a consequence, partisan differences regarding real variables such as output and unemployment will have disappeared by the end of an administration in such a world. Under rational expectations theory, it is still believed that there are natural rates of unemployment and output. However, policy makers are seen as having even less control over unemployment under this theory, which argues that policy makers can influence real variables such as unemployment and output only by surprising or fooling people. Because people are presumed to be too rational to be repeatedly fooled, policy makers have little control over unemployment and output, which are assumed to be normally in equilibrium at these natural rates.

---

[20] Chappell and Keech (1986b) used two models of the economy, the "St. Louis" model and a rational expectations model. Alesina and Sachs (1988) and Chappell and Keech (1988a) used rational expectations models to study partisanship in income growth and unemployment, respectively. Elsewhere, Chappell and Keech (1988b) used the Fairmodel (Fair, 1984).

Several scholars have shown that it is still possible to have party differences in the equilibrium world of rational expectations. According to one leading view of this, Democrats should produce higher growth and lower unemployment, and Republicans should produce the reverse pattern, but such differences should be transitory and should come early in an administration.[21] As supportive evidence, note the following figures; they are averages of GNP growth rates for each year of Republican and Democratic administrations from 1949 through 2008[22]:

	Year			
	1	2	3	4
Democrat	3.67	5.90	4.17	3.65
Republican	3.32	0.68	3.30	3.77

Consistent with rational expectations theory, the differences come early in an administration, and they disappear toward the end. On average, they are small to negligible; in the second year, they are striking, but transitory.

Table 4.3 shows that unemployment figures do not follow quite the same pattern, even though in theory the two variables are inversely related through "Okun's law." The unemployment figure is actually higher in the first year of a Democratic administration. However, the difference returns to those predicted by conventional wisdom for the second, third, and fourth years, with the maximum difference coming in the third year. For unemployment, the parties are most different in the second half of the terms, whereas for income growth, they are most different in the first half.

The scope for differences in unemployment and growth rates has narrowed steadily as our analysis has moved through successive developments in macroeconomic theory. The natural rate hypothesis narrowed the scope from the stable menu of choices on a static, naïve Phillips curve, and the

---

[21] The explanation is based on the assumption that partisan differences in monetary policy are predictable and that wage contracts overlap electoral periods. Because there is uncertainty before an election regarding which party will win, any election outcome will involve a surprise regarding the rate of money growth and, therefore, the rate of inflation. Because labor contracts are set before the election, expectations of inflation cannot be adjusted immediately with the outcome of the election. See Alesina and Sachs (1988) and Chappell and Keech (1988b).

[22] These figures are taken from Table 4.3, following. They are modeled on Alesina (1995), who gives figures from 1949 through 1992.

Party	UNEM1[a]	UNEM2	UNEM3	UNEM4	GDP1[a]	GDP2	GDP3	GDP4	CPI1[a]	CPI2	CPI3	CPI4
Total	5.68	5.78	5.72	5.53	2.98	2.77	3.65	3.72	3.34	3.70	3.90	3.83
Democrat	6.47	5.22	4.73	4.72	2.54	5.90	4.17	3.65	1.83	2.83	4.77	4.55
Republican	5.06	6.16	6.38	6.08	3.32	0.68	3.30	3.77	4.52	4.28	3.32	3.34

Administration	Year	UNEM1	UNEM2	UNEM3	UNEM4	GDP1	GDP2	GDP3	GDP4	CPI1	CPI2	CPI3	CPI4
Truman (D)	1949	5.90	5.30	3.30	3.00	-0.50	8.7	7.7	3.8	-1.2	1.3	7.9	1.9
Kennedy/Johnson (D)	1961	6.70	5.50	5.70	5.20	2.3	6.1	4.4	5.8	1.0	1.0	1.3	1.3
Johnson (D)	1965	4.50	3.80	3.80	3.60	6.4	6.5	2.5	4.8	1.6	2.9	3.1	4.2
Carter (D)	1977	7.10	6.10	5.80	7.10	4.6	5.6	3.1	-0.3	6.5	7.6	11.3	13.5
Clinton (D)	1993	6.90	6.10	5.60	5.40	2.9	4.1	2.5	3.7	3.0	2.6	2.8	3.0
Clinton II (D)	1997	4.90	4.50	4.20	4.00	4.5	4.4	4.8	4.1	2.3	1.6	2.2	3.4
Obama (D)	2009	9.30	9.60	8.90		-3.5	3.0	1.7		-0.4	1.6	3.2	
Average		6.47	5.84	5.33	4.72	2.39	5.49	3.81	3.65	1.83	2.66	4.54	4.55
Average		6.16		5.02		3.94		3.73		2.24		4.55	
Average			5.59				3.83				3.39		
Eisenhower (R)	1953	2.90	5.50	4.40	4.10	4.6	-0.6	7.2	2	0.8	0.7	-0.4	1.5
Eisenhower II (R)	1957	4.30	6.80	5.50	5.50	2	-0.9	7.2	2.5	3.3	2.8	0.7	1.7
Nixon (R)	1969	3.50	4.90	5.90	5.60	3.1	0.2	3.4	5.3	5.5	5.7	4.4	3.2
Nixon/Ford (R)	1973	4.90	5.60	8.50	7.70	5.8	-0.6	-0.2	5.4	6.2	11.0	9.1	5.8
Reagan (R)	1981	7.60	9.70	9.60	7.50	2.5	-1.9	4.5	7.2	10.3	6.2	3.2	4.3
Reagan II (R)	1985	7.20	7.00	6.20	5.50	4.1	3.5	3.2	4.1	3.6	1.9	3.6	4.1
Bush (R)	1989	5.30	5.50	6.70	7.40	3.6	1.9	-0.2	3.4	4.8	5.4	4.2	3.0
GW Bush (R)	2001	4.70	5.80	6.00	5.50	1.1	1.8	2.5	3.6	2.8	1.6	2.3	2.7
GW Bush II (R)	2005	5.10	4.60	4.60	5.80	3.1	2.7	1.9	-0.3	3.4	3.2	2.8	3.8
Average		5.06	6.16	6.38	6.07	3.32	0.68	3.28	3.68	4.52	4.28	3.32	3.34
Average		5.61		6.22		2.00		3.48		4.40		3.33	
Average			5.91				2.74				3.87		

[a] UNEMI, unemployment in first year; GDP1, gross domestic product in first year; CPI1, consumer price index in first year.
Source: Bureau of Labor Statistics, Bureau of Economic Analysis, *Economic Report of the President*

rational expectations version of the natural rate hypothesis narrowed the scope still further. Although partisanship theory is alive and well in studies of the politics of macroeconomic policy, it does not explain much of the substantial variation in outcomes such as unemployment and growth rates.

CONDITIONAL PARTISANSHIP AND SECONDARY PARTISANSHIP[23]

Thus far, we have treated party differences as if they were based on fixed targets. In fact, it is likely that partisan goals are more fluid and conditional. For example, Tufte (1978, pp. 101–2) identified two rules:

1. If there is a single highly visible economic problem that is very important to the electorate, seek re-election improvements on that problem regardless of the economic priorities of the party platform.
2. If no single economic problem is dominant, seek to improve the pre-election economy in the direction of party platform priorities.

Hibbs also acknowledged that both parties will relax unemployment goals with rising inflation (1987, p. 253), and presumably they will also relax inflation goals with rising unemployment.[24]

One study took account of varying economic conditions using historical data. Chappell and Keech (1988b) estimated "typical" Republican and Democratic fiscal and monetary policies over the period from 1953 through 1984. Using a multi-equation model of the U.S. economy, they simulated what a typical Republican and a typical Democrat would have done in each administration and compared those results with the performance of the actual incumbent. They found that the differences in outcomes caused by party differences were invariably small in size, and sometimes counter-intuitive in direction.[25]

The most explicit model of contingent goal formation is that of Hibbs (1994), which builds directly on the idea that there is a sustainable rate of output growth akin to a natural rate, and that output above that sustainable

---

[23] Not to be confused with "conditional party government" (Aldrich and Rohde, 2000).

[24] See also Frey and Schneider (1978) and Mosley (1984) for suggestions of contingent partisanship.

[25] The method of inferring typical partisan policies is to estimate "reaction functions" in which choices of policy instruments are regressed on economic conditions and partisan-ship. See Alt and Woolley (1982) for a discussion of the assumptions and limitations of that strategy. The model of the economy was the Fairmodel. For a description, see Fair (1984).

path is inflationary.[26] In this newer Hibbs theory, the differences between the parties is in the degree to which they will risk inflationary growth: "Democratic Administrations entertain higher output growth targets than Republican ones, because Democrats are more averse to needless shortfalls of output growth from potential and less averse to the risks of higher inflation that up-side mistakes might generate" (Hibbs 1994, p. 7).

The parties are uncertain about what the sustainable path is, and they are both concerned about inflation. Hibbs argues that the parties' variable targets for nominal output "depend on fixed ('politically deep') preference parameters" and on actual and expected inflation (1994, p. 8). Thus, Hibbs creates a viable theory of how immediate partisan goals vary with conditions, while maintaining that these varying targets are functions of unvarying underlying preferences. This idea of fixed underlying partisan preferences is asserted without defense and can safely be viewed as simply a provisional assumption.

Such an interpretation makes much more sense for electorally motivated parties than does the idea of fixed and unconditional goals. Any party is likely to take the stance of a general problem solver and try to deal with the prominent problems at hand. Success or failure in doing so may have lasting influence on the identity, reputation, and even the electability of parties. The idea that the Democrats were the party of prosperity and the Republicans the party of economic stagnation was surely due in small part to various accidents of history from the late 1920s through the late 1960s, including who was in office when adverse shocks occurred.

Party Differences as Secondary Consequences

The importance of partisanship in economic policy is not contingent on the size or regularity of systematic differences in outcomes such as unemployment. Parties may have more clearly defined policy differences regarding the distribution of income. Hibbs and Dennis (1988) documented the differences in income shares for the top and bottom segments of the population under Democratic and Republican administrations, showing that the distribution was more egalitarian under Democrats. Bartels (2008,

---

[26] This newer contribution by Hibbs quietly drops his earlier claim concerning differences between parties on the question of sustainably divergent unemployment rates. He does observe that the divergent output paths he graphs (1987, p. 228) are in levels, rather than growth rates, and thus roughly compatible with the Alesina figures noted earlier (personal communication).

ch. 2) documents differences between the parties in income growth patterns by income quintile, to the same effect.

Some of those patterns may have derived from tax and transfer policies that were designed to redistribute income downward. Havrilesky (1987) argues that redistribution has disincentive effects that produce adverse electoral consequences and that governments create monetary surprises to stimulate output so as to compensate for the decline in output associated with redistribution. Through this process or others like it, some of the observed party differences in macroeconomic performance may be secondary consequences of other partisan goals. These ideas are at least superficially compatible with research based on the idea that parties have different targets for inflation and unemployment.[27]

REVERSIBILITY AND LIMITING THE CHOICES OF SUCCESSORS

Thus far in this chapter, we have considered a model in which the policy choices of defeated, outgoing governments were reversible by their successors, who could move to their goals without cost. According to another model, it was painful and costly for the new party to correct the mistakes of its predecessor, but even in that case, the outgoing party made no *intentional* effort to restrict the choices of its successor. However, several studies have built on the observation that incumbent governments can influence the nature of the policy that will be implemented after they are out of office, and they have presented models of how parties might do so strategically.

For example, in an article entitled "Why a Stubborn Conservative Would Run a Deficit," Persson and Svensson (1989) show that a conservative party that expects not to win the next election can impose its preferences on its liberal successor. The key is that government consumption is negatively related to inherited debt. The losing conservatives may seek to restrict the spending proclivities of their successors by increasing indebtedness.[28]

Notable politicians (such as Senator Daniel Patrick Moynihan) and distinguished academics (such as Professor Aaron Wildavsky) have observed that that may have been a strategy of the Reagan administration. I find it doubtful that President Reagan intended to run up the deficits he produced, but a restriction on new Democratic programs may well have been seen as a welcome side effect of the huge increase in government debt

[27] See Cukierman (1992, pp. 341–3) for a commentary.
[28] See also Alesina and Tabellini (1990) and Tabellini and Alesina (1990).

in the 1980s. And clearly that debt limited the options available to the Clinton administration.

However, perverse and cynical strategies such as the one identified by Persson and Svensson are not the only ways in which politicians can ensure that their preferences will live on regardless of who succeeds them. An early example of this was the Social Security system, set up by the Social Security Act of 1935. Social Security was a Democratic program opposed by Republicans, and different from programs Republicans would have preferred. It may seem ironic, but the Republicans preferred a program that would be targeted at the poor, that would have been funded with general tax revenues on a pay-as-you-go basis, and that would have provided immediate universal coverage for the needy. In contrast, the winning Democratic program was intended ultimately to include everybody, not just the poor; it was to be funded with earmarked taxes held in a trust fund, and it would be phased in slowly.

Why would the Republicans have wanted to target the poor, who were not part of their basic constituency? Why would the Democrats seek to incorporate the entire workforce, including the upscale classes that were part of the Republican constituency? The parties appear to have reversed roles again when the Democrats preferred saving insurance contributions in a trust fund, whereas the Republicans favored the use of general revenues for the poor.

The answer, I think, has to do with the remarkable foresight that both parties seem to have shown concerning the long-term consequences of their preferences. Republicans seem to have anticipated that a program with annual appropriations for the poor and needy could easily be kept small, whereas a trust fund would be more difficult to limit. Democrats seem to have known that if people believed that insurance contributions were being held in a trust fund, they would feel entitled to these benefits and would retain higher self-esteem than if they were receiving tax revenues doled out to the needy. Obviously, it would be much more difficult to restrain or scale down the Democratic program in times of budgetary stringency.

Subsequent history has shown that both the Democrats and the Republicans were probably correct in supporting the programs that fit with their preferences for large and small government, respectively. The Democrats, of course, won that battle. The Republicans campaigned against Social Security in 1936 but subsequently gave up opposition to that increasingly popular program. As Republicans predicted, the trust fund was not allowed to grow to a level at which people would be receiving benefits closely geared to their individual contributions plus interest. Instead, the trust fund was tapped through a series of amendments that moved the system to a pay-as-you-go arrangement, under which most early beneficiaries received back large multiples of their contributions.[29] Because of the extravagant rhetoric surrounding the system, people began to believe that they had earned their benefits, quickly losing sight of the fact that (in the early experience, at least), they were receiving a great deal more than they had ever paid in.

For a time, the government provided increases in Social Security benefits in a pattern that suspiciously followed even-numbered years. That was one of Tufte's leading examples of an electoral cycle for an instrument under government control, until a 1972 bidding war among presidential aspirants finally exhausted the slack in the trust fund (Tufte 1978, pp. 29–36). Since then, benefits have been indexed to go up with the consumer price index, and Social Security became known as the "third rail" of American politics (touch it and you die). Clearly, the Democrats of the 1930s succeeded in creating a program that quickly became too big, too popular, and too entrenched to be vulnerable to future efforts to reduce or eliminate it.[30]

Social Security is a leading example of a program that limited the choices of succeeding administrations. It shows that a partisan model of political economy must take into account more than the reversible movements in inflation and unemployment, and it shows that the environment of choice that parties face changes over time, even if there are no changes in the identities and goals of the parties. I see no reason to assume that partisan stances on policy innovations will always show as much foresight as was evident in the Social Security example.

Of course, Social Security is no longer the third rail of American politics. Early in his second term, President George W. Bush proposed a privatization of the program that went nowhere in Congress. Republican presidential contenders felt free to criticize Social Security as a Ponzi scheme in the 2012 party debates. And the Social Security system does at best need some tinkering to be sustainable for more than twenty years.[31]

---

[29] "For example, the average 65-year-old retiree in 1982 (with a nonworking spouse) recovers his lifetime contributions within nine months after retiring" (Federal Reserve Bank of New York, *Quarterly Review*, Autumn 1982, pp. 1–2).

[30] The shift to automatically indexing benefits to the rate of inflation in 1974 can be seen as conservative, relative to the previous practice of discretionary increases that were greater than the rate of inflation. However, it can also be seen as liberal relative to the possibility that in some circumstances of budgetary stringency, there might have been no increases at all. See Weaver (1988).

[31] The Trustees report of April 2012 says that without revision of the law, full benefits can be paid only through 2033. See http://www.ssa.gov/oact/TRSUM/index.html. Soneji and King (2012) argue that the problem is much worse than the Social Security actuaries realize.

Sometimes we go down a path that reduces our alternatives in a way that is neither deliberate nor shrewd, though it may be opportunistic in the short run. In describing "how we became the choiceless society," Peter Peterson argues that the American people never made a deliberate choice for the policies that have resulted in deficits and slow growth: The choices were never framed honestly and seriously. The American people were never provided with realistic assessments of the costs and benefits of different courses of action" (1993, ch. 2, p. 69).

DIMENSIONS OF CHOICE IN A WORLD OF ASYMMETRIC INFORMATION

The most thorough treatment of macroeconomic policy making in a framework of asymmetric information between policy makers and the public is Cukierman's *Central Bank Strategy, Credibility, and Independence* (1992). Systematic and predictable partisan differences are discussed in only a small part of that book, but Cukierman analyzes a variety of dimensions on which policy makers may differ and over which voters may have some choice, even though their information about the nature of those choices is imperfect. Cukierman points out that policy makers differ in their relative emphasis on price stability and employment, and such preferences may change over time, even for a given policy maker. They may differ in their ability to commit to a noninflationary strategy, and they may differ in their forecasts about the state of the economy and the persistence of inflation.

All of these differences are likely to confound the clarity of otherwise predictable party differences, and these are issues on which policy makers may differ without regard to party. Therefore, this chapter on models of choice must acknowledge that partisanship is only one of the bases for choice, though it is surely the most fundamental. In Chapter 3, in discussing electoral cycles, we found that asymmetric information rendered elections imperfect institutions for accountability. In this chapter, we see that asymmetric information also renders elections imperfect institutions for choice.

COSTS OF DEMOCRACY IN PARTISAN MODELS

Partisan models have not paid much attention to the public welfare consequences of party competition and alternation. Many models use social welfare functions in which the weights on output or inflation differ by party, but no partisanship model contrasts that sort of welfare function with a nonpartisan social welfare function, or with such a function for a benevolent dictatorship. The closest the literature comes to modeling the costs of bipartisan alternation in power can be seen in the work of Alesina (1987, 1988a). In his model, voters prefer a position that is between the platforms of the two parties. The parties themselves, because of risk aversion, would also prefer some averaging of their two positions, rather than the continual policy changes that result from their alternation in office. But because of credibility problems, they cannot commit to the more moderate position. As a result, they fail to converge on the position most preferred by the voters, and alternation between polarized parties continues.

This kind of oscillation, as a result of the parties' failure to converge to a moderate best outcome as defined by the position of the median voter, may be considered a cost of democracy. It is the cost entailed in having choices, wherein the existence of meaningful choices implies uncertainty about the outcomes. But because all of the outcomes are on a Pareto frontier,[32] the costs derive from the uncertainty, rather than from a basis for considering the outcomes inferior, from everyone's point of view, to an alternative that is feasible. Costs are entailed in having choices and having an open process of defining alternatives.[33] A more convincing case that partisan conflict can have adverse consequences can be derived from models that go beyond the context of relatively small differences in inflation, unemployment, and growth caused by changes in partisan control of the American presidency. The context of partisan conflict can vary in several ways that will have welfare consequences. These include polarization of the alternatives, dispersal of power across political institutions, and the congruence of partisan alternatives with economic institutions.

Polarization

If there is a cost that derives either from uncertainty about partisan outcomes or from oscillation between alternatives, that cost will increase with increasing distance or polarization between the alternatives. However, some of the models that show adverse consequences of polarization involve a failure to agree on programs that could make everybody better off by dealing with pressing problems or avoiding adverse long-term consequences. These models involve situations in which different partisan actors have a veto

---

[32] That is, there is no alternative than can make someone better off without making someone else worse off.
[33] Cukierman (1992) models the welfare cost of uncertainty about the outcomes.

power that can be used to prevent implementation of a painful but potentially beneficial policy change.[34]

Since the first edition of this book, polarization between the two main
American parties has increased substantially.[35] This is especially true in
Congress, where its consequences have for the most part not been good
(Fiorina 2009, ch. 7). The national legislature increasingly approximates a
situation in which the leftmost Republican is to the right of the rightmost
Democrat. The consequences for macroeconomic performance have been
especially bad because partisan polarization has obstructed fiscal policy
agreements that would avoid the fiscal crises the United States has been
facing in recent years. These matters will be taken up in Chapter 9.

Beyond these spatial movements in expressed policy preferences among
the parties, civility and respect for the other party's goals and motivations
have declined. Mann and Ornstein attribute this mostly to Republicans
(2012, chs. 1–2). Grunwald calls Republicans "The Party of No" (2012,
ch. 7). Senator Mitch McConnell (R-KY) repeatedly said that Republicans'
main goal was to make Barack Obama a one-term president.

Now this may appear unseemly. Compromise, mutual respect, and cooperation are all valued in American culture. Republicans are not saying that
they want to do what is best for the country, whether or not it is equivalent
to what Democrats happen to want. They are not trying to compromise and
move a policy in their direction. Republicans have been taking a lot of
criticism for being obstructionist, and there is something less than dignified
about opposing something that you once were for because you do not want
the other party to get credit for it.[36]

How might this be reasonable? If an opposition party wants to win office,
a reasonable strategy may well be to use its influence to have things go badly
for the incumbent party. The risk is that voters will punish behavior that
they see as obstructionist, but it may work. And what if a party is seeking a
future majority that will radically restructure American public policy?
Having things go badly for incumbents may work to this party's advantage,

---

[34] See Alesina and Drazen (1991), who show that polarization of parties has consequences for
the possibility of carrying out stabilization policy in the face of massive debt or hyperinflation. Their model helps us understand political problems that are more dire than those
that have historically been faced in the United States.

[35] See McCarty, Poole, and Rosenthal 2006; Fiorina 2009; Theriault 2008.

[36] Mann and Ornstein give as an example the January 26, 2010, Senate Republican filibuster
against a deficit reduction task force that several Republicans had cosponsored. "Why did
they do so? Because President Barack Obama was for it, and its passage might give him
political credit" (2012, pp. ix–x). "If he was for it, we had to be against it" (quoted in
Grunwald (2012, p. 19).

either by retrospective voting against an incumbent or by radicalizing enough of the electorate for the out party to win a future election.

This is a risky strategy, because it may or may not work. And even if it does work, in the American constitutional system, the party that lives by this sword and wins office may face comparable obstructionist tactics by the formerly incumbent party it defeated in this way. Earlier, I reviewed some models in which parties traded off policy and office goals, but these were oriented mainly to the next election. As in a democracy, all goals and preferences are in principle legitimate, the possibility of using this long-term strategy may be considered a strength of democracy, in that it opens up possibilities of dramatic change.

Dispersal of Power

The polarization over the distribution of the burdens of a stabilization program would not be a problem if agreement between the actors were not needed. If winning meant that the successful party would be completely dominant, it would not matter (within the context of the model) which party won. However, many countries have multiple parties and no single majority party. In those countries, coalitions are likely to be necessary to form a government and to carry out policy. When that is the case, polarization can make agreement between partisan actors more difficult and less likely. Also, the institutions that embody the separation of powers in the American sense can make partisan disagreement or polarization consequential. Roubini and Sachs argue that "when power is dispersed, either across branches of the government (as in the U.S.) or across many political parties in a coalition government (as in Italy), or across parties through the alternation of political control over time, the likelihood of intertemporally inefficient budgetary policy is heightened" (1989a, p. 905). These themes will be picked up in Chapter 9, where budgetary policy is explicitly considered.

Congruence between Partisan Alternatives
and Economic Institutions

Alvarez, Garrett, and Lange (1991) have shown that various partisan alternatives may be more effective and may lead to better performance under different patterns of organization of the domestic economy. Specifically, they have shown that Left governments deliver better performance in terms of growth, inflation, and unemployment in countries with strong and centralized unions, and Right governments perform better in those areas when the labor movement is weak. However, in countries that do not have that congruence between winning parties and economic institutions, economic performance is worse. This suggests that there may be another dimension to the costs inherent in having choices. One kind of partisan alternative may be inferior and inefficient in some settings, but the determination of which one is inferior will vary across countries.

Partisan models seem to be far more robust theoretically and empirically than are the electoral cycle models. Both are models of routine politics. As this chapter shows, there is considerable variety in the nature of partisan conflict. Partisan conflict is routine if it is repeated again and again in the same context. In fact, the context is rarely static, as succeeding chapters will show. Even partisan conflict is likely to be fluid, rather than predictable, according to an equilibrium model.

5

Unintended Consequences, Moral Hazard, and Time-Consistency

This chapter uses the recent financial crisis to identify and illustrate three risks of politics and government in general that are not captured by models of routine democratic politics: political business cycles (Chapter 3) and models of partisan competition (Chapter 4). The first is the simple and intuitive possibility that programs that reflect good intentions may have unintended and unanticipated consequences and that some of these consequences may be undesirable. The second is moral hazard, wherein insuring against risk may lead agents to behave less prudently than they would if they were to bear the full costs of the consequences of their behavior. The third is the time-consistency problem, in which there may be a conflict between the right thing to do for all times and the right thing to do at a particular time. These are problems to which all governments are subject, whether authoritarian or democratic, whereas the models of routine politics are unique to countries that choose their leaders through elections.

We focus on the financial crisis of 2007–9, with its aftermath of sluggish growth and high unemployment. The financial crisis exacerbated the deficit and debt problem that preceded it, which will be briefly introduced here and taken up further in Chapter 9. Each of these problems happened independently, but the financial crisis has made the fiscal situation even worse than it would have been without it.

We will evaluate the formal and constitutional democratic institutions of elections and limited government for their role in creating the problems, and for their role in addressing if not resolving them. As the formal democratic institutions are a constant, they cannot be a direct or unconditional cause of the deterioration in economic conditions. The impact of democratic institutions on economic performance is not generic, but it depends among other things on the nature of secondary institutions that may be formal in the sense that they are legislated or otherwise official. Or the secondary institutions may be informal in the sense that they are not written down but are patterns of behavior or norms. Alternatively, the preferences of citizens may have changed. Or random events may have shocked the system.

I argue that both economic problems (debt and financial crisis) could have been avoided or at least made less consequential if different actions had been taken by policy makers and by economic agents. Still, there is not one single responsible agent or party, a fact that blurs accountability. Yet, the chapter will distinguish mistakes and foibles that are part of ordinary human nature from those that are exaggerated or made more consequential by democratic institutions. Specifically, the chapter will distinguish mistakes that could easily be made by both democratic and authoritarian leaders from those that can be specifically linked to democratic institutions, such as regular elections or the legislative process.

Obviously, democratic institutions are compatible with good economic performance. The world's richest nations are almost uniformly democratic, and most of them have become rich under democratic institutions. The United States has been a leading example of growth and prosperity under democratic institutions. This was a central message of the 1995 edition of this book. But things are not as they were.

To what extent are the decisions that put the United States into and are keeping it in this adverse situation attributable in whole or in part to the fundamental democratic institutions of regular elections and limitations on government such as separation of powers? To what extent are they due to secondary formal or informal practices associated with the formal democratic institutions? To what extent are they just human nature? To what extent are they the result of adverse random shocks, or bad luck?

One important feature of democratic institutions is that they process the preferences of citizens in two ways. One is through popular elections, and a central feature of democratic institutions is that no restrictions should be placed on the nature or range of opinions expressed. That is to say that the opinions and values behind voting can be sophisticated or ignorant, wise or unwise, informed or uninformed. As the possibility always exists that opinions can be ignorant, unwise, and uninformed, democratic institutions do not always ensure that the choices voters make will be good ones. In this way, the policy consequences of democratic electoral institutions are contingent on the preferences that are fed into them.

Similarly, the limitations on the power of any given institution in a system of separated powers and individual rights provide a possibility of blocking constructive change. There is a bias in favor of the status quo in any system that provides institutional means of blocking new initiatives. This feature can work against good solutions that threaten or undermine existing groups or privileges. But the feature can also protect a desirable status quo against misguided initiatives.

These two features can interact, as well. If the results of the electoral process are policies that are unwise, they can become the status quo. Then the limits on government feature can work against constructive solutions. In sum, electoral contests that are simplistic or misleading and lawmaking procedures that permit the blocking of constructive changes are just as democratic as electoral contests that are enlightening and fair and law-making procedures that solve problems and make Pareto improvements. The relationship between democratic institutions and the quality of policy is an open question, and it surely varies across time and political geography.

I suggest that democratic institutions have contributed more to the current economic problems in the United States through irregular mechanisms such as the three that are the focus of this chapter than through opportunistic models of routine politics such as the political business cycle. These mechanisms include generic and general problems such as unintended consequences, and they include more precise problems such as moral hazard and time-consistency. These problems are faced by all governments, and not unique to democracy, but democracy may bring unique vulnerabilities to them.

DEMOCRATIC INSTITUTIONS AND FISCAL PROBLEMS BEFORE THE FINANCIAL CRISIS

For most of U.S. history, federal revenues have exceeded expenditures or been within sight of covering them. With the major exception of wartimes, there has been a bipartisan commitment to balanced budgets, and an approximate balance between years of deficit and years of surplus up until the 1960s. This was done without formal mechanisms to ensure a coordination of taxing and spending. Since then, this informal fiscal discipline has broken down.[1]

The Clinton administration left the country with four years of federal budget surpluses, the first since 1969. This was good news about the performance of democratic institutions that would have fit with the message of the first edition of this book. In spite of attention to these issues in the 2000 presidential campaign, several major events occurred in the George

---

[1] See Ippolito (2012) for an authoritative history of fiscal policy in the United States.

W. Bush administration to undermine the surplus. First, major cuts in taxes were passed in 2001 and 2003. Second, wars were started in Afghanistan and Iraq. Third, the pay-as-you-go institutions were dropped. In addition, Medicare was expanded to include a prescription drug benefit, without provision for covering the costs. The net result of these actions was that deficits soared.

So even before the financial crisis began in late 2007, the United States faced a looming fiscal crisis that would get worse the longer action was postponed. To illustrate the serious nature of the fiscal situation before the budgetary costs and the macroeconomic impact of the financial crisis became clear, I draw on a report by David M. Walker, then comptroller general of the United States (Walker 2008). Walker pointed out that between fiscal years 2000 and 2007, explicit present liabilities of the U.S. government had risen from $6.9 trillion to $10.8 trillion, or 57 percent. These included publicly held debt, military and civilian pensions, and retiree health care. The implicit future liabilities in terms of Social Security and Medicare benefits had risen from $13 trillion to $40.8 trillion, or 213 percent.

Electoral Politics and Deficit Spending

What did these developments have to do with democratic institutions? In my view, they were driven by the generic incentives of electoral politics. As Buchanan and Wagner pointed out in 1977, the main incentives of budget policy are twofold: the public likes public programs, and it dislikes paying taxes. Before Keynes gave an economic rationale for intentional deficit spending, the informal norms of balanced budgets prevailed for the most part against the temptation to spend beyond what was taxed.

The feature of democracy that has the most to do with the fiscal problems is the incentives of electoral politics. This is not the electoral cycle that involves spurts to spending or growth close to elections, or the partisan theory that shows different results for inflation, unemployment, and growth after elections in which parties change. The operative incentives are the natural desire to have public expenditures that one does not fully pay for and to pay less in taxes.

In addition, there is a bias in favor of the status quo. When public programs exist, it is much more difficult to pare them back or take them away than to just let them continue. When taxes are insufficient to cover expenditures, it is much more difficult politically to raise them than to continue them as they are.

Fiscal policy under democratic politics can run well under formal or informal rules. Since at least 2000, it has been running in an ad hoc way that is without discipline or principle. Much previous experience shows that such indiscipline is not inevitable in a democracy in general, and not in the United States in particular. In that country, the more irresponsible and shortsighted possibilities of democracy have come to the fore.

These possibilities reflect dangers and risks of democracy but not inevitability. The United States has lost its sense of fiscal discipline and the formal and informal institutions that support it. It remains to be seen whether the bipartisan National Commission on Fiscal Responsibility and Reform (2010), and other forces of long-term sustainability in fiscal policy can reestablish such discipline. The prospects are not encouraging.

DEMOCRATIC INSTITUTIONS AND PROCESSES AND THE EMERGENCE OF THE FINANCIAL CRISIS

The crisis that began in the United States in the summer of 2007 and reached its greatest intensity in the fall of 2008 is the most significant financial crisis since the Great Depression. Reinhart and Rogoff (2009, p. 203, passim) call it the "Second Great Contraction." It began in the United States and spread worldwide, especially to Europe. It has caused enormous losses of wealth, income, and employment.

Democracy and Financial Crises in General

Democracy is neither necessary nor sufficient for financial crises. The subtitle of Reinhart and Rogoff's survey is indicative regarding necessity: "Eight Centuries of Financial Folly" reflects the fact that financial crises existed well before modern democracies emerged. As to sufficiency, Gary Gorton identifies what he calls the "Quiet Period," a span of more than seven decades lasting from 1934 to 2007 in which there were no banking panics in the democratic United States (2010, p. 54, passim). Of course, some financial crises did occur in the United States in that period, such as the savings and loan crisis, the brief stock market crash of 1987, and the bursting of the dot.com bubble. But these crises were contained and did not have major systemic consequences. They did not lead to a banking panic on the order of 1907, 1929 to 1933, or 2007 to 2009.

Although he leaves the question open, Gorton suggests that we might think of this long period as exceptional and based on special conditions that no longer hold, rather than something that we know how to recreate. One key to an explanation of why the United States went for so many years without banking panics could be deposit insurance, which was established in the Banking Act of 1933.

Deposit insurance is a mechanism that illustrates both the constructive possibilities of democratic institutions and also the risks. Because banks take short-term deposits and use them to make long-term loans, even well-run and strong banks cannot remain solvent if many of their depositors demand their money within a short period. Deposit insurance contributes to confidence in banks by avoiding the risk that rumors of bank weakness will become self-fulfilling, even for strong banks. This confidence is the constructive possibility of democracy: making rules that create Pareto improvements and solve collective action problems.

But the risk of such constructive possibilities is moral hazard, the possibility that people or organizations that are insured against risks will act less prudently and take more risks. This problem was handled with regulation. To become a bank, an organization had to acquire a charter from the federal or state government, and these were not easy to obtain. According to Gorton, the privilege of being a bank was like the privilege of being a monopoly, and it provided an incentive to self-regulate (2010, p. 54). Under broad congressional supervision, various agencies administer deposit insurance and have the capacity to impose capital requirements and to take over undercapitalized banks.

Moral Hazard and Democracy

Democracies provide a systematic, institutionalized incentive to do things that will please mass publics and interest groups. Deposit insurance is a good example of a program that will do so. It will please the public whose deposits are insured and remove from them the need to monitor carefully the soundness of their bank. Banks should like it, because it makes them less vulnerable to panics and runs on their assets. But the problem of moral hazard exists from a systemic perspective, and resolving the problem of moral hazard is unlikely to have as direct a constituency in a democracy as depositors or banks.

There is not a clear counterfactual to democracy here. A benevolent authoritarian government might well introduce deposit insurance to achieve the benefits for both depositors and bankers. A wise and benevolent authoritarian ruler might also worry about moral hazard. It is human nature to yield to moral hazard and take more risks if one knows that he or she will not bear the full costs of failure. So moral hazard is not a problem that is unique to democracy, but I will show how democratic institutions have been used explicitly in electoral and legislative processes in ways that have enhanced moral hazard. But first, I provide some background on housing, which was one of the root causes of the crisis.

Housing Policy in the United States: Unintended Consequences of Good Intentions

It is widely acknowledged that housing was one of the main sources of the financial crisis. The majority report of the Financial Crisis Inquiry Commission (FCIC) concluded that "collapsing mortgage lending standards and the mortgage securitization pipeline lit and spread the flame of contagion and crisis" (2011, p. xxiii). The Republican minority report also identifies housing as one of ten causes of the crisis: a housing bubble (not just in the United States), a proliferation of nontraditional mortgages, and deterioration in lending standards (FCIC 2011, pp. 417–9, 422–5). These Republicans say that mainly private actions "were supplemented by government policies, many of which had been in effect for decades, that subsidized homeownership but created hidden costs to taxpayers and the economy. Elected officials of both parties pushed housing subsidies too far" (FCIC 2011, p. 424).

Peter Wallison, a Republican who dissented from both of these reports, argues that the U.S. government's housing policy was "the *sine qua non* of the financial crisis." He continues, "If the U.S. Government had not chosen this policy path – fostering the growth of a bubble of unprecedented size and an equally unprecedented number of weak and high risk residential mortgages – the great financial crisis of 2008 would never have occurred" (FCIC 2011, p. 444).

So the majority and minority of the FCIC agreed that housing practices were at the root of the crisis, though they differ in the degree to which they blame the U.S. government and its housing and other policies for the crisis.

The U.S. government has influenced private housing markets in three basic ways. The first is in tax preferences for housing. The second is by insuring home mortgages, and the third is by additional efforts to encourage home ownership and increase the amount of "affordable housing." Tax preferences for housing may have encouraged overinvestment in housing, at the expense of more growth-oriented investments, but otherwise it had nothing to do with the financial crisis. The practice of insuring mortgages, although innocuous enough in its own right, was extended into practices that distorted markets and made the American taxpayer vulnerable to massive bailouts. The effort to increase the amount of affordable housing has led to deterioration in the standards used in lending, and to massive defaults and foreclosures.

All of these policies have been motivated to at least some degree by good intentions, and usually they have been reinforced by the incentives of democratic politics. But these intentions and incentives often have unintended consequences.[2] Sometimes, these consequences are arguable, subtle, and highly contestable, such as the suggestion that tax preferences for housing have led to less growth than a more neutral tax policy regarding housing and other investment.

The other two patterns of policy, insuring mortgages and the effort to encourage homeownership existed for years without major adverse consequences. But implementation of these well-meaning programs was extended into consequences that can be traced to catastrophes such as the recent financial crisis. In this way, the incentives of democratic politics enhanced moral hazard.

Democratic government is responsible and somewhat responsive to mass publics through popular elections and to interest groups through elections and legislative processes. Such responsiveness can lead to good or to bad policies. Democratic (and other) governments can be good for economic performance when they solve collective action problems. They can be bad for economic performance when they create moral hazard or when they create (or fall into) time-consistency traps. They may do these bad things in the process of solving collective action problems. So did the U.S. government play a role in causing the financial crisis by creating moral hazard or time-consistency traps? And if so, did it do so in response to the incentives of democratic politics?

The U.S. government has been indirectly or directly subsidizing homeownership since the modern income tax was ratified in the Sixteenth Amendment. The very first 1040 form for 1913 allowed deduction from gross income of "All interest paid within the year on personal indebtedness of taxpayer."[3] So the government was subsidizing borrowing to buy homes (along with borrowing for investment and consumption). When the deductibility of all interest was ended in the Tax Reform Act of 1986, the popular deductibility of interest for mortgages was left intact, along with a

---

[2] See Merton (1936); Hayek (1967), ch. 6; Smith (1976/1776).

[3] Form 1040 for 1913, accessed at http://www.irs.gov/pub/irs-utl/1913.pdf, on January 14, 2011. The federal government also supported housing by allowing the deduction of property taxes.

new possibility of "home equity loans," which allowed taxpayers to borrow against the value of their homes for any purposes, and to deduct that interest from their taxable income. In this way, housing got preferential tax treatment relative to other kinds of consumption and investment in 1986.

In addition to these tax subsidies, the U.S. government has been insuring some home mortgage loans through the Federal Housing Administration and other entities since 1934. Normally, the borrower pays a premium at closing for this insurance, but the government is liable in case of default. Fannie Mae (Federal National Mortgage Association, founded 1938) and Freddie Mac (Federal Home Loan Mortgage Corporation, founded 1970) are government-sponsored enterprises (GSEs) that provide a secondary market for mortgages. They repackage loans into mortgage-backed securities that they resell and provide more money for the mortgage market. Although they are private, profit-making corporations, their implicit backing by the government has allowed them advantages in the marketplace.

The Financial Crisis Inquiry Commission found that the GSE's "had a deeply flawed business model as publicly traded corporations with the implicit backing of and subsidies from the federal government and with a public mission ... They used their political power for decades to ward off effective regulation and oversight – spending $164 million on lobbying from 1999 to 2008" (FCIC Report 2011, p. xxvi).

They became insolvent after the housing bubble burst and were taken over by the government in September 2008. Thomas Sowell estimated that the cost to the taxpayer for bailing out Fannie and Freddie would be more than the bailouts of Bank of America, Citigroup, J.P. Morgan Chase, and Wells Fargo combined (2010, p. 75).

The federal government has for some time been actively encouraging "affordable housing" and endeavoring to broaden access to credit for purchasing homes. In 1992, Congress passed the Federal Housing Enterprises Financial Safety and Soundness Act (FHEFSSA), which authorized the Department of Housing and Urban Development to set affordable housing goals for Fannie and Freddie to give prospective homeowners of modest resources better access to mortgage credit (FCIC 2011, p. 41). This soon became a set of requirements for the relevant GSEs (i.e., Fannie Mae and Freddie Mac) to lower their standards for underwriting mortgages (FCIC 2011, pp. 451–4 in online version, Wallison dissent). In 1995, President Bill Clinton announced an initiative to increase home ownership from 65.1 percent to 67.5 percent of families by 2000. One element of his plan was to raise the affordable housing goals for Fannie Mae and Freddie Mac. President George W. Bush continued the push to expand home ownership (FCIC 2011, p. 41).

Loans were made available to borrowers whose credit would previously have made them ineligible for a mortgage. The agencies making these loans were no longer dominated by banks and savings and loans, which are regulated by the federal government. And the connection between the borrower and the agency that originated the mortgage was soon broken by the fact that the mortgage was resold and securitized.

As long as house prices kept going up, the weakness in borrowers' ability to meet their mortgage could be addressed by refinancing. And go up they did: "Since 1891, when the [Case-Shiller] price series began, no housing price boom has been comparable in terms of sheer magnitude and duration to that recorded in the years culminating in the 2007 subprime mortgage fiasco" (Reinhart and Rogoff 2009, p. 207).

Another government-related reason for the housing bubble was excessively loose monetary policy, which kept interest rates lower than economic conditions warranted. Between 2001 and 2006, the Federal Reserve had kept interest rates below those consistent with rules that guide the economy in response to interest rates and output (Taylor 2009, ch. 1).

Links to Democratic Institutions

The effort to increase affordable housing and to broaden home ownership had very wide public appeal. For the Democrats, it appealed to the low-income and minority part of their supporters. For the Republicans, the "ownership society" rang with traditional conservative values. And there was almost no direct federal expenditure or other obvious budgetary consequence.

Raghuram Rajan has suggested that these policies were a response to the rising inequality in American society (2010, ch. 1). The rich have been getting much richer, while the middle class and the poor have barely kept pace with their previous incomes. This is, according to Rajan, due to the returns from education, which increase with technological advance. In a country with little popular support for direct redistribution, or even for a denser safety net, easy credit is a way to enhance the living standards of those whose incomes are not rising. The result, of course, is mounting private debt, along with risk to the government in some cases of default.

Mian, Sufi, and Trebbi (2010a) show a more directly democratic process that involves legislation. They indicate that campaign contributions from mortgage-oriented financial institutions and subprime borrowers in congressional districts contributed to policies that led to the subprime crisis, and also to relaxing of regulation. Mian et al. show how elections, electoral competition, and constituency interest all combine into a pattern that created moral hazard.

Similarly, Igan, Mishra, and Tressel (2009) suggest that lobbying of Congress involves moral hazard and rent seeking. Specifically, they start with articles in the *Wall Street Journal* and the *Financial Times* that assert that mortgage lenders fought legislation that would work against predatory lending, and that subprime originators sought to prevent tighter regulations of the subprime market (2009, p. 4). In a careful empirical investigation, they find supportive evidence for the hypothesis that lobbying of Congress between 1999 and 2006 was by firms that were disproportionately risk taking ex ante and performed more poorly ex post.

Of course, lobbying is a First Amendment right: "Congress shall make no law ... abridging ... the right of the people ... to petition the Government for redress of grievances." But there is no assurance or requirement that lobbying be constructive, or that it not be a part of rent seeking or moral hazard. Here is a case without a clear counterfactual. No system is invulnerable to moral hazard, but Mian et al. show how processes associated with democratic legislative institutions led to outcomes that involved moral hazard. Democracy is consistent with moral hazard in that moral hazard resulted from decisions made through explicitly democratic institutions and processes.

One important link between democratic institutions and processes and the underlying causes of the financial crisis is as follows. The general subsidization of home ownership was a way to appeal to voters in the middle class and later to minorities and poor people who were not in the middle class. These policies can be founded in beliefs about responsible citizenship and firming ties to the community as enhanced by home ownership. They are also policies that are well designed to appeal for votes in a democracy. So they fit democracy but are not necessary or unconditional products of democratic institutions. For example, Canada is a democracy that did not go in this direction.

The Failure to See Danger Signs Is Human Nature

The financial crisis of 2007–9 is in some ways the result of unanticipated consequences of normal democratic processes. But the fact that they were not anticipated does not mean that they could not have been anticipated. Reinhart and Rogoff identify four characteristics of conditions leading up to financial crises and find that all were present in the United States before 2007: real housing prices rose, real equity index prices rose, current account deficit as a percentage of GDP was very high, and public debt was high. Now, admittedly, they were sampling on the dependent variable and do not give the fraction of countries or country-years in which such conditions were present, but no financial crisis occurred. However, these were characteristic of all modern financial crises above a certain threshold of seriousness.

Reinhart and Rogoff's title and theme are that countries that are otherwise vulnerable to crises have reasons, arguments, and pretexts to say that "this time is different" for them, and they quote Alan Greenspan, Ben Bernanke, and others to show how knowledgeable policy makers believed that their situation excused them from the risks. This stance of denying vulnerability to crisis is human nature, and not a phenomenon that is unique to democracy. As Reinhart and Rogoff point out, U.S. officials and economists used "this time is different" (TTID) in at least six ways (2009, pp. 214–15). But this pattern seems to be less democratic institutions than human nature. The experience reminds us that democratic institutions do not always protect us against the foibles of human nature.

DEMOCRATIC INSTITUTIONS AND PROCESSES AND THE RESPONSE TO THE FINANCIAL CRISIS

Reinhart and Rogoff show that the consequences of major financial crises are very great and long lasting. In the context of history, the United States may have recovered to positive (though not potential) growth remarkably fast.[4] But its currently high public debt and high unemployment are not unusual for a country that has experienced a financial crisis. In any case, the costs of the financial crisis are so great that one would hope that everything possible would be done to avoid a recurrence (Reinhart and Reinhart 2009, 2010). It is not clear that that is happening under the democratic institutions of the United States.

The Time-Consistency Problem

The financial crisis of 2007–9 is a good example of the time-consistency problem, which was crystallized by Kydland and

---

[4] According to the NBER, this recession lasted from December 2007 to June 2009, a duration of 18 months, which was longer than any recession since the Great Depression, which lasted 43 months from August 1929 to March 1933. There were two 16-month recessions, from November 1973 to March 1975, and from July 1981 to November 1982. *Source:* http://www.nber.org/cycles.html, accessed April 1, 2011.

Prescott (1977).[5] It is important to distinguish between the best thing to do for all times and the best thing to do at a specific time. There are two ways to evaluate the reaction to the financial crisis, and in particular the bailouts of Bear Stearns, Fannie Mae and Freddie Mac, AIG, and Citigroup.

The time-consistency problem is one in which not doing the right thing at time t creates expectations that the right thing will not be done at time t + 1. The quoted passage that follows gives the decision calculus faced by policy makers in 2008. I find the logic presented for bailing out the financial institutions in the situation described compelling, and the responsible thing to do at that time and under those conditions. But what makes it a time-consistency problem is that there had been bailouts going back to Continental Illinois in 1984, if not to the Reconstruction Finance Corporation of 1930. If banks had been allowed to fail before, their behavior would have changed to make them less vulnerable to the financial shocks.

The Republican minority report of the Financial Crisis Inquiry Commission gives a good case for the thinking of the members of Congress who voted for the Emergency Economic Stabilization Act of 2008 (EESA) and that of Secretary of the Treasury Henry Paulson, Federal Reserve Chairman Ben Bernanke, and New York Federal Reserve President Timothy Geithner:

> Policymakers were presented, for example, with the news that "AIG is about to fail" and counseled that a sudden and disorderly failure *might* trigger a chain reaction. Given the preceding failures of Fannie Mae and Freddie Mac, the Merrill Lynch merger, Lehman's bankruptcy . . . market confidence was on a knife's edge. A chain reaction could cause a run on the global financial system. They feared not just a run on a bank, but a generalized panic that might crash the entire system – that is, the risk of an event comparable to the Great Depression.
>
> For a policymaker, the calculus is simple: if you bail out AIG and you're wrong, you will have wasted taxpayer money and provoked public outrage. If you don't bail out AIG and you're wrong, the global financial system collapses. It should be easy to see why policymakers favored action – there was a chance of being wrong either way, and the costs of being wrong without action were far greater than the costs of being wrong with action. (FCIC 2011, p. 433)

Given the situation as described, this certainly makes sense. Under the circumstances, which include previous bailouts, voting for EESA and approving the bailouts did provoke public outrage and even look courageous when one considers the risks of inaction. But this is not the whole story. This was perhaps doing the right thing at a particular time, but it was

---

[5]   See Chapter 2.

not the best policy for all times. Previous comparable actions may have made the situation worse.

The U.S. government had been bailing out major banks since Continental Illinois in 1984. In hearings on the rescue of that bank, the comptroller of the currency actually said that the government would not let the eleven largest "money center banks" fail. This led immediately to a new phrase, "too big to fail" or TBTF. This and other actions created moral hazard in the banking system (FCIC 2011, pp. 36–7. See also pp. 57–8, 431–2).

All of these rescues created the expectation of future rescues. This expectation encouraged risk taking that might not have occurred if it were not for the expectation of bailout. This was a clear case of government causing moral hazard, and of the time-consistency problem. The best thing for all times would have been to allow failing banks to fail. The systemic risks of contagion and TBTF were encouraged by previous rescues.

A "Greenspan Put"?

Another contributor to moral hazard was the "Greenspan put." The chairman of the Federal Reserve had famously wondered in 1996 how we would know when the stock market was reflecting "irrational exuberance."[6] Not only did he not do anything to temper the exuberance, he later intimated that although the Fed would not intervene on the high side, it would recognize a downturn when it happened and "ease the transition to the next expansion." In other words, the Fed would not limit gains when traders took risks but would limit adverse consequences when things went badly (Rajan 2010, pp. 112–14; FCIC 2011, pp. 61–2; Meltzer 2009, pp. 1248, 1250; Miller, Weller, and Zhang 2002).

Now democracy does not have any monopoly on moral hazard or on the time-consistency problem. An authoritarian system could also be comparably vulnerable to these problems. But Mian, Suffi and Trebbi (2010b) have shown how EESA got through Congress. They say that "it was clear that the legislation represented a large wealth transfer from U.S. taxpayers to the financial services industry" (2010b, p. 1973). They analyze differences between votes in the House of Representatives on September 29, when the bill failed, and on October 3, when it passed. Between the two dates was the largest one-day drop in stock market value since the 1987 Black Monday (2001b, p. 1991). The first vote was mainly influenced by campaign contributions from the financial

---

[6] See http://www.federalreserve.gov/boarddocs/speeches/1996/19961205.htm, accessed May 17, 2013.

industry and by ideology. Among the 228 members who switched from no to yes, the causal patterns differed between the parties. For the 95 switching Democrats, the main factors were the mortgage default rate in their district and the fraction of constituents with more than $200K in income. For the 133 Republicans, the main factor was the fraction of constituents working in finance (2010b, pp. 1991–2).

The authors conclude that their "results are consistent with the hypothesis that politicians voted in favor of the EESA in part because of special interest campaign contributions from the financial services industry" (2010b, p. 1997). The policy that made bailouts possible was made in democratic institutions as a result of democratic processes.

The fact that the crisis did happen and that the bailouts were necessary was itself a policy failure, linked to previous bailouts. Banks and other financial institutions had gotten so large that their failure would have huge adverse ramifications beyond their own creditors, stockholders, and customers. The fact that the major banks except Lehman were bailed out by the government reinforced the moral hazard that already existed in the system. It was a violation of time-consistency, the idea that doing the right thing at any given time should be consistent with doing the right thing for all times.

Reforms That Would Minimize Vulnerability to Comparable Crises in the Future

In his dissent from the Financial Crisis Inquiry Commission Report, Peter Wallison says he is often asked why Congress bothered to authorize the commission at all, as Congress passed the Restoring Financial Stability Act (the Dodd-Frank Act) in July 2010, months before the commission's report came out (FCIC 2011, p. 443). The report does not give a single coherent explanation of why the crisis occurred and how it could have been avoided. The majority report is a lengthy history of what happened. The main minority report is much more analytical. And Wallison's personal dissent blames the crisis entirely on government housing policies.

Although I agree with those who argue that the full explanation will not be known for some time, I also think that there will never be a single widely accepted explanation. Surely some of the political pressure to pass "reform" legislation quickly can be attributed to the incentives of democratic politics to "do something now" and to act before public interest dissipates.

In the remainder of this section, I compare two analyses. The first is *The Squam Lake Report: Fixing the Financial System*. It is a product of a meeting of fifteen top financial economists, who first met at a New Hampshire resort in the fall of 2008. It draws together their collective wisdom about the causes of the financial crisis and makes numerous recommendations, which are reflections of two central principles. The first principle is that "when developing and enforcing regulations, government officials must consider the implications not only for individual institutions but also for the financial system as a whole" (French et al. 2010, p. 135). The second principle is that "regulators must create conditions that minimize the likelihood of bailouts of financial firms by forcing them to internalize the costs of failure that they have been imposing on taxpayers and the broader economy" (French et al. 2010, p. 137). A central substantive recommendation is that capital requirements should be larger for larger banks, banks with less liquidity, and those with more short-term debt (French et al. 2010, ch. 5). In spite of its distinguished collective authorship, this report seems to have received almost no public attention.[7]

The second (Carpenter 2010) takes the Obama administration's proposal for reform and analyzes what happened to it in Congress on the way to becoming the Restoring Financial Stability (Dodd-Frank) Act that passed in July 2010. Carpenter focuses on five features of the original proposal: minimal capital requirements, regulation of derivatives, unification of systemic financial regulation in a new agency, a consumer financial protection agency, and fees for the regulation of large banks (2010, p. 827). Although Carpenter does not explain or directly defend the desirability of these proposals, the article implicitly endorses them and makes the case that they were watered down or cast aside on the way to the passage of the Dodd-Frank law.

Carpenter's explanation is not simply in terms of the well-known constitutional veto points in the American political system. His article expresses an interpretation of "institutional strangulation" that is presented as more insidious than it would be if simply based on the classical ideas of limited government and checks and balances. He points out that many of the institutional veto points, such as the filibuster, were not part of the original institutional design of checks and balances. He also observes that new ideas and proposals may be discounted because they come from people outside of privileged professional networks. Carpenter also observes that a "culture of partisanship and vituperation" has emerged in a way that worked against financial reform. Finally, he identifies bureaucratic politics and struggle over turf as obstacles to the Obama proposals. Clearly, Carpenter does not like

---

[7]   But see Goodhart (2011) and Hoshi (2011).

what happened to the Obama administration's proposals. He makes a strong case that important parts of them were watered down and cast aside by a process of negation that went beyond the original intents of the framers of the Constitution.

Carpenter's analysis has a somewhat stronger political valence than the articles of Igan et al. (2009) or Mian et al. (2010a, 2010b), but they all call attention to features of the legislative process that make it responsive to the preferences of special interests that are established or powerful or have a substantial financial stake in a policy that involves moral hazard, time-consistency, or both. This is to say that the legislative process in a democracy can be used to create these generic problems as well as to resolve them.

CONCLUSIONS

Democratic institutions in the fundamental sense of regular elections of public officials and limitations on government do not necessarily cause any particular type of policy. In terms of Plott's fundamental equation [preferences ($\times$) institutions $\rightarrow$ outcomes], it depends on the preferences that are processed by the institutions. These preferences can be shortsighted or not, and highly polarized or not.

In terms of long-term budgetary sustainability, there have been regimes in which the democratic institutions of the United States have performed better than they have in recent years. This good performance is due to informal practices that can be inferred econometrically[8] and it is not due to the presence or absence of formal rules of budgeting.

The United States first drifted into an unsustainable fiscal situation, basically because of political leaders pandering to voters with policies that brought short-term benefits with long-term costs.[9] These were appealing enough to the public to have been rewarding to the politicians who proposed them. This is a fairly simple story of promising lower taxes and more benefits with the costs shifted to future generations through borrowing. The corrective would be a return to fiscal discipline, whether through political will or formal rules such as those reviewed in Auerbach (2008). One hopeful sign is that several commissions and an increasing number of scholars and public figures are calling for reform. But the case for pessimism seems

---

[8] See Hoover and Sheffrin (1992) and Hoover and Siegler (2000), which will be taken up in Chapter 9.

[9] For an insightful treatment of pandering, see Canes-Wrone (2006).

strong, given the lack of attention to the long-term problems even after the November 2010 election that seemed to hinge on deficits and debt.

The financial crisis of 2007–9 is more complicated. To the extent that it was rooted in U.S. housing policy, it is a leading example of adverse unintended consequences of efforts to do good things by extending the benefits of home ownership to more and more people. These policies were efforts to please constituencies that are directly linkable to the incentives of democratic politics. Unfortunately, they have lessons for how good intentions can have bad consequences.

To the extent that even members of the Federal Reserve thought that "this time is different," the financial crisis was caused by human nature discounting danger signs for prudent behavior. But the financial crisis was in part facilitated by democratic institutions and processes that exacerbated the dangers. Mian et al. (2010a) document that special interests representing the mortgage industry and subprime borrowers influenced housing legislation in the period leading up to the subprime crisis in ways that made the country more vulnerable to the crisis that resulted. Mian et al. (2010b) also show that the bailouts were a response to lobbying by the financial industry.

We still do not know the full impact of the Dodd-Frank law, but we do know that the banking industry successfully blocked higher capital requirements for banks, and also requirements that banks reduce their size so as not to be too big to fail. It is not at all clear that had Dodd-Frank been in effect before the recent financial crisis, that the crisis would have been avoided.

Democratic institutions are compatible with just about any pattern of policy. It is not just regular elections or limitations on government that lead to the good economic performance that is often associated with democratic politics. It is the ancillary institutions and practices, such as the unwritten rules of the budgetary process, that guide behavior and policy making in democracies.

Systematic models of routine politics as developed in the political economy literature have contributed enormous insight into the ways in which politicians and voters interact with each other and among themselves. Yet for the most part, they overlook some more serious problems that may be less routine and more like one-time developments and path dependent processes. Public choice and political economy models of democratic politics should consider more seriously ways in which formal and informal democratic institutions relate to generic problems such as moral hazard and time-consistency.

PART THREE

THE SOURCES AND AUTHORITY OF MACROECONOMIC GOALS

Democracy is about process, rather than goals. Chapter 6 discusses the degree to which macroeconomic goals are part of the Constitution and laws of the United States. It also treats the status of such goals in the economics profession and shows that even in the absence of professional consensus on goals, some compelling danger signs have emerged.

Voters are the ultimate authority in a democracy and no less so in the United States. Chapter 7 assesses the dynamics of voting behavior and ways in which voters may be reliable or, alternatively, vulnerable to misjudgments.

6

The Authority of Macroeconomic Goals

In Chapters 3 and 4, dealing with models of routine politics, we treated parties and voters as oriented to identifiable goals regarding inflation, unemployment, and income growth. We drew on the familiar misery index and showed how it could be modified to represent different preferences, and even to represent a conception of social welfare or the public interest. In doing so, we accepted goals and preferences as given, as predetermined, and as clearly defined. In this chapter and the next, we step back and ask where goals and preferences come from and how well defined and authoritative they are. In this chapter, we consider official public definitions of national economic goals, as well as what economists say about various targets of macroeconomic policy.

These chapters present the argument that there is no basis for an unambiguous or uncontestable definition of the public interest, and no basis for an authoritative welfare function.[1] This argument undermines assertions that democracy has costs and pathologies. Without authoritative definitions of what public policy ought to be, we have no solid basis for comparing the outcomes of democratic politics to the best or most appropriate outcomes. It is difficult to argue that democratic political processes lead systematically to inferior outcomes when superior outcomes resist precise and authoritative definition. In fact, the goals of public policy are defined and redefined in a continuing and fluid political process.

However, I suggest that even though uncontestable targets may not exist, there are ranges of outcomes beyond which results are clearly inferior. The

---

[1] Note the difference between social welfare functions as used here, that is, objective functions, and Arrow-type social welfare functions that might emerge from the aggregation of preferences. See Mueller (2003, chs. 23–24). See Asher, DeFina, and Thanawala (1993) for a treatment of alternatives to the misery index.

leading examples are hyperinflation and unsustainable increases in public indebtedness. The democratic political process might involve dynamics that take outcomes beyond the ranges of acceptability, and democratic institutions might obstruct the stabilization programs that would correct them. This, I think, is what has happened in the Great Recession that followed the financial crisis of 2007–9.

OFFICIAL DEFINITIONS OF NATIONAL GOALS

Could some kind of objective definition of national economic goals, some social welfare function be made public law? Should it? How close do the existing laws come to expressing specific goals? The U.S. Constitution contains a basic stance on this issue. It is quite specific on the procedures through which law and policy will be made, but quite vague on goals. The closest it comes is in the Preamble, where "to promote the general welfare" is articulated as a goal.

The concept of "general welfare" is broad and vague enough to provide no guidance at all in choosing specific goals. Implicitly, the Constitution seems to provide for continuing definition and redefinition of public purposes in a fluid political process. The Constitution is a general document with general goals, and it is difficult to imagine what might have been adopted in 1787 that would appropriately provide more specific guidance for modern economic policy making.

The Federal Reserve Act of 1913 is much more specifically oriented to economic issues and performance than is the Constitution, and it is comparable in that it established decision-making bodies and procedures but was vague on goals. The act specified that the Fed was designed "to furnish an elastic currency, to afford means of rediscounting commercial paper, to establish a more effective supervision of banking in the United States, and for other purposes." These goals are notably imprecise.

The first law to focus specifically on macroeconomic goals was the Employment Act of 1946, whose purpose was to promote "maximum employment, production and purchasing power." The act itself was watered down considerably from the initial bill, which was "to establish a national policy and program for assuring continuing full employment in a free and competitive economy." The phrase "full employment" was dropped in the legislative process, as was the following assertion:

All Americans able to work and seeking to work have the right to useful, remunerative, regular, full-time employment, and it is the policy of the United States to assure the existence at all times of sufficient employment opportunities to enable all Americans who have finished their schooling and who do not have full-time housekeeping responsibilities freely to exercise this right. (Bailey 1950, p. 243)

In a classic book-length case study of the legislative process, Stephen K. Bailey described and bemoaned the dilution of the original bill in the congressional process, which he described as a "kaleidoscopic and largely irresponsible interplay of ideas, interests, institutions and individuals" (1950, p. 240). In fact, the legislative process was not always inspiring, and "there were few cases of mature economic debate between a Congressman and a witness" (p. 160). However, the process did provide an official forum for public deliberation about national goals.[2]

The Employment Act did establish the Council of Economic Advisors, to ensure that the president has ready access to professional economic advice, and provided for the annual *Economic Report of the President*. As such, it made lasting contributions in providing for systematic reporting of economic performance and providing a basis for accountability for economic performance.

A similar bill was passed in 1978 after likewise being watered down by its opponents. The Full Employment and Balanced Growth Act of 1978, also known as the Humphrey-Hawkins Act, had originally proposed that government provide "last resort" jobs for the unemployed and work toward a goal of 4 percent unemployment by 1983. The government jobs provision was deleted in the legislative process, though the 4 percent goal was retained. The critics of the original bill also succeeded in adding specific inflation targets of 3 percent by 1983 and zero by 1988.

The real-world experience following the passage of the Humphrey-Hawkins Act raised questions about the realism of the targets, and even about the wisdom of setting numerical goals for macroeconomic outcomes. In 1983, unemployment was more than double the target rate, at 9.5 percent, whereas inflation was close to the target for that year, at 3.9 percent. By 1988, inflation had dropped to 3.3 percent and unemployment was down to 5.4 percent, which might be considered tolerably within range of the targets. Such variations in performance have considerable political consequences in their own right, as Chapter 7 will elaborate. But the fact that they succeed or fail in approximating numerical targets in the Humphrey-Hawkins Act is almost totally ignored in public discourse, being left for consideration in books such as this one.

---

[2] See Bailey (1950, pp. 127–8) for four interpretations of the meaning of the Senate bill, and how the subsequent House deliberations narrowed to a contest between two of them.

As we saw in Chapter 2, macroeconomic theory provides no assurance that targets for outcomes such as these can be met. Without such assurance, and without better guidance on how to achieve them, the incorporation of specific numerical goals into public law renders the laws mere expressions of preferences, without regard to their realism.[3] When we consider that the act also specified the goals of a balanced federal budget, reduced federal spending, and primary reliance on the private sector, it is obvious that the Humphrey-Hawkins Act was a close approximation to the incorporation of wishful thinking into law. We have failed to achieve the targets, and many economists would tell us that they were impossible to begin with. A cynic might observe that the act was a charade that allowed members of Congress to take popular positions without following through, providing symbolic rather than concrete benefits to their constituents.

However, some provisions in the Full Employment and Balanced Growth Act had lasting and probably constructive effects. Title III recognized that some of the goals and timetables might not be realistic, and it identified a series of procedures that Congress might use to deliberate goals and the means to achieve them. These included schedules for regular reporting to Congress by the Council of Economic Advisors and by the Federal Reserve. Those reports provide the basis for semiannual public hearings and debate. They are institutions for public accountability of those responsible for economic policy.[4]

The most recent examples of the effort to identify specific, official macroeconomic goals in legislation are the Balanced Budget and Emergency Deficit Control Acts of 1985 and 1987, known after their sponsors as Gramm-Rudman-Hollings (GRH). The original act of 1985 was declared unconstitutional on a technicality, and a new version was passed in 1987. The numerical targets in these laws are for the federal budget deficit. Because the federal budget is much more directly controllable by the government than are unemployment and inflation rates, the GRH law is, in a sense, more realistic than the Humphrey-Hawkins Act, at least from the point of view of economic theory.[5]

That is, no one seriously claims that outcomes such as inflation and unemployment rates are under direct government control. At best, they can be influenced by monetary or fiscal policy instruments, which are under

[3] However, inflation targeting is a widely approved strategy for monetary policy. See Chapter 8.

[4] See *Congressional Quarterly Almanac*, vol. 34 (1978), pp. 272–9.

[5] The Budget Control Act of 2011 incorporated numerical targets.

Table 6.1. *Gramm-Rudman-Hollings deficit targets and actual deficits*

Deficit	Fiscal Years							
	1986	1987	1988	1989	1990	1991	1992	1993
GRH-I targets	172[a]	144	108	72	36	0		
GRH-II targets			144	136	100	64	28	0
Actual deficits	221	150	155	153	221	269	290	255

[a] Billions of dollars

direct control. Federal budget deficits are, in contrast, much more nearly under direct government control through taxing and spending laws. Even though federal tax receipts and expenditures are themselves products of the interaction of laws that are under government control and economic fluctuations that are not, budget deficits are far more directly subject to government control than are inflation and unemployment rates.

However, the effort to enforce a balanced budget has been even less successful than the Humphrey-Hawkins effort to achieve 4 percent unemployment. Table 6.1 identifies the deficit targets in the two versions of the GRH law and compares them with actual experience. The gaps between the targets and the actual deficits have become larger and larger, in spite of the fact that the laws had specific enforcement mechanisms designed to carry out automatic cuts if the government did not achieve the targets through its discretionary decisions. Although these targets may have been economically realistic, they apparently were not politically realistic.

The GRH law demonstrates that numerical targets with enforcement mechanisms provide no assurance of success even when the targets are, in principle, under the control of public officials. The problem with achieving the unemployment targets of the Humphrey-Hawkins Act was that they probably were not economically realistic; that is, they were not feasible under the constraints of economic reality. The problem with the budget targets of the GRH law was one of political rather than economic feasibility. Congress and the president were not able to agree on a program of expenditure cuts and/or tax increases that would reduce the deficit by degrees that would approximate the targets. These authorities seem to have been operating under political constraints that limited their capacity to achieve the targets. Such constraints involved failure to reach agreements across parties and across branches of the government that would reduce expenditures or increase taxes. They involved the fear that proposals to cut specific expenditures or to raise taxes not only would not achieve agreement and cooperation but also would be exploited by partisan opponents in the next election. Specific actions to reduce the deficit often appear to be politically suicidal.

Under recent circumstances, then, voluntary agreement on taxing and spending decisions that would reduce deficits seems not to have been politically feasible. But the fact that continuing large deficits are not always features of democratic politics suggests that the conditions of political feasibility may vary. We will return to an analysis of the political incentives surrounding deficit creation and reduction in Chapter 9.

The GRH declining deficit targets were quietly abandoned in the Budget Enforcement Act of 1990. In signing that agreement into law, President George H. W. Bush undermined his credibility by violating his famous pledge: "Read my lips: no new taxes." The law was actually a substantive victory for the president in several respects (Collender 1992, ch.2), but the fact that it was accompanied by a tax increase made it seem a major political and symbolic defeat, given his campaign pledge. Although the 1990 act does not state visible and inflexible targets for anything, it may have been more realistic in terms of achieving certain goals, such as a limitation on the growth of federal spending.

This record of experience with laws that identified specific numerical goals for unemployment and budget deficits should, at the very least, give pause to anyone who would advocate a constitutional amendment that would require a balanced federal budget. Regardless of the worthiness of the goal, experience has made it clear that identification of goals in public laws provides no assurance of their achievement. Those who would propose such laws should consider carefully whether or not it is within the power of the government to meet those goals, whether or not they can design a credible enforcement mechanism, and whether or not the identification of one official goal will entail costs by detracting from other goals.

A deeper problem with legislated goals for public policy is captured in the title of a classic article: "Congress Is a 'They,' Not an 'It': Legislative Intent as Oxymoron" (Shepsle 1992). Drawing on social choice theory, Shepsle points out that any given majority is likely to be one of many possible majorities based on the same preferences. As Jerry Mashaw has put it, "statutes are . . . the vector sum of political forces expressed through some institutional matrix which has profound, but probably unpredictable and untraceable, effects on the policies actually expressed. There is no reason to believe that these expressions represent either rational, instrumental choices or broadly acceptable value judgments" (Mashaw 1989, p. 134).

Legislated goals for public policy could reflect a broad, well-informed, and stable consensus on values, but there is no assurance that they will. They may reflect an arbitrary stopping point in the legislative process that could be defeated by some other proposal if the process were allowed to continue, or they may reflect superficial agreement on goals that would appear questionable if the full costs and implications of their achievement were seriously considered. The American experience in placing specific macroeconomic goals into law has reflected little well-informed, stable consensus, but many arbitrary stopping points and superficial agreements.

GOALS AS UNDERSTOOD IN ECONOMIC ANALYSIS: OUTCOMES

In this section, we review a series of macroeconomic goals in their own right, as well as some of the considerations that a genuine national deliberation on goals should address. The main, standard goals for macroeconomic outcomes have to do with growth in income, output, and consumption, and with unemployment and inflation.

Income, Output, and Consumption Growth

Probably the most comprehensive and consensual contemporary measure of economic performance is growth, specifically growth in national income, total output, or consumption, all of which are empirically related. In contemporary economics, growth is largely an uncontested goal, but it was not always so in the past and may not always be so in the future. In *The Rise and Fall of Economic Growth*, H. W. Arndt (1978) found an interest in growth and material progress among classical economists from Adam Smith to John Stuart Mill, but that "hardly a line is to be found in the writings of any professional economists between 1870 and 1940 in support of economic growth as a policy objective." In that intervening period, most attention went to problems such as "the theory of value and distribution, welfare economics, monetary and trade cycle theory, all these treated almost entirely on static assumptions" (1978, p. 13).

"Economic growth" returned as a major objective of public policy, and as a preoccupation of economists, after World War II. During that period, the literature acknowledged that growth involved some issues of preference for the present, to the neglect of the future, and that growth might well impose costs in terms of inflation, the international balance of payments, and inequality, as well as noneconomic goals. But even at that peak of interest, according to Arndt, "no economist was foolish enough to think of economic growth as an 'end in itself'" (1978, pp. 80–1).

Arndt characterizes the arguments of those with major reservations about the goal of economic growth (the critics, the revolutionaries, and the prophets) and concludes that "what the debate over economic growth has achieved is wider recognition that the trade-offs between the objective of a high rate of economic growth and some of the other objectives need to be reconsidered" (1978, p. 153). In my reading of the contemporary scene, this recognition has been lost from public discourse and from economic analysis.

There is one major exception to this observation. In 2008, President Nicholas Sarkozy of France appointed Joseph Stiglitz, Amartya Sen, and Jean-Paul Fitoussi to create a commission to identify the limits of GDP as an indicator of economic performance and social progress. A year later, a distinguished commission issued a report (Stiglitz, Sen, and Fitoussi 2009). A third of the report is on classical GDP issues, a third on quality of life, and a third on sustainable development and the environment. The report is more about measurement than policy, and the first ten recommendations are an effort to merge classical GDP measurement with concerns about the quality of life.

Growth issues now dominate both the partisan debate and macroeconomic analysis. Perhaps growth as a goal is questioned most sharply when growth performance is the strongest, as in the 1960s. Since the early 1970s, growth in American national income has stagnated, and as growth performance has deteriorated, it seems to have risen as a topic of economic analysis and of political debate. Growth of national income is now a central concern of economists, politicians, and the public, but historical perspective makes it clear that growth comes and goes as a goal. As Tibor Scitovsky has said, "the national income is at best an index of economic welfare, and economic welfare is a very small part and often a very poor indicator of human welfare" (1992, p. 145).

Growth is a central issue today because it has risen to the top of the agenda in a fluid political process, not because anyone has made an authoritative case that maximizing growth should be a central goal of public policy without regard to trade-offs with other concerns. What those concerns are and how their trade-offs are defined are questions with no single, lasting, authoritative answers. In a democratic system, these are questions that are answered in different ways at different times, depending on what the most significant problems of the day seem to be. If the rates of national income growth were higher, I expect that the prominence of the goal would fade, to be replaced by issues of equity or the environment or other alternatives, in ways that are not easy to predict.[6]

Amartya Sen (1993) has pointed out that some basic indicators of well-being, such as infant mortality, life expectancy, and famine, are only loosely related to national income. His argument makes it clear that maximization of income growth at the expense of distributional considerations can be a limited and perhaps limiting goal, rather than an appropriate index of all good things.

Unemployment

Minimum feasible unemployment is another leading goal of economic policy. Unemployment is well known to be inversely related to income growth, and policies designed to reduce unemployment are often the same as those designed to increase growth. The rate of unemployment is the fraction of the labor force out of work and looking for jobs. Note that this rate is relative to the size of a base that is not fixed. The size and composition of the labor force as a fraction of the total U.S. population has changed substantially (from 58.9 in 1965 to 64.1 in 2011) with a decrease in the participation of men and an increase in the participation of women.[7] Thus, the unemployment rate is imperfect as a constant measure of the economy's capacity to provide jobs.

The unemployment rate is also imperfect as a constant measure of human suffering. At any given time, some of the unemployed will have been out of work for extended periods, whereas others will have only recently joined the ranks. Also, people enter and leave the labor force for a variety of reasons, and the search for a job may reflect different degrees of need. In addition, the pain of unemployment may be cushioned to various degrees by unemployment compensation or public assistance.

Still, unemployment is a more direct indicator of human suffering than is a low rate of economic growth. Even though minimizing unemployment seems desirable, other things being equal, zero unemployment is not a reasonable target, as was explained in Chapter 2. One way to understand this is to recognize that much unemployment is *frictional unemployment*, wherein people sometimes are voluntarily unemployed while looking for better jobs. For such people, unemployment might not seem as bad as

---

[6] For an analysis of the fluidity of national political agendas, see Kingdon (1984) and Baumgartner and Jones (2009).

[7] See *Economic Report of the President* (2012), Table B-39, p. 365.

working at a job that did not suit their talents or interests. A free society will always have some unemployment of this type, and this fact alone justifies not having a goal of zero unemployment.

Structural unemployment is defined on the basis of a mismatch between the skills and training of available workers and the demands of available jobs. An example of this is the unemployment that has resulted from the declining number of manufacturing jobs in the contemporary economy, leaving pockets of unemployment in former manufacturing regions. This is a serious economic problem, but it is not highly amenable to solution by the monetary and fiscal stabilization policies that are the concerns of this book.

Cyclical unemployment, a third type, is the kind of unemployment that comes with recessions and disappears with expansions of the business cycle. It is the kind that has been thought to be responsive to monetary and fiscal stabilization policies. As shown by the review of macroeconomic theories in Chapter 2, a great deal of controversy has arisen in economics over just what, if anything, can be done to correct cyclical unemployment.

There is no doubt that unemployment has serious costs. These costs can be measured in terms of lost output for the economy as a whole. They can be measured in terms of lost income for the individuals and families directly affected. These costs have been borne disproportionately by those in the lower economic strata. Finally, the costs can be measured in terms of psychological consequences, as measured by various indicators of mental health.[8]

Even though little good and much bad can be said about unemployment, there are no clear, objective answers about how low unemployment ought to be, and what public officials should do about it. That there is a "natural" or equilibrium rate of unemployment at any given time is little disputed, but there is considerable dispute about where it is, what causes it, and what should be done about it.[9] Ironically, Democratic programs designed to benefit the working class are likely to raise the natural rate. Minimum wage laws raise the price of labor and are likely to reduce the demand for it. Generous unemployment compensation reduces the incentive for the unemployed to accept jobs they do not like. Both policies place upward pressure on the natural rate of unemployment. Economist have deep and legitimate disagreements about what can and should be done through economic stabilization policy to reduce unemployment. These

[8] See Schlozman and Verba (1979) for a book-length treatment of the political consequences of unemployment. See also Summers (1990).
[9] See Summers (1990, chs. 8 and 9).

disagreements are largely scholarly and intellectual, but in an important sense, they are political as well, because they involve differences in values and judgments that often cannot be resolved outside of a political process.

Inflation and Price Stability

Minimizing inflation is the last of the three leading public goals for macroeconomic performance. The fact that it is the last to be considered does not necessarily imply that it is last in priority. Inflation is a general increase in the money prices of goods and services and a decline in the purchasing power of the currency. As such, it has to do with numerical values for prices and wages, with no necessary connection with "real" variables such as unemployment or income growth.

The most common indicator of inflation is the rate of change in the consumer price index (CPI), a number that represents the dollar price of a standard bundle of goods and services that are thought to represent typical tastes and needs. This index is normalized to 100 for a base year, and inflation is calculated as the annual rate of change in this index. The CPI currently used by the U.S. government is based on 100 for the period 1982–4; it had risen to 225 by the end of 2011.[10] In recent years, inflation rates for all items (including food, energy, and medical services) have been as high as 13.3 in 1979, and as low as 0.1 in 2008.[11]

Annual rates of inflation in the United States rose to double digits in 1974, 1979, 1980, and 1981.[12] Rates can be negative, indicating deflation, or a general decrease in prices and an increase in the purchasing power of money. This is rare in the contemporary era, having happened last in the mid-1950s.

Inflation is not the same as the cost of living. If inflation is truly general, there will be the same percentage increase in the price of everything, including wages and salaries earned and goods and services purchased. If this is so, high rates of inflation can be compatible with a constant capacity to purchase and a constant standard of living, so long as incomes keep pace with prices. To see this, think of the value of the dollar being arbitrarily doubled or halved or being multiplied or divided by ten. There would be no "real" difference in the purchasing power of the dollar. The change would be "nominal" rather than real.

[10] *Economic Report of the President* (2012), Table B-60, p. 387.
[11] Ibid., Table B-63, p. 391.
[12] Year to year. December to December gives slightly different results.

What are the costs of inflation? What difference would it make if these arbitrary numbers are changing? These questions can be answered in several ways, and most of them imply that inflation has real costs even though it fundamentally involves only numerical values. Douglas Hibbs (1987, ch. 3) conducted a massive data analysis in which he empirically estimated the consequences of inflation for real income growth, for the distribution of income, for corporate profits, and for savings. For the most part, he found that the consequences and costs of inflation were minimal.

For example, his findings for the post–World War II American experience showed that inflation had negligible consequences for growth in real disposable income. He showed that inflation was moderately advantageous for the income shares of lower-income strata relative to higher-income strata, and that it adversely affected corporate profits only after taxes. Hibbs used those findings to make an interesting and subtle argument about the "true costs" of inflation. He argued that "it is unlikely that the measureable consequences of inflation . . . explain satisfactorily the common belief that rising prices pose a serious problem . . . less tangible and partly psychological factors are probably more significant in accounting for concern about inflation than are easily identifiable objective costs" (1987, p. 118).

Hibbs was suggesting that inflation not only measures nominal rather than real wages, but also has psychological rather than real consequences. Note the difference between this use of the term "psychological" and the earlier use regarding unemployment. Here, psychological implies that the costs of inflation are imagined, rather than real or objective. In the previous usage, the psychological costs of unemployment in terms of family stress, admissions to hospitals, and even suicides were very real. I argue later that the costs of inflation can be real, though not easily measured.

Hibbs makes an interesting, almost tongue-in-cheek argument about the costs of inflation: "The biggest costs are *indirect* costs, flowing from the consequences of monetary and fiscal policy reactions to inflation, rather than the direct effects of rising prices *per se*" (1987, p. 123, emphasis in original).

That is, he argued that inflation entails large costs because policy makers induce recessions to get rid of inflation. The costs come from the recessions (through unnecessary unemployment and lost income) rather than from the inflation itself. Hibbs suggested that society would be better off if the public and public officials would ignore inflation and not incur the costs of reducing it by inducing recessions.

The public aversion to inflation is well documented, and I contend that it reflects real rather than imaginary consequences. It is true that the costs of inflation are difficult to measure precisely, but this does not mean that they do not exist. Inflation interferes with the efficiency of prices as indicators of relative value and as signals for what people should do to use their resources efficiently.[13]

Think of prices as carrying information about the relative values of things that are bought and sold in the market. When the demand for or supply of these things shifts, their prices will change in ways that will reflect an increase or decrease in value relative to other things that have prices. These kinds of changes are continually taking place because of changes in tastes and in the availability of the factors of production.

When inflation occurs, the general increase in prices can easily be confused with the relative changes in prices that are continually taking place. This confusion leads to inefficiencies in the economy that are difficult to measure but are nevertheless likely to be real and consequential. Because they are so difficult to measure, their evaluation becomes a matter of judgment, and quite likely a subjective and contestable judgment. As such, this judgment can be called *political*, for two reasons: it is likely to be associated with a person's values and interests, and there is no authoritative source for a public, objective evaluation.

Considered without regard to other goals, a zero target for inflation makes sense in a way that a zero target for unemployment does not.[14] Other things being equal, lower inflation is generally better than higher inflation. But the effort to reduce inflation, or to achieve a target of zero, is not likely to be unambiguously desirable, because other things are not equal. Reductions in inflation are likely to come at the expense of (temporary) costs in real variables such as unemployment, as was illustrated in the figures presented in Chapter 3 regarding the misery index in the 1980s. Chapter 2 showed that these trade-offs can be defined in several ways.

High, Very High, and Hyperinflation

There is no precise definition of where hyperinflation begins and inflation that is merely very high ends, but both represent a pathological condition. When prices increase at rates of thousands of percent per year, the utility of money as a means of exchange breaks down, and an economy retreats into a barter system. Hyperinflation was experienced in several European

---

[13] See Fischer (1986) for analysis and assessments.
[14] There are sophisticated arguments that optimal rates of inflation should be above zero, for example, as a nondistorting tax (Barro 1979), or as a way to change relative wages without reductions in nominal income.

countries after World Wars I and II, in Latin America and Israel in more recent years, and in Zimbabwe in the twenty-first century.[15] The elimination of hyperinflation makes virtually everybody better off.[16]

But is hyperinflation a pathology of democracy? It would be if democratic institutions and processes had an inflationary bias that led to hyperinflation. Democratic institutions may well have an inflationary bias under some (but obviously not all) circumstances. However, so far as I know, the case has not yet been made that democratic institutions have had a causal influence in the creation of the hyperinflations that have existed. There is reason to believe, however, that democratic institutions may obstruct the implementation of painful stabilization programs that are designed to eliminate hyperinflation (Alesina and Drazen 1991).

Growth, unemployment, and inflation are all legitimate and appropriate areas for macroeconomic policy making. The public and politicians have good reasons to want to increase growth and reduce unemployment and inflation. However, even if there were no trade-offs between these and other goals, there are no obvious, authoritative, numerical targets that public policy ought to aim for, with the possible exception of inflation. The fact that these three goals may conflict with one another, as well as with other goals, is not discussed here.

With no external authority for individual goals or for objective functions that could define optimal combinations among goals, we must consider that public goals are to be formulated and reformulated in a public political process. Each formulation is likely to be subject to subsequent reformulation. This fluid dynamic is likely to be an inevitable feature of macroeconomic policy making in a democracy.[17]

GOALS AS UNDERSTOOD IN ECONOMIC ANALYSIS: INTERMEDIATE TARGETS

Growth, unemployment, and inflation will continue to be the outcomes of interest in this book, because they are the ultimate indicators of macroeconomic performance. However, economists and the public often recognize

---

[15] In Zimbabwe, inflation reached a monthly rate of 79.6 billion percent in November 2008 (Hanke and Kwok 2009), which made it second to Hungary in 1946 among the world's great hyperinflations. See also Bernholz (2003).

[16] See Fischer et al. (2002) for a complete and enlightening treatment of high and hyperinflation.

[17] This argument may sound like one in favor of discretion as opposed to rules. It is not. Perhaps the main theme of this second edition is that a commitment to rules for monetary and fiscal policy is very desirable. See Shepsle (1991).

other variables as indicators of the health of an economy. Among these are the balance of the government's budget, interest rates, the balance of trade, and the exchange rate. These are sometimes thought of as intermediate targets, because they are more subject to government control than are the ultimate goals regarding growth, unemployment, and inflation, and also because they are of less intrinsic interest and value.

The balance of the federal budget has been the intermediate target that receives by far the most attention in the United States. Almost everyone has an opinion about it. A very large gap exists between the opinions of the public and those of economists on the issue of whether or not the budget should be balanced. For the public, the goal of a balanced budget has been strongly supported as long as opinion surveys on the topic have been taken. Furthermore, the public also consistently favors an amendment to the Constitution to require a balanced budget.[18]

Although the balance of a government's budget is a common goal in conventional wisdom, it is less important in economic analysis. Macroeconomists are, in fact, quite divided in general over the desirability of balanced budgets and the consequences of deficits. These differences follow the various schools of macroeconomic theory.[19] The classical school favored balanced budgets, whereas the Keynesians saw intentionally created deficits as appropriate means to stimulate the economy out of a depression or recession. Keynesians have advocated balance of budgets over the business cycle, rather than annually. Monetarists disagreed; they favored a balanced budget as one of the rules that should guide government policy. Supply-siders have never really acknowledged that they preferred low taxes to balanced budgets. At least some new classicals think that deficits do not really matter, because rational agents will simply save to cover the future tax liabilities implied by deficits.[20]

No firm level of debt as a fraction of national income means the same amount of danger for different countries. For example, Reinhart and Rogoff point out that "default often occurs at levels well below the 60 percent ratio of debt to GDP enshrined in Europe's Maastricht Treaty, a clause intended to protect the euro system from government defaults" (2009, p. 21).

---

[18] See Bratton (1994); Blinder and Holtz-Eakin (1984); Modigliani and Modigliani (1987).
[19] See Salsman (2012) for a comprehensive treatment of the history of thought on debt, deficits, and credit.
[20] The idea that economic agents will not increase consumption but rather save to cover the future tax price of current deficit spending is called Ricardian equivalence. See Seater (1993) and Elmendorf and Mankiw (1999).

Table 6.2. *Selected data on U.S. federal deficit and debt, fiscal years 1946–2012*

Year	Surplus (+) or Deficit (-)[a]	Surplus or Deficit as percentage of GDP	Interest[a]	Interest as percentage of expenditure	Interest as percentage of GDP	Interest as percentage of deficit	Total debt[a, b]	Total debt as percentage of GDP[b]
1946	-15,936	-7.2	4,111	7.4	1.8	-25.8	270,991	121.7
1947	4,018	1.7	4,204	12.2	1.8	104.6	257,149	110.3
1948	11,796	4.6	4,341	14.6	1.7	36.8	252,031	98.2
1949	580	0.2	4,523	11.6	1.7	779.8	252,610	93.1
1950	-3,119	-1.1	4,812	11.3	1.8	-154.3	256,853	94.1
1951	6,102	1.9	4,665	10.2	1.5	76.5	255,288	79.7
1952	-1,519	-0.4	4,701	6.9	1.3	-309.5	259,097	74.3
1953	-6,493	-1.7	5,156	6.8	1.4	-79.4	265,963	71.4
1954	-1,154	-0.3	4,811	6.8	1.3	-416.9	270,812	71.8
1955	-2,993	-0.8	4,850	7.1	1.2	-162.0	274,366	69.3
1956	3,947	0.9	5,079	7.2	1.2	128.7	272,693	63.9
1957	3,412	0.8	5,354	7.0	1.2	156.9	272,252	60.4
1958	-2,769	-0.6	5,604	6.8	1.2	-202.4	279,666	60.8
1959	-12,849	-2.6	5,762	6.3	1.2	-44.8	287,465	58.6
1960	301	0.1	6,947	7.5	1.3	2308.0	290,525	56.0
1961	-3,335	-0.6	6,716	6.9	1.3	-201.4	292,648	55.2
1962	-7,146	-1.3	6,889	6.4	1.2	-96.4	302,928	53.4
1963	-4,756	-0.8	7,740	7.0	1.3	-162.7	310,324	51.8
1064	-5,915	-0.9	8,199	6.9	1.3	-138.6	316,059	49.3
1965	-1,411	-0.2	8,591	7.3	1.2	-608.9	322,318	46.9
1966	-3,698	-0.5	9,386	7.0	1.2	-253.8	328,498	43.5
1967	-8,643	-1.1	10,268	6.5	1.3	-118.8	340,445	42.0
1968	-25,161	-2.9	11,090	6.2	1.3	-44.1	368,685	42.5
1969	3,242	0.3	12,699	6.9	1.3	391.7	365,769	38.6
1970	-2,842	-0.3	14,380	7.4	1.4	-506.0	380,921	37.6

1971	−23,033	−2.1	7.1	14,841	1.4	−64.4	408,176	37.8
1972	−23,373	−2.0	6.7	15,478	1.3	−66.2	435,936	37.1
1973	−14,908	−1.1	7.1	17,349	1.3	−116.4	466,291	35.6
1974	−6,135	−0.4	8.0	21,449	1.5	−349.6	483,893	33.6
1975	−53,242	−3.4	7.0	23,244	1.5	−43.7	541,925	34.7
1976	−73,732	−4.2	7.2	26,727	1.5	−36.2	628,970	36.2
TQ	−14,744	−3.2	7.2	6,949	1.5	−47.1	643,561	35.0
1977	−53,659	−2.7	7.3	29,901	1.5	−55.7	706,398	35.8
1978	−59,185	−2.7	7.7	35,458	1.6	−59.9	776,602	35.0
1979	−40,726	−1.6	8.5	42,633	1.7	−104.7	829,467	33.2
1980	−73,830	−2.7	8.9	52,533	1.9	−71.2	909,041	33.4
1981	−78,968	−2.6	10.1	68,766	2.2	−87.1	994,828	32.5
1982	−127,977	−4.0	11.4	85,032	2.6	−66.4	1,137,315	35.3
1983	−207,802	−6.0	11.1	89,808	2.6	−43.2	1,371,660	39.9
1984	−185,367	−4.8	13.0	111,102	2.9	−59.9	1,564,586	40.7
1985	−212,308	−5.1	13.7	129,478	3.1	−61.0	1,817,423	43.8
1986	−221,227	−5.0	13.7	136,017	3.1	−61.5	2,120,501	48.2
1987	−149,730	−3.2	13.8	138,611	3.0	−92.6	2,345,956	50.4
1988	−155,178	−3.1	14.3	151,803	3.0	−97.8	2,601,104	51.9
1989	−152,639	−2.8	14.8	168,981	3.1	−110.7	2,867,800	53.1
1990	−221,036	−3.9	14.7	184,347	3.2	−83.4	3,206,290	55.9
1991	−269,238	−4.5	14.7	194,448	3.3	−72.2	3,598,178	60.7
1992	−290,321	−4.7	14.4	199,344	3.2	−68.7	4,001,787	64.1
1993	−255,051	−3.9	14.1	198,713	3.0	−77.9	4,351,044	66.1
1994	−203,186	−2.9	13.9	202,932	2.9	−99.9	4,643,307	66.6
1995	−163,952	−2.2	15.3	232,134	3.2	−141.6	4,920,586	67.0
1996	−107,431	−1.4	15.4	241,053	3.1	−224.4	5,181,465	67.1
1997	−21,884	−0.3	15.2	243,984	3.0	−1114.9	5,369,206	65.4
1998	69,270	0.8	14.6	241,118	2.8	348.1	5,478,189	63.2
1999	125,610	1.4	13.5	229,755	2.5	182.9	5,605,523	60.9

(continued)

Table 6.2. (*continued*)

Year	Surplus (+) or Deficit (-)[a]	Surplus or Deficit as percentage of GDP	Interest[a]	Interest as percentage of expenditure	Interest as percentage of GDP	Interest as percentage of deficit	Total debt[a, b]	Total debt as percentage of GDP[b]
2000	236,241	2.4	222,949	12.5	2.3	94.4	5,628,700	57.3
2001	128,236	1.3	206,167	11.1	2.0	160.8	5,769,881	56.4
2002	-157,758	-1.5	170,949	8.5	1.6	-108.4	6,198,401	58.8
2003	-377,585	-3.4	153,073	7.1	1.4	-40.5	6,760,014	61.6
2004	-412,727	-3.5	160,245	7.0	1.4	-38.8	7,354,657	63.0
2005	-318,346	-2.6	183,986	7.4	1.5	-57.8	7,905,300	63.6
2006	-248,181	-1.9	226,603	8.5	1.7	-91.3	8,451,350	64.0
2007	-160,701	-1.2	237,109	8.7	1.7	-147.5	8,950,744	64.6
2008	-458,553	-3.2	252,757	8.5	1.8	-55.1	9,986,082	69.7
2009	-1,412,688	-10.1	186,902	5.3	1.3	-13.2	11,875,851	85.2
2010	-1,293,489	-9.0	196,194	5.7	1.4	-15.2	13,528,807	94.2
2011	-1,299,595	-8.7	229,968	6.4	1.5	-17.7	14,764,222	98.7
2012[b]	-1,326,948	-8.5	224,784	5.9	1.4	-16.9	16,350,885	104.8

[a] Millions of dollars.
[b] End of year.
[c] Estimate.

Source: Table 1.1 – Summary of Receipts, Outlays, and Surpluses or Deficits (-): 1789–2018 at http://www.whitehouse.gov/omb/budget/Historicals (for the surplus and deficit data)

Table 1.2 – Summary of Receipts, Outlays, and Surpluses or Deficits (-) as Percentages of GDP: 1930–2018 at http://www.whitehouse.gov/omb/budget/Historicals (for the surplus or deficit as a percentage of GDP data)

Table 3.1 – Outlays by Superfunction and Function: 1940–2018 at http://www.whitehouse.gov/omb/budget/Historicals (for interest, interest as percentage of expenditure, and interest as percentage of GDP data)

Table 7.1 – Federal Debt at the End of Year: 1940–2018 at http://www.whitehouse.gov/omb/budget/Historicals (for total debt and total debt as percentage of GDP data)

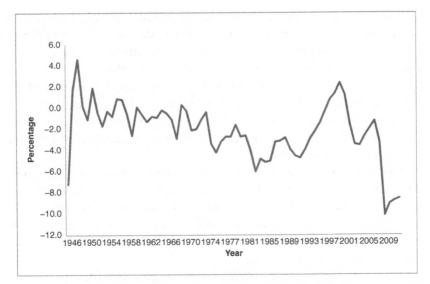

Figure 6.1. U.S. federal deficit as a percentage of GDP
Source: Table 1.2 – Summary of Receipts, Outlays, and Surpluses or Deficits (–) as Percentages of GDP: 1930–2018 at http://www.whitehouse.gov/omb/budget/Historicals

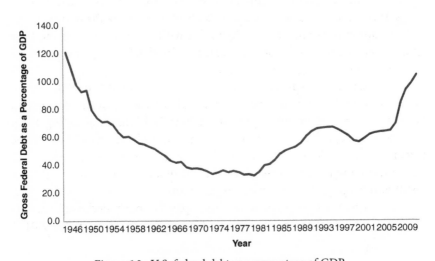

Figure 6.2. U.S. federal debt as a percentage of GDP
Source: Table 7.1 – Federal Debt at the End of Year: 1940–2018 at http://www.whitehouse.gov/omb/budget/Historicals

Default is not a danger in the United States, unless it were to be chosen through the democratic political process, and in that sense, it may well be a danger. The democratic political process has contributed to rising annual debt and to rising debt to GDP ratios in the United States. The debt limit fiasco of 2011 shows how default might well emerge from choices made in American democratic institutions. This is to say that the United States is not near the economic stress of Argentina in 2001 or Greece in 2011–12. The United States has an enormous capacity to borrow, and interest rates are remarkably low at present.

Dealing with rising deficits presents two main democratic political problems. The first is getting elected public officials to agree on spending and taxing levels that would reduce annual deficits The second is dealing with future patterns of revenue and expenditure that are determined by the combination of demographic changes and the fact that entitlement expenditures are set in law by formula.

In the half century since 1960, there have been five fiscal years with surpluses: FY 1969, based on the last Johnson budget, and FY 1998 through 2001, based on Clinton budgets. (See Figure 6.1 and Table 6.2 for details.) Since FY 2009, deficits have risen above 10 percent of GDP. A better indicator of budgetary health is debt as a fraction of GDP. This was above 120 percent of GDP right after World War II and declined fairly steadily since then to the low thirties in the transition between Carter and Reagan. By the end of the Reagan administration, the debt level had risen into the fifties. It continued to rise to approximately 67 percent by the middle of the Clinton administration but started to fall with the surpluses of the later Clinton years. Then, as the Bush tax cuts took hold, it began rising again and has not stopped, as Figure 6.2 indicates.

The causes of U.S. deficits and debt are well understood and are the result of the dysfunction of the democratic political process. As of 2000, there had been several years of surpluses, and the debt to GDP ratio was falling. Hard to believe, the problem was too much surplus, which would reduce the leverage that the Federal Reserve had to conduct monetary policy. There was at the same time a foreseeable problem of a crisis in entitlements as a result of the aging of the baby boom generation.

Federal Reserve Chairman Alan Greenspan famously endorsed tax cuts in testimony before the Senate Budget Committee on January 25, 2001.[21]

---

[21] http://www.federalreserve.gov/boarddocs/testimony/2001/20010125/default.htm#page-top, accessed May 17, 2012.

The problem Greenspan saw a need to address was the possibility that the federal debt would be reduced to zero before the end of the first decade of the twenty-first century. Without cutting taxes, the accumulation of surpluses might risk federal accumulation of private assets.

Although this document seems quaint and even possibly naïve with the hindsight of the current debt crisis, nothing in it does not make sense in terms of conditions at the time the chairman spoke. Moreover, it should be noted that Greenspan specified that tax cuts "cannot be open-ended," and "conceivably, [the tax plan] could include provisions that, in some way, would limit surplus-reducing actions if specified targets for the budget surplus and federal debt were not satisfied. Only if the probability was very low that prospective cuts or new outlay initiatives would send the budget accounts into deficit would unconditional initiatives appear prudent."

In fact, the Bush tax cuts of 2001 and 2003 were unconditional. The deficits quickly returned, and gross federal debt mounted from 56.4 percent of GDP in FY 2001 to 69.7 percent in FY 2008, which ended just after the failure of Lehman Brothers. Gross federal debt has subsequently risen to more than 100 percent of GDP (see Table 6.2).[22]

The nominal federal surplus or deficit is based on the relative sizes of revenues and expenditures. Even if public policy is designed to produce a balance between the two, business cycles and exogenous shocks can throw them out of balance. For example, an economic downturn automatically leads to increases in expenditures for unemployment compensation and decreases in revenues, because of lost income among the newly unemployed. These "automatic stabilizers" operate in a countercyclical fashion to cushion the impact of a recession, whereas balancing the budget every year would have an opposite, pro-cyclical effect.

Liberal and Keynesian economists have always seen these automatic stabilizers as desirable, but even leading conservative economists have come to accept them, including their implications of occasional deficits. For example, Milton Friedman's famous article, "A Monetary and Fiscal Framework for Economic Stability" (1953a) advocated automatic stabilizers based on transfer payments and a progressive income tax. Robert Barro

---

[22] Gross debt includes debt owed to federal trust funds, such as the Social Security Trust Fund. Another figure commonly used is "debt held by the public," which does not include such debt. I find gross debt a more meaningful figure, because money borrowed from trust funds represents real obligations.

(1979) defended occasional deficits on grounds of the revenue-smoothing hypothesis, which states that governments can and should plan equal marginal tax rates over time to minimize distortionary effects on people's incentives to work and consume. Such rates will be set to cover the expected stream of expenditures, which will be exogenously determined, presumably in a political process. Because unanticipated shocks such as wars and recessions will affect the path of expenditures, deficits will be allowed to fluctuate in a way that will meet government budget constraints over time, without demanding distortionary adjustments in taxes.

A nominal balance of the government's revenues and expenditures is a thoroughly arbitrary target, although it is very appealing politically because it is simpler than any other target and thus is more widely understood among voters.[23] A cash flow deficit of zero is a focal point for agreement in a way that no other goal is likely to be.

Only a few of the arguments in favor of a balanced budget present this goal as an end in itself. Such arguments are likely to be based on aphorisms, such as Adam Smith's analogy with households: "What is prudence in the conduct of every private family, can scarce be folly in that of a great kingdom." The most convincing arguments that deficits are harmful hinge on the their consequences, rather than on deficits as a goal in their own right. Deficits are said to cause inflation and rising interest rates in the short run, and reductions in growth in the long run: they may cause inflation, because increases in aggregate demand relative to a supply that is fixed in the short run are likely to increase prices. They may cause interest rates to rise, because increases in deficits increase the demand for lendable funds, the price of which is the interest rate. These arguments have lost force because the enormous increases in deficits in the Reagan-Bush, George W. Bush, and Obama eras have been associated with very low rates of both inflation and interest. It would be a mistake to assume that this condition will continue indefinitely.

Deficits and the associated indebtedness are said to be at the expense of long-run growth and the capacity to produce, because savings that might be invested in productive capital are diverted to government borrowing. Although that belief is widespread among economists, there is considerable

---

[23] Economists on the left, such as the late Robert Eisner, and on the right, such as Robert Barro, agree on certain accounting issues that imply that zero is a meaningless and arbitrary target. See Eisner (1986).

disagreement about what level of deficits will seriously threaten the other, more important economic goals (Rock 1991).

The idea that a budget should be balanced for every period, such as every year, is based on conventional wisdom, such as that quoted earlier from Adam Smith. It has no sounder basis than its inherent appeal and than its analogy with households. But the analogy is misleading, because of the differences between governments and households. It is also misleading because even conservative and prudent households have always gone into debt for certain purposes, such as the purchase of housing.

Budget balance over the business cycle was a more relaxed standard that received attention in the years after the Keynesians began advocating intentional deficits. Thus, a deficit in a recession would be inevitable, because of the automatic stabilizers and the desirability of a countercyclical policy. A prominent suggestion in the postwar era was that such deficits be balanced with surpluses in good times. Budget balance at full employment was a still more relaxed standard. It recognized that deficits were desirable in recessions, but avoided the issue of paying off the debt. That standard made the definition of full employment implicitly important, but failure to agree on a definition made the standard ineffective as a guide.[24]

Rising Debt to GDP Ratio

Most targets for deficits are contestable by reasonable and informed people. However, a compelling "minimum standard for deficit reduction is that federal deficits should be low enough that an unchanging fiscal policy should *not* result in steadily rising debt or interest burdens" (Gramlich 1991, p. 184, emphasis in original). Such a condition of steady rise would be a good candidate for a pathology. A steadily rising ratio cannot be sustained without adverse consequences. In spite of some models that illustrate how the normal political process may have a bias in favor of deficits, there is too much history of budget balance to think that such is an inevitable feature of democratic government. In parallel with the arguments regarding hyperinflation, mentioned earlier, the case has not been convincingly made that democratic institutions cause rising debt to GDP ratios. We have enough experience with such institutions to be confident that any such connection is not simple and deterministic.

---

[24] See Stein (1969, 1994). For an authoritative discussion of the demise of just about any standard for balancing the budget, see Part 2 of Stein (1996), an updating of Stein (1969).

Exogenous shocks have had much to do with rising debt to GDP ratios in the Organization for Economic Cooperation and Development nations since 1970 (Roubini and Sachs 1989a, 1989b). However, there is reason to believe that certain features of democratic institutions systematically obstruct stabilization programs that are designed to resolve such situations. Specifically, divided government and fractionalized party systems are associated with failure to resolve them.[25]

Rising debt to GDP ratios have called attention to a major fiscal crisis in the United States that is not just business as usual. The problem was caused by the Bush tax cuts of 2001 and 2003, and the fact that they were not matched with spending cuts. In fact, federal spending increased substantially in the Bush administration, with wars in Afghanistan and Iraq and a new Medicare drug benefit. Then, the financial crisis of 2007–9 hit, with a deep recession beginning in December 2007. Although the recession associated with this crisis was officially over in June 2009, growth in GDP has been sluggish and unemployment has remained high.

Whether or not they were good ideas, the Troubled Asset Relief Program, which began in the Bush administration, and multiple fiscal stimulus laws, culminating in the American Recovery and Reinvestment Act of 2009, have added substantially to the federal deficits and debt. All of this takes place in the context of projections that entitlement spending will rise automatically because of the retiring of the baby boom generation, and the inexorable rise in medical costs.

As the federal deficit climbed from more than 3 percent of GDP in FY 2008 to nearly 13 percent of GDP in FY 2009, the fiscal situation became too threatening to ignore. President Obama appointed a National Commission of Fiscal Responsibility and Reform, whose charge was to identify "policies to improve the fiscal situation in the medium term and to achieve fiscal sustainability over the long run." The commission, sometimes called the Simpson-Bowles or Bowles-Simpson commission, after its co-chairs, had eighteen members, twelve of whom were members of Congress, evenly divided by legislative branch and by party, and six presidential appointees, plus an executive director.

The commission used Congressional Budget Office projections from its Long-Term Budget Outlook, which include current law, which included an end to the Bush tax cuts, and current policy, which involved extending

[25] See Roubini and Sachs (1989a, 1989b); Grilli, Masciandaro, and Tabellini (1991); Poterba (1994).

them. The extension of current policies implied that debt as a fraction of GDP could rise to around 200 percent by 2035. The Simpson-Bowles Commission proposed a plan that would cut mandatory and discretionary expenditures, cut tax rates and tax loopholes, balance the budget by 2035, and reduce federal debt as a fraction of GDP to 40 by that time.

The relationship between revenues and expenditures is an intermediate target for which there are many legitimate views. Many different budgetary outcomes can be considered to be legitimized by a democratic political process, without being pathological. But the long-term projections of U.S. federal debt are now so foreboding that the fiscal situation has become pathological. Congress's inability to make hard decisions is a sign of weakness and ineffectiveness of democratic procedures in the United States at this time.

THE NATURE OF GOALS IN A SYSTEM OF DEMOCRATIC ACCOUNTABILITY

This chapter has shown that no obvious sources in law or in economics for definitions of public economic goals are fundamentally authoritative. We have found no source of authority for single goals or for objective functions such that we can use them as benchmarks for evaluating the performance of the political process. There are no authoritative social welfare functions.

The closest we might come to a consensual goal is balance in the federal budget, because that has been an official goal in legislation (e.g., Gramm-Rudman-Hollings) and is widely and consistently supported by the public. Ironically, fiscal balance is where the democratic political process in the United States has most clearly broken down. Even though both parties pay lip service to balanced budgets, Republicans have seemed to care more about low taxes than about balanced budgets, but they have softened their position after the 2012 elections. Democrats are concerned about preserving government programs but seem to be willing to trade off spending cuts with tax increases "on the wealthiest Americans."

Public purposes are defined within the political process, not outside of it. To paraphrase Arthur Okun, a nation's constitution (and perhaps even its laws) should not try to settle forever the precise weighting on economic goals. The constitutional arrangement "should rely on the democratic political process it establishes to select reasonable weights on specific issues as they arise" (Okun 1975, pp. 93–4). This stance presumes that the political process operates in a reasonable and healthy fashion. In Chapters 3 and 4, models of electoral cycles and partisanship did not provide compelling arguments or evidence that the political process is unreasonable or patho-logical. Chapter 5 was more disturbing, and this chapter continues the theme that something is wrong. The next three chapters will consider the political process in regard to voting and the making of monetary and fiscal policies.

7

Voters, Elections, Accountability, and Choice

Voters are the ultimate authority in a democracy. Their preferences and behaviors are the fundamental sources of legitimacy for policy makers, who get their power through elections. Their preferences and behaviors also place constraints on what elected politicians can do. The electorate is the source for the authority of constitutional rules of procedure and for the authority of official statements of public goals. When there is ambiguity about what goals are appropriate for public policy, voter choices can resolve it at least provisionally. When there is ambiguity about which potential officeholders have correct or appropriate beliefs about the way the economic world works, voter choices can determine which ones will get to test their views against experience.

All this would be true in a world of ideal democratic citizens, but it is true in the real world as well. Yet the effort by candidates for office to maximize their share of the votes of even ideal citizens can lead to opportunism, according to some of the models of political economy we have reviewed. Whereas ideal citizens may be public spirited and fully informed, real-world voters may not have either of these qualities. This chapter will assess what we know about how voting behavior is affected by macroeconomic issues, as well as the implications for policy making. It will also raise some questions about how voter behavior may have contributed to the poor contemporary state of American political economy.

Most real-world voters are not well informed about political issues; they sometimes are characterized as being vulnerable to cynical manipulation by opportunistic politicians. However, I suggest that politicians do not need to be opportunistic to succeed: voters will tolerate a wide variety of policies and outcomes, and politicians have considerable latitude for alternative choices, many of which are consistent with successful electoral careers. Pandering to voters' worst instincts is a realistic possibility, and it may even be rewarded.

But such pandering is not a necessity for political survival. It is, of course, easy to conceive that responsible policy making will be punished at the polls, but that is not necessarily so. Voters do not necessarily or even usually *demand* irresponsible policy making.

THE HEAVY BURDEN OF THE SIMPLE ACT OF VOTING

An individual's vote must settle on a single choice following the consideration of many preferences and judgments that may be in tension or even incompatible. Thus, a vote may be only a crude reflection of a great deal of information. Because they allow voters to "throw the rascals out," elections enable voters to hold incumbents accountable for the past performance of the government. (This is what was going on in the electoral cycle models discussed in Chapter 3.) At the same time, the election is the institution through which voters choose among alternative future governments. (This is what was going on in the partisan choice models discussed in Chapter 4.)[1]

Consider the information that might be communicated in a single vote in a presidential election between two candidates, an incumbent and a challenger. If the voter approves of the past economic performance of the incumbent and also prefers the choices offered by the incumbent to those offered by the challenger, the choice is clear. The same is true if the voter disapproves of the past performance and prefers the challenger. In both cases, the meaning of the vote is unambiguous, even though the vote is carrying two kinds of information.

However, suppose the voter disapproves of the incumbent's performance but does not prefer the options presented by the challenger. A vote for either candidate garbles this message, and such a vote is indistinguishable from the votes in the simpler unambiguous cases.[2] If we knew that voters always voted retrospectively, essentially by evaluating the performance of incumbents, we could interpret the meaning of elections accordingly. Or if we knew that voters always voted prospectively, by choosing among the expectations for future policy and performance, that fact would also simplify the

---

[1] James Fearon (1999) distinguishes models that involve pure selection and pure sanctioning and a model in which the two methods interact. Duch and Stevenson (2008) build on this distinction in a massive comparative study of economic voting.

[2] A less likely possibility is that the voter prefers the policy preferences of the incumbent but believes that the challenger will be more competent to guide the economy. A single vote cannot carry this message clearly either. One reason I expect that this possibility is less likely is that judgments of competence and judgments of the appropriate policy preferences are likely to be closely intertwined.

interpretation of elections. But evidence exists for both patterns, and we cannot assume that all voters use the same decision rule or even that any one voter uses the same rule all of the time.[3] Not voting might be a way of expressing both disapproval of the incumbent and dislike of the challenger, but nonvoting because of distaste for both alternatives is not on its face distinguishable from nonvoting that derives from the indifference of those who would be satisfied with either alternative.

The addition of new alternatives does not necessarily help, because this may simply divide a majority that disapproves of the incumbent, so that he or she may win anyway. If the simple act of voting is overburdened in an artificially simple case such as this, imagine how many more complex opinions must be distilled in an ordinary election in which considerations of partisan loyalty, candidate appeal, and other policy issues are also relevant. All these considerations may combine in ways that vary from voter to voter. When we consider the rich set of institutional alternatives regarding parliamentary and presidential systems, two-party and multi-party systems, the possibilities for ambiguity become still greater.

No wonder it is difficult to infer mandates from elections. In fact, I contend that in a narrow sense, mandates almost never exist. The narrow sense of "mandate" is an authoritative command or instruction, presumably regarding a policy choice. Referenda give such commands by virtue of clear popular majorities choosing between the binary alternatives of a proposal and a status quo. For an election of persons to give such a command, a clear majority would have to express itself clearly about the policy choice through its choice among persons. The majority would have to choose the person because of a policy position with which he or she was identified. I know of no concrete case of such a mandate.

The term "mandate" will not go out of use because of this argument, however. A weaker definition is also meaningful: an "authorization given by a political electorate to its representative" (*American Heritage Dictionary*, 1992). Public officials who win elections have mandates, in this sense, to do what they see fit, subject to the authority of the office. This interpretation means that even if some of the support received by a winning candidate came in spite of their stands on certain issues, they are still "authorized" to carry out their goals. Otherwise, public officials would be virtually paralyzed by the absence of mandates in the narrow sense: "The voice of the people

---

[3] See Sniderman, Brody, and Tetlock (1991, ch. 9) for a report of research that shows that different groups use different decision rules. See also Rivers (1988).

can be about as readily ascertained as the voice of God" (Huntington 1968, p. 106).[4]

RETROSPECTIVE AND PROSPECTIVE VOTING

In spite of all of this complexity, I argue in this book that the most consequential feature of elections can be understood in a simple way. Elections are meaningful exercises in accountability even when they are not inspiring exercises of public discourse. It is now conventional wisdom to understand presidential elections as being influenced by retrospective evaluation of the economic performance of the incumbent administration. Many studies have reported "unmistakable" evidence that voting in presidential elections responds to economic performance, and one study has reported that economic performance is an even better predictor of the outcome than is a measure of the relative personal appeal of the presidential candidates (Erikson 1989).

Some scholars go so far as to claim that information about economic performance allows them to predict the outcomes of presidential elections better than public opinion polls intended to directly measure voters' intentions (Fair 1988; Hibbs 2012b). There is something to this, along with reason for humility among forecasters.[5] But even when different defensible models provide different predictions, as is sometimes the case, almost no careful student of the issue would deny that past economic performance is an important determinant of election outcomes. There is, however, a considerable range of interpretations of the meaning of this fact.

Two leading alternative interpretations go back to those of V. O. Key Jr. (1966) and Anthony Downs (1957). The leading student of retrospective voting (Fiorina 1981) has designated the Key view as the traditional reward-punishment theory. This view imposes little burden on the electorate: "The patterns of flow of the major streams of shifting voters graphically reflect the electorate in its great, and perhaps principal, role as an appraiser of past events, past performance, and past actions. It judges retrospectively: it commands prospectively only insofar as it expresses either approval or disapproval of that which has happened before" (Key 1966, p. 61).

---

[4] See Kelley (1983, ch. 7) and Conley (2001) for useful discussions of mandates in concrete contexts.

[5] The October 2012 issue of *PS: Political Science and Politics* has a symposium that includes thirteen articles forecasting the 1912 election.

Key recognizes that voters have policy preferences, but he discounts the importance of policy choice in elections. He does address the contrast between the experience of the past and promises for the future: "Voters may reject what they have known; or they may approve what they have known. They are not likely to be attracted in great numbers by promises of the novel or unknown. Once innovation has occurred, they may embrace it, even though they would have, earlier, hesitated to venture forth to welcome it" (Key 1966, p. 61).

Thus, Key recognizes that voters may take a leap in the dark when they reject incumbent parties. His interpretation was presented as a realistic description of American voters, but it was not meant to denigrate. In fact, the title of Key's book makes that doubly clear: *The Responsible Electorate: Rationality in Presidential Voting, 1936–1960*. The charitable quality of his view was further clarified by his statement that the "perverse and unorthodox argument of this little book is that voters are not fools" (1966, p. 7).

In contrast to Key's use of empirical data for inferences about how voters actually decide, Anthony Downs articulates a theoretically grounded argument about "The Basic Logic of Voting" (1957, ch. 4). In his theory, the vote is a future-oriented comparison of the streams of utility income to be expected from government activity under alternative parties. Downs is explicit about the future orientation of his theory: to "ignore the future when deciding how to vote ... would obviously be irrational, since the purpose of voting is to select a future government" (1957, p. 39).

However, the most solid basis for an assessment of future utility under the incumbent party is its performance in the current period, "assuming that its policies have some continuity" (1957, p. 39). Downs continues: "As a result, the most important part of a voter's decision is the size of his *current party differential*, i.e. the difference between the utility income he actually received in period t and the one he would have received if the opposition had been in power" (1957, p. 40, emphasis in original). Downs's theory of the logic of voting is emphatically future oriented. But note that both elements of the information that Downs's voter would use are based on the past: the utility "received" in the past and the utility the voter "would have received" in the past.

Downs implicitly assumes that the future will be a projection of the past, whether the projection is based on a continuation of the incumbents' policies and performance or a continuation of the counterfactual conditions that would have prevailed if the opposition had been in power. For Downs, the past is important because he sees it as the most useful available guide to the future. The relationship between past and future is seen as simple extrapolation or projection. Downs shows no awareness of the possibility that opportunistic incumbents might manipulate conditions before elections in ways that would mislead voters about the conditions that would obtain after the election. That is, a Downsian voter could be quite vulnerable to a Nordhaus-type electoral cycle. Of course, there is no reason to be sure that voters as characterized by Key would not also be vulnerable to such manipulation, though Key's vagueness about standards leaves the question more open.[6]

It would be a mistake to exaggerate the differences between the views of Downs and Key. Downs (1957) cites Key's earlier work three times, though Key (1966) does not mention Downs and does not seem to be aware of his relevance. Each scholar acknowledges, at least implicitly, the central theme of the other: Downs discounts the value of platforms and promises relative to actual performance, and Key implicitly acknowledges that some voters might respond to promises. But still, as Fiorina asserts, the difference is important: "under the Downsian view elections have policy implications . . . Downsian retrospective voting is a means to prospective voting . . . But under the traditional theory, elections have no policy implications other than a generalized acceptance or rejection of the status quo" (1981, p. 13).

In fact, as a general rule, most judgments about the future are related somehow to the past, and most judgments about the past are not totally divorced from implications for the future. We should not expect to find that voting is purely retrospective or purely prospective. Most votes will involve some mixture of the two elements, and the mixture is likely to vary among voters. The next sections present an overview of the evidence regarding the importance of the past and the future in voting as it relates to the economy. Even though ample evidence shows that voters are at least somewhat future oriented when they vote, I argue that some important features of elections are better understood from Key's perspective. This is partly because, as Downs readily acknowledges, information about the past is much more solid than information about the future. But there is another reason. Sometimes elections produce innovations that are quite surprising by almost any standard.[7]

---

[6] The idea that incumbents would manipulate the economy in this way was not common among political scientists or economists when Downs and Key wrote. The idea, probably inspired by the 1972 election, became widespread only after the publications of Nordhaus (1975) and Tufte (1978).

[7] See, for example, Cukierman and Tomassi (1998), Stokes (2001), and Keech (1999).

EVIDENCE OF RETROSPECTIVE JUDGMENTS

Considerable evidence shows that past economic performance affects the vote share and the popularity of incumbent presidents. This is, at least superficially, evidence in support of Key's view that voters are retrospectively oriented. But there is also reason to believe that information about the past is used as a guide to the future, which implicitly supports a Downsian view. The most basic evidence of the importance of past performance is that a measure of recent real national income growth is a very powerful predictor of the vote share of the incumbent party's presidential candidate. For example, Erikson argues that "one can better predict the presidential vote divisions from income change during the previous administration than from the voters' relative liking of the two candidates! ... Evaluations of candidate personal characteristics aside, the vote is determined almost entirely by the amount of prosperity that the incumbent party delivers" (1989, p. 568).

The economic performance variable that Erikson uses is a quarterly measure of per capita growth in disposable income, discounted over the presidential term so that recent performance counts most heavily. Erikson's model does include a measure of candidate appeal, which is also significantly related to vote share, but not more strongly than economic performance.

Ray Fair has been relating American national election outcomes to economic votes since 1978 (Fair 1978, 1988, 1990, 2009). His models include inflation, the party of the incumbent, whether or not the incumbent is running, and income growth. Income growth and inflation both consistently influence presidential elections, and somewhat less consistently influence Congressional elections as well, all in the intuitive and predictable ways.

Douglas Hibbs has the most parsimonious and elegant model of the impact of the economy on presidential and congressional elections, called "Bread and Peace" (Hibbs 2012b). Presidential elections since World War II can be explained by just two variables: "(1) weighted-average growth of per capita real disposable personal income over the term, and (2) cumulative US military fatalities due to unprovoked hostile deployments of American armed forces in foreign wars. No other objectively measured exogenous factor systematically affects postwar aggregate votes for president" (2012b, p. 635).

Four coefficients are estimated from 15 elections between 1952 and 2008: the intercept (45.7) and the geometric lag coefficient (0.90), and the two substantive bread (3.64) and peace (−0.05) variables. All four are highly significant (p-value less than 0.00) (2012b, p. 636). Figure 7.1 shows the scatter plot of the weighted income growth and vote share of two-party vote.

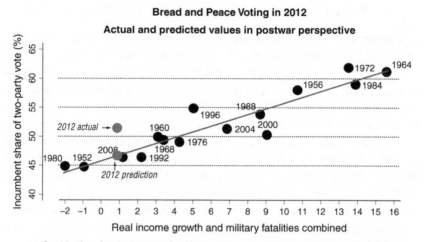

Bread and Peace Voting in 2012

Actual and predicted values in postwar perspective

Combination of real growth and fatalities weights each variable by its estimated coefficient.
Estimated effects of fatalities on vote shares: –0.7% in 2008 (Iraq), –7.4% in 1968 (Vietnam),
–9.7% in 1952 (Korea): negligible in 1964, 1976, 2004, 2012, and null in other years.
Source: www.douglas-hibbs.com November 11, 2012.

Figure 7.1. Economic performance and vote for incumbent party's
presidential candidate

Economic conditions such as those just discussed seem not to have the
same impact on congressional elections that they have at the presidential
level. The seminal study of the effect of economic performance on voting
(Kramer 1971) was a study of congressional elections. In a memorable
exchange, George Stigler (1973) challenged Kramer's findings on both
theoretical and empirical grounds.[8] Subsequent research leaves little doubt
that voting for president is influenced by economic performance, but controversy continues regarding the impact of the economy on congressional
elections. Erikson argues that "with proper specification, per capita income
growth is not significantly related to the congressional vote" (1990, p. 373),
but Jacobson (1990) contests that finding. Fair (2009) found that not all of
his economic variables affected congressional elections in presidential
years and off years estimated separately. Hibbs found that the vote in

---

[8]   Stigler argued that economic performance should not be a basis for voters' decisions, but if
it were, it should be based on the entire electoral period, rather than just one year. He
showed that Kramer's finding evaporated when economic performance was measured over
the two-year electoral period, and he used that fact as evidence in support of his assertion
that economic performance should not be a basis for political competition, because
prosperity is not a partisan issue. He contended that distributional issues should be a
basis for partisan competition.

presidential-year congressional elections was influenced by cumulative income growth over the congressional term, and the vote share of the previous congressional election won by the president's party, but not war casualties. At best, evidence of the impact of the economy on congressional elections is sensitive to specification decisions in a way that its impact on presidential elections is not.

Most quantitative studies of the impact of economic performance on American elections have focused on the twentieth century. However, there is reason to believe that incumbents have been punished for poor economic performance well before anyone would think that they could have had any influence over it. For example, incumbent presidents or their parties' nominees were defeated after several of the major economic downturns of the nineteenth century, in the elections of 1840, 1860, 1884, and 1896.[9]

More Refined Inferences of Voter Preferences

Elections are the authoritative expressions of voters' wishes, but there is a limit to the information that can be squeezed out of them, because American national elections are held at two-year intervals. Presidential approval has been measured in a series of public opinion polls that began in 1935. Since 1953, the question, "Do you approve of the way [president's name] has been handling his job as president?" has been asked at a rate that averages more than once a month (Edwards 1990). These polls yield a data series that provides a much richer source of inference about the connections between different economic conditions and political responses than can be inferred from elections.

For example, Hibbs has used these studies to infer the relative aversion of the public to inflation and unemployment, among other issues. Consider an equation that relates presidential popularity to unemployment and inflation rates:

$$\text{approval} = a - b(\text{inflation}) - c\,(\text{unemployment})$$

The coefficients b and c, which we expect to be negative, show how popularity varies with inflation and unemployment, respectively. If the coefficients were the same, that would imply that the public was equally averse to inflation and to unemployment. That would indicate an indifference

---

[9] See Keech and Lynch (1992). See Miller and Wattenberg (1985) for survey-based measurements of the balance of retrospective and prospective judgments in elections from 1952 to 1980.

curve with a slope of −1 in the Phillips curve space described in Figure 4.1. If *b* were twice the size of *c*, that would imply that voters found a point of inflation to be twice as distasteful as a point of unemployment, indicating a slope of −0.5. We can call the lines defined by these ratios "indifference curves"; they reflect the relative aversion to inflation and unemployment.

Hibbs found that the slopes of such "marginal rates of substitution" differed among partisans. He found that for Democrats, the slope was −1.1, and for Republicans it was −0.65 (Hibbs 1987, p. 177). If possible combinations of unemployment and inflation were characterized by a static Phillips curve, that would imply that Democrats would choose a point such as *D*, and Republicans would choose a point such as *R*, in Figure 4.1.

Inferring Incentives for Manipulation by Vote-Motivated Politicians

Just as the approval polls permit a more refined assessment of voters' tastes regarding inflation and unemployment, they provide a more refined measure of the time horizon over which citizens evaluate past performance. This issue has confused some of the controversies over the impact of economic conditions. For example, Kramer (1971) had originally assessed the impact of the most recent year's economic performance on congressional votes, whereas Stigler (1973) had assessed the impact of performance over the entire two-year term. Stigler thought that his unweighted two-year measure was an obviously superior measure of performance, but he did not consider the possibility that voters might discount the past in the spirit of the ancient question, "What have you done for me lately?"

Hibbs and other scholars have used the presidential approval series to infer the relative weights that citizens place on conditions that vary in their distance from the present. The standard that has become widely accepted is a weight that declines quarterly from a full weight for conditions in the quarter before an assessment to approximately 0.8 for the quarter before that. The weighting formula is a geometric lag, where the parameter $0 < g < 1$, which is 0.8 in this case, is multiplied by itself one additional time for each additional quarter back into the past. Because the parameter can vary between zero and one, a value of 0.8 might seem relatively high. However, when multiplied by itself several times, it rapidly approaches zero. The weight for the first quarter of the year before the election year would be *g* to the sixth power, or 0.26. The weight for the first quarter of a presidential term would be close to zero.

If that is the rate at which voters discount the past, even Downsian future-oriented voters might seem very much like those characterized in

Nordhaus's model of vote-maximizing politicians manipulating naïve voters. The crucial features are that they evaluate incumbents in terms of past economic performance, with the greatest emphasis on the recent past, and then project forward. The temptation Nordhaus identified for vote-maximizing politicians was to exploit a presumed possibility of making things look misleadingly good just before the election and the expense of being worse after the election. For example, a misery index would be lower before the election than after, and a Downsian projection of past performance into the future would be misleading. Voters who heavily discounted the early part of the term would be vulnerable to such manipulation.

The reason that the past might be a misleading indicator of the future is the complicated and time-dependent trade-off between unemployment or income growth on the one hand and inflation on the other. In the natural-rate world that Nordhaus modeled, unemployment below its natural rate or income growth above its natural rate would have delayed inflationary consequences. The main reason that voters were seen as vulnerable to manipulation was that the models used to estimate their preferences assumed that voters would reward reductions in unemployment and increases in income growth without regard to their natural rates, and without regard to their inflationary consequences. That feature was not an explicit assumption in the scholarship, but it was the simplest and most direct way to model voter responses to economic conditions.

The implication that voters are naïvely retrospective and vulnerable to manipulation was tested against an alternative hypothesis by Chappell and Keech (1985a), who conceptualized a model of voters who would reward reductions in unemployment or increases in income growth only to their natural rates. In that model, voters would not reward unemployment reduction or income growth that had inflationary consequences, and they would even tolerate economic slack that brought about reductions in inflation. For such voters, vote-maximizing policy is not irresponsible and does not generate inferior outcomes. Chappell and Keech tested and compared their model of sophisticated voters against the standard model that implicitly assumes vulnerability to manipulation. In those tests, the model that presumed voters to be sophisticated performed at least as well as and sometimes better than the alternative. Those findings cannot be interpreted as robust support for the hypothesis that voters are sophisticated and invulnerable to manipulation, but they do strongly suggest that voters will not necessarily punish responsible policy making.

As a theory of voting behavior, the strength of the sophisticated voter model left a puzzle. The performance of this model was only marginally better than the naïve voter model. Direct evidence about voter information and understanding of the relevant trade-offs is not strongly supportive of the sophisticated voter hypothesis.[10] These facts suggest that the sophisticated voter hypothesis is most compelling when considered as a suggestion that voters behave "as if" they were sophisticated. But this leaves open the question of why voters are able to act in a sophisticated way without sophisticated cognitive processes.

Motoshi Suzuki (1991) has illuminated this puzzle by suggesting that under certain conditions, the two models are observationally equivalent. The responsiveness of output growth to unanticipated demand shocks or inflationary surprises may vary across countries and across time within a country. In settings (or regimes) in which unexpected policy shifts have large impacts on output, vote-motivated politicians might have an incentive to manipulate the economy. In those settings, the difference between naïve and sophisticated voters will be consequential. However, in settings in which government policy has little impact on real growth, voter sophistication does not matter very much.

Suzuki (1991) distinguished two such settings or regimes in the United States. The period from 1961:I through 1974:II was characterized as a stable period in which the two models of voting behavior could not be distinguished, whereas the period from 1974.III to 1985.IV was characterized as an unstable period in which they could. In empirical tests, Suzuki found that the two models performed comparably well and were indeed indistinguishable in the first period. However, he found that the sophisticated model was outperformed by the naïve or adaptive model in the second period. Directly, these results imply support for "nonrationalist" perspectives on voting behavior. However, Suzuki suggested that voters may learn only what they need to learn to hold incumbents accountable for economic performance. Because the economic regime since 1985 has returned to the stability that characterized the earlier period, voters may not have been rewarded for the effort to learn new decision rules that would make them less vulnerable to manipulation (Suzuki 1991). In a study of Japanese voting, Suzuki suggested that voters were able to learn strategic behavior in response to the emergence of manipulative behavior by politicians.[11]

Suzuki's important work suggests that an observed pattern of economic voting behavior is likely to be conditional. If the economy does not respond to policy manipulation, or if politicians do not try to manipulate it, naïve

---

[10] See Gramlich (1983).
[11] Suzuki (1994). See also Richards (1986).

and sophisticated voting will be difficult to distinguish. And even if economic and political conditions make sophisticated voting appropriate, it
may take time for voters to learn. We are far from having conclusive
observations on voter vulnerability to cynical manipulation of economic
performance.

Both the model of naïve performance evaluation and that of sophisticated
performance evaluation are based on past performance and are in that sense
retrospective, and in keeping with Key's views. But the model of sophisticated performance evaluation is implicitly future oriented, in that it is
consistent with behavior that would avoid adverse future consequences.
This feature makes it consistent with a reformulated Downsian view in
which information about the past is used as a guide to the future.

The impact of voters on economic policy making should be viewed less in
terms of what voters demand than in terms of what they will tolerate and
reward. Voters are not the initiators of public policy; they are more like an
audience whose approval is necessary for a show to continue. The question
is not what kind of show they demand, but whether or not the shows that are
produced will receive good reviews and continued support.

There is no compelling evidence that voters characteristically punish
responsible policy making that is not opportunistic. We have seen that no
single best economic policy is uncontested among fair-minded people.
Many policies may be legitimately defensible and receive voter support.
Only some of these should be considered irresponsible, and the case is yet to
be made that there is strong voter demand for inferior policy.

"Reagan Proved That Deficits Don't Matter" (for Elections)[12]

Although voters regularly support balanced budgets, they do not seem to
take them into account when voting. President Reagan was reelected in 1984
even though the tax cuts he had sponsored had led to considerable deficits.
(I have argued that in terms of the basic macroeconomic outcome variables
of unemployment, inflation, and income growth, his performance was
good.) Similarly, George W. Bush was reelected in 2004 in spite of his two
major tax cuts of 2001 and 2003.

President George H. W. Bush was defeated in 1993 in spite of having
raised taxes and cut expenditures, which were designed to improve the
deficit situation. President Clinton was not rewarded in the 1994 election
for his package of tax increases and budget expenditures, which would bear

---

[12] Attributed to Vice President Richard B. Cheney (Johnson and Kwak 2012, p. 69).

fruit in his second term with the first federal surpluses since 1969. Nor was Vice President Al Gore rewarded in 2000 for the Clinton surpluses. These elections are explained well by the Hibbs bread and peace model, which pays no attention to deficits and debt.

PROSPECTIVE VOTING

Several studies have found evidence that voters are forward looking as well as retrospective.[13] For example, in his study of *Economics and Elections*, based largely on western European voters (i.e., those in Britain, France, Germany, Italy, and Spain), Michael Lewis-Beck found that "future expectations about what economic performance a government will deliver emerge as a decisive individual vote determinant" and that "prospective economic policy evaluations have at least as strong an immediate effect on individual vote choice as retrospective economic evaluations do" (Lewis-Beck 1988, pp. 82–3, 122, 133). The evidence for that inference came from sample surveys in which voters were asked for their evaluations of past economic performance and their expectations about future economic conditions. Lewis-Beck presented regression analyses in which he compared future-oriented and past-oriented judgments in terms of their capacity to predict vote choice.[14]

If prospective judgments are important determinants of voter choice, where do they come from? How valid are they? How do voters know what to expect about the future performance of government? There are several possible grounds for judgment about the future consequences of alternative choices. One is that future expectations are based on a simple extrapolation from past performance, as Downs suggested. Another is that they are based on a more sophisticated way of forecasting the future. A third possibility, that future expectations are based on campaign promises, is considered in a later section of this chapter.

If judgments are based on a simple extrapolation from the past, a clear distinction between retrospective and prospective voting cannot be made. Models based on such inferences are quite respectable. For example, when Kramer (1971) formulated the seminal study of the relationship between economic performance and voting behavior, he did so in an explicitly

---

[13] Fearon (1999) calls this selection of good types, as opposed to sanctioning poor perform-ance. See also Besley (2006) and Woon (2012).

[14] For related evidence on the United States, see Kuklinski and West (1981) and Lewis-Beck (1988).

Downsian future-oriented framework. The measure of future economic performance to be expected from reelection of the incumbent party was a measure of actual recent past performance (in the election year), which was considered to be the best available indicator. Because the inference was made from aggregate economic data (and did not involve surveys), we do not have direct evidence of how voters were using that information; we also do not know whether past performance was consciously used as a basis for judgments about the future. The more sophisticated and strategic standard of voting modeled by Chappell and Keech (1985a) is implicitly future oriented, in that such voters do not reward policy that seems desirable at the time but implies undesirable consequences in the future.

MacKuen, Erikson, and Stimson (1992) present an argument that voters are future oriented in a sophisticated way. They assert that "economic conditions affect presidential popularity only to the extent that economic conditions alter expectations of the economic future" (1992, p. 603). They show that expectations of the future are not simple extrapolations of past performance, however. They argue that there is independent informational content in these expectations, which comes from the leading economic indicators, as filtered through news media. This remarkable finding makes a case that the orientation of voters toward the future depends on the economic news, which in turn depends on the index of leading indicators of economic performance. In a more recent article, Erikson, MacKuen, and Stimson update and expand their analysis. Using the Index of Consumer Sentiment, they argue that the electorate "efficiently weighs retrospective and prospective knowledge of the economy" (2000, p. 304). Furthermore, this efficient use of information means that the electorate is not vulnerable to being fooled by short-term and opportunistic manipulation of the economy for electoral gain (2000, pp. 309, 311).[15]

Party Identity and Policy Voting

All of the models in the foregoing accounts of voting have treated incumbents as if they had no identity that was independent of their performance, but we know that that is an oversimplification. Parties have reputations as being best able to deal with particular problems. There is a theory of "policy" voting that is to be distinguished from retrospective voting. In that theory, voters react to conditions by choosing the party that has the best record of

---

[15] For a careful effort to model the differences and similarities between retrospective and prospective voting, see Hibbs (2006).

concern and performance regarding the most salient problems. For example, voters might support Republicans in conditions of high inflation, because that party is known for being effective in dealing with that problem. John Wright (2012) argues that unemployment is an issue that is "owned" by Democrats, and that Democrats are advantaged by high unemployment, even if they are in office when it occurs.[16]

RETROSPECTIVE VOTING AND INNOVATION IN ECONOMIC POLICY

American presidential elections are simultaneously contests between challengers and incumbents (or their heirs) and contests between candidates from parties with identities and histories. But these identities can change substantially. The identity of the Democratic Party changed substantially in 1896, when the gold standard advocate Grover Cleveland was replaced by the free silver advocate William Jennings Bryan as the party's candidate for president. The most dramatic, lasting change in the identity of the Democratic Party came with the election of Franklin D. Roosevelt in 1932. President Roosevelt presided over a revolution in American government and policy making that was so fundamental that one leading scholar has designated the period since then as the Second Republic.[17]

The identity of the Republican Party may never have changed so dramatically as had that of the Democrats in these two instances, but there is little doubt that the Reagan presidency marked a significant departure from previous Republican administrations. In some respects, Reagan's election represented victory for a conservative wing that had been losing all the postwar nominating contests except that of 1964, when the conservative Barry Goldwater was soundly defeated in the general election. But Reagan's program showed more innovation than simply the proposals and policies of the party's Taft-Goldwater wing. Supply side economics and the predominance of the goal of reducing taxes over the goals of reducing expenditures and balancing the budget were new features of Republican economic policy.[18]

---

[16] See Kiewiet (1981, 1983). Petrocik (1996) first identified the phenomenon of issue ownership.

[17] Lowi (1979).

[18] Ippolito (2012) suggests that it is easy to overestimate the degree of departure of the Reagan supply side policies from earlier tax-cutting preferences of conservative Republicans.

The policy innovations of Roosevelt's New Deal and of Reagan's supply side revolution were dramatic departures from their previous partisan identities, as well as from the policies of the party that each replaced. Still, I contend that those innovations are best understood in terms of Key's point that voters "are not likely to be attracted in great numbers by promises of the novel or the unknown. Once innovation has occurred, they may embrace it, even though they would have, earlier, hesitated to venture forth to welcome it" (1966, p. 61). That observation is least controversial with respect to the 1932 election, but I argue that it is also true for 1980.

In 1932, Roosevelt ran a remarkably conventional campaign. He promised to balance the budget, which Herbert Hoover had failed to do, but in general he gave no indication of the flood of innovations that were to come. The 1932 election is easily interpreted as a negative retrospective judgment of the Hoover administration. In 1936, after four years of new policies that radically changed the nature of American government and policy, voters again had a chance to approve or disapprove, and Roosevelt was reelected in a landslide. Voters approved in retrospect what they had not actively chosen four years before.

One need not argue that voters did not think about or care about what kind of president Franklin Roosevelt would be. Choosing him involved taking a substantial risk, perhaps even a "leap in the dark." Knowing what we know now, we could even argue that the 1932 campaign was misleading in suggesting that Roosevelt was not a radical innovator. In retrospect, the risk of major innovation was much greater than it seemed at the time.

The first Reagan administration was more predictably innovative than the first Franklin Roosevelt administration. Governor Reagan was outspoken in advocating change, promising major cuts in taxes and domestic expenditures and increases in defense spending, along with a balanced budget. But it would be too facile to conclude that the American public actively chose these changes, even though they seemed to endorse them in the landslide election of 1984. Just as Roosevelt's victory in 1932 can best be understood as a rejection of Hoover, so Reagan's victory in 1980 can best be understood as a rejection of Carter.[19]

Both of these elections involved retrospective voting against incumbents whose performance was seen as inadequate, and they both involved some risk in the choice of the alternative. Quattrone and Tversky (1988) provide some insight into the reasons why voters might take such risks without clear knowledge of what to expect. They argue that risk aversion is common for

[19] See Hibbs (1982).

people who expect positive outcomes. For example, during a period of prosperity, voters will be less inclined to take a risk and vote for a challenger whose policies and skills are not well known.

However, as negative outcomes become more likely, risk aversion gives way to risk acceptance. In political terms, as incumbents become associated with economic downturns, voters may be more likely to seek risks in the form of the unknown economic leadership of the challenger. Quattrone and Tversky observe that

incumbents are usually regarded by voters as less risky than the challengers, who are often unknowns and whose policies could drastically alter the current trends, for better or for worse ... the less risky incumbent should fare better when conditions are good ... in contrast the election of the challenger offers a *political gamble that is worth taking when "four more years" of the incumbent is viewed as an unsatisfactory state*. (1988, p. 724, emphasis in original)

When conditions are satisfactory, a challenger may seem like too much of a risk, but as conditions deteriorate, the risk involved in rejecting an incumbent for an unknown challenger may seem more and more palatable.

If these interpretations are correct, major changes in policy are likely to be somewhat like mutations in evolution. From the point of view of the electorate as a whole, such changes are not actively chosen from a clearly defined set of alternative future programs. Instead, they "happen" as a result of the rejection of incumbents. They happen at the initiative of those who take over, and only sometimes can their direction be foreseen by even careful study of what challengers say they will do.

CAMPAIGNS, INCENTIVES, AND ACCOUNTABILITY

The foregoing observations do not lead to a claim that electoral campaigns are meaningless exercises. Systematic studies have shown a connection between platforms and promises on the one hand and policy innovation on the other.[20] In spite of this, there are several reasons to discount the predictive value of campaign promises:

1. They typically are so vague as to predict very little. For example, candidate John F. Kennedy proposed "let's get this country moving again." Candidate Richard Nixon proclaimed that "I have a plan to end the war." Candidate Bill Clinton promised "change." Candidate George W. Bush spoke disparagingly of "nation building." Candidate

---

[20] See Budge and Hofferbert (1990); Conley (2001).

Obama promised "hope and change," and President Obama's slogan in 2012 was "forward."

2. They are often not credible. President Franklin Roosevelt assured the public in 1940 that "your boys will not be sent into any foreign war." Both Jimmy Carter in 1976 and Ronald Reagan in 1980 promised to balance the federal budget in the next four years. Candidate George H. W. Bush reached a new height in explicitness: "Read my lips: no new taxes."

3. Some of the most dramatic policy innovations come from people who might be most expected to oppose them. In a sense, Richard Nixon built his career on cultivating hostility toward Communist China; yet he was the president who took the initiative to lay the groundwork for opening diplomatic relations and bringing the People's Republic into the community of nations. Any cooperation with China would once have been a politically risky move that would have made the initiator vulnerable to charges of being "soft on communism." Because Nixon had impeccable credentials as an anti-Communist, he was in a safer position to take that initiative than someone who did not have such strong credentials.[21] Nixon's establishment of price and wage controls in 1971 showed similar ironies.

A complete and reasonable view of elections should at least provide room for potential influence from each of the elements we have been discussing: a place for retrospective evaluations, for consideration of promises, and for independent sources of information about the future. There is no reason to believe that any of these elements should always have the same impact regardless of circumstances. In fact, it is quite likely that the relative balance of retrospective and prospective judgments will be affected by conditions. Very bad conditions are likely to prompt negative retrospective voting regarding incumbents. Very good conditions are likely to prompt positive retrospective voting. In between the very bad and the very good may be more careful attention to comparisons between the record and promises of the incumbent and the promises of the challenger.[22]

Consider the implications of my interpretation of the electoral process. This view implies that the accountability aspect of elections is more meaningful than the choice aspect, partly by default. Voters can know well what

---

[21] See Cukierman and Tommasi (1998).

[22] I am grateful to Peng Lian for a number of these suggestions about the conditional nature of retrospective and prospective voting.

they are accepting or rejecting when they vote on an incumbent. But forward-looking choices often are not clear, and often they are even misleading, for the reasons stated. Elections, at best, offer only a blunt instrument of popular control.

But this interpretation is far from implying that elections are meaningless just because they do not always offer clear choices, or because their outcomes do not always allow unambiguous interpretation of their meaning. The anticipation of possible rejection at the polls is a powerful motivator for politicians. It is often, if not always, a constructive incentive. Recall from Chapter 1 the liberal interpretation of democracy presented by William Riker. In his interpretation, "all elections do or have to do is to permit people to get rid of rulers ... The kind of democracy that thus survives is not, however, popular rule, but rather an intermittent, sometimes random, even perverse popular veto" (1982, p. 244). According to Riker, even democracy that is no more inspiring than that is the most desirable *realistic* form of government. This book's interpretation of American democracy in practice is compatible with Riker's view, but in mapping performance regarding economic issues, I am developing a picture that is less negative.

Retrospective voting is compatible with innovation in politics in two ways. The backward-looking rejections of incumbents can enhance the prospect for innovations that might not be chosen by an otherwise risk-averse electorate. I contend that retrospective voting makes possible more innovation than would purely prospective voting. The fact that innovations themselves will be subject to retrospective evaluation makes the process of innovation accountable. The anticipation of possible rejection at the polls is a powerful (though not always constructive) mechanism of accountability.

This book began with an analysis of a model that showed how this anticipation might lend itself to opportunistic behavior that would reduce public welfare through creation of an electoral business cycle. That hypothesis was based on the possibility that vote-maximizing incumbents would exploit naïve retrospective evaluations by voters with short memories. The evidence in favor of that model is not strong, to say the least. Some of the reasons for the weak evidence have to do with the fact that the economy is not so easy to manipulate. Few analysts still believe that public officials have the capacity to manipulate the economy with the precision needed to create an electoral cycle in outcomes.

Other reasons have to do with the motivations of politicians. They may not, in fact, all be vote maximizers, and even among those who are, not all may think that the way to do it is through manipulating the economy. We saw in Chapter 4 that partisan politicians may have policy goals that they try to implement in office, and they may appeal for votes to the extent that it helps them win office and implement other policy goals.

However, the strong evidence that voters respond to recent economic performance does not necessarily make a strong case that voters are manipulable, or that politicians could get away with opportunistic electoral cycles if they could actually create them. It is doubtful that voters provide a strong incentive for politicians to attempt manipulation, and even if they did, there is reason to believe that voters could learn what was happening and would change their behavior. The simplest reading of the bulk of studies of retrospective voting suggests that voters respond most strongly to income growth and that they pay attention to recent experience at the expense of the more distant past. This is exactly the kind of voter whose support Nordhaus's opportunistic politician would maximize. But the studies of economic voting by Chappell and Keech and by Suzuki also raise questions about voter vulnerability to repeated manipulation over the electoral cycle.

Still, occasional examples of cynical manipulation can be seen as a response to electoral incentives. When this does happen and leads to inferior outcomes, what comes first, voter demand or politicians pandering? Do voters really demand irresponsible behavior? Nothing in my reading of the extensive literature on voting on economic performance provides a strong case that voters will not reward performance that involves a sustainable noninflationary path of economic growth. I contend that irresponsible behavior by public officials is a conditional rather than an inevitable response to voter incentives.

Voters do respond to superficial appeals, and they do heavily discount the past. This could make them vulnerable to manipulation from time to time. But whereas voters may reward irresponsible behavior, they do not generally demand it. In fact, there is no reason to believe that any single level of economic performance is demanded for economic success. Voters learn to want what they know they can get. Voters and the electoral process may contribute to or support national conditions for growth and development or those for stagnation and decline.

In one respect, retrospective voting with short memories allows politicians to do constructive things that can improve outcomes. Recall the path of the misery index through the first Reagan administration as described in Chapter 4. The recession early in the Reagan administration permitted inflation to fall in a way that made for a much lower misery index by election time. If voters had weighted all periods equally, they might not have tolerated that. Similarly, painful austerity programs designed to eliminate deficits or inflation may be feasible only with long electoral periods, in which the pain might be forgotten by election time. Key's view of retrospective voting suggests that voters may well accept sacrifices they would not choose. Would voters have prospectively chosen the 1980s recession to reduce inflation if that had been promised in the 1980 campaign? Krugman (1992, ch. 5) says no, and I agree. But would they retrospectively approve of the choice? Clearly they did. Slack between principal and agent can be used constructively as well as perversely.

PART FOUR

INSTITUTIONS AND PROCESSES

This section treats the institutions and processes by which macroeconomic stabilization policy is made. Chapter 8 deals with political control of the money supply and interest rates, or monetary policy. Chapter 9 deals with the politics of taxing and spending, or fiscal policy. In both cases, the immediate pressures and demands of policy making take place in the context of an overall debate about rules versus discretion. Although policy makers are not always conscious of that overall debate, their actions may lean one way or the other. Until the recent financial crisis, I believe that monetary policy had moved in the direction of rule-based behavior since the 1980s, whereas fiscal policy had become increasingly discretionary and ad hoc.

In the period since World War II, there was a time when fiscal policy was seen as the main instrument of stabilization, but it has since been eclipsed by monetary policy. And for the period of the "Great Moderation" between about 1984 and 2007, it seemed that problems of stabilization policy had been resolved, that is, until the financial crisis of 2007 and after. Ad hoc fiscal policy has been used repeatedly in the twenty-first century, culminating in the massive stimulus bill passed in February 2009. Yet the standard view is and remains that "the central bank *should* and *does* have a dominant role in stabilization policy (Blinder 2006, p. 26, emphasis in original).[1]

Mankiw and Weinzierl (2011) have suggested a four-step hierarchy of conditions for the use of monetary and fiscal stabilization policy. The first level of action in conditions of insufficient aggregate demand is conventional monetary policy, such as reducing the short-term interest rate. If the zero lower bound constrains short-term rates, the second strategy is to

---

[1] It is telling that this statement is made in an article entitled "The Case Against the Case Against Discretionary Fiscal Policy."

target long-term interest rates. In both cases, fiscal policy is to be determined by classical principles of benefit–cost analysis rather than Keynesian principles of demand management.

If both of these strategies are unavailable, fiscal policy becomes relevant, but only to do what monetary policy would if it could, that is, "incentivizing interest-sensitive components of spending, such as investment" (Mankiw and Weinzierl 2011, p. 246). Only when none of the first three works is conventional aggregate demand management fiscal policy appropriate.

The argument in Mankiw and Weinzierl is developed in terms of maximizing the welfare of households rather than multipliers and "bang-for-the-buck" questions that normally are used in analyzing fiscal policy. The comments and discussion (Mankiw and Weinzierl 2011. pp. 250–72) make it clear that this is not the last word on how fiscal and monetary policy should be used.[2] Still, I use the hierarchy loosely as an organizing device for the chapters on monetary and fiscal policy.

Both the monetary (8) and the fiscal chapter (9) give some background on the basic formal institutions and show how patterns of policy making have varied over time. These patterns are, in my view, not far from satisfactory in monetary policy. But in fiscal policy, the fundamental institutions of democracy are now obstructing constructive and necessary change. There was a time when patterns of fiscal policy making did not lead to undesirable outcomes, because the informal "rules of the game" constrained behavior. This is no longer so, but effective rules are harder to create in fiscal than in monetary policy.

---

[2]   See Leeper (2010) on the relative strengths of our understanding of monetary and fiscal policy.

8

Rules, Discretion, and Accountability in the Monetary Policy Process

Monetary policy is the control of the money supply and of interest rates to stabilize the economy. For decades, it has been the main instrument of stabilization policy in the United States. Fiscal policy, the use of taxing and spending powers to guide the economy, receded into the background, though it has had a resurgence in the 2000s (Auerbach et al. 2010). Normally, the possible actions available to monetary authorities have to do with the levels of interest rates and the rate of growth of the money supply, which in turn may affect the level of economic activity and the rate of inflation.

Good and successful monetary policy can bring an appropriate balance between economic growth and stable prices, but, of course, the meaning of "appropriate" is contestable. Poor or unsuccessful monetary policy runs two main risks. If the money supply grows much faster than real economic activity, the result will be inflation or even hyperinflation. The opposite risk is that there will not be enough financial liquidity to support the real economic activity that would take place if credit were more readily available. The United States has never experienced hyperinflation, but monetary policy has been at least partly responsible for the sustained increases in price levels since World War II.[1] The second risk was experienced in the banking panics and recessions of the nineteenth and early twentieth centuries, and the Great Depression itself has been attributed to poor monetary policy.[2]

---

[1] With 1967 = 100, the price index varied between 30 and 60 for the 80 years between 1860 and 1940, but it has been in the 600s since 2007. *Source:* http://www.bls.gov/ro3/fax_9160.htm, accessed May 26, 2011. Broz (1993) described the experience of the "Continental" paper currency of the Revolutionary War as hyperinflation. See also Sachs and Larraín (1993, p. 728); Bernholz (2003).

[2] Friedman and Schwartz (1963) is the classical source. See Meltzer (2003), especially ch. 5, and Fishback (2010) for a contemporary review of evidence and arguments.

RULES, DISCRETION, AND STABILIZATION POLICY

Just as two main risks are inherent in poor monetary policy, there are two basic alternative strategies for good policy. One of these is to make monetary policy rule based. Rules can be doctrines or systems of thought such as the now discredited "real bills doctrine" that guided monetary policy before the Great Depression. The gold standard can be thought of as a system of rules. An extreme case of rules is a policy that is automatic, in the same sense that formula-defined entitlements to Social Security benefits or marginal income tax rates are automatic fiscal policy. The other basic alternative is for policy makers to use their discretion in manipulating the instruments available to them.

As Taylor (1993) points out, it is useful to think about rules and discretion in terms of the time-consistency problem. Rules should embody the best policy for all times and conditions. Discretion is what seems to be the best thing at the time. Discretion may or may not be time inconsistent, and in some conditions, such as a transition to a rule, discretion may be appropriate. But if discretion is time inconsistent, following a rule is the way to solve that problem. A rule is relevant when long-term policy is described as optimal, systematic, or something for which precommitment is desirable. Undesirable discretion would be described as shortsighted, inconsistent, or even cheating (Taylor 1993, pp. 198–9).

Historically, the best-known rule for monetary policy is surely Milton Friedman's recommendation that the money supply grow at a fixed rate. Research on policy rules has moved away from advocating fixed settings of policy instruments, as did Friedman, to rules that respond to relevant economic conditions.[3] A leading example is the Taylor Rule, which relates a controllable short-term interest rate to inflation and output. Meltzer (1987) and McCallum (1988) propose similar rules regarding growth of the monetary base.

At the extreme, a rule that responds in detail to a wide range of conditions becomes hard to distinguish from discretion. But as John Taylor, a leading advocate of rules, says, "it is important to preserve the concept of a policy rule even when in an environment where it is practically impossible to follow mechanically the algebraic formula economists write down to describe their preferred policy rules" (1993, p. 197). Taylor makes it clear that the rule need not be so rigid that a computer could apply it. Human judgment may be used to decide how to implement the rule.

---

[3] This section draws heavily on Taylor (1993).

The strategy of discretion, of course, involves no single set of procedures, but rather an enormously mixed bag that incorporates virtually all of American monetary history, including the successes and the failures. Some of the reasons for such an eclectic mixture are that policy makers' understanding of the alternative instruments available for discretionary choice has changed over time, their conceptions of the possibilities for active discretionary stabilization and control have varied with macroeconomic theory and over time, and the institutions through which discretionary choices are made have also changed.

Monetary policy can go wrong with either rules or discretion, and it has done so with each. Following the wrong monetary rules had a lot to do with the severity and length of the Great Depression, and activist discretionary policy had a lot to do with the great inflation of the seventies. The argument of this book is very sympathetic to the use of rules, and to transparency in both monetary and fiscal policy. A clear and widespread understanding of rules helps avoid time-consistency problems by keeping publics and policy makers aware of the general principles that make for good policy at all times.

Several of these observations will be documented and elaborated in this chapter, with examples from the span of American history. Most of the chapter will focus on the Federal Reserve System, the current institution for monetary policymaking, which was established in 1913. Rules and discretion will be a recurring theme throughout this chapter.

INSTITUTIONS AND ISSUES IN MONETARY POLICY

Article I of the Constitution gives the Congress the power to "coin money and to regulate the value thereof," but it goes no further in specifying how such actions should be carried out. There are many institutional alternatives for handling monetary policy. Some of the most fundamental considerations concern the backing of the currency, the existence of central banks, and the independence of central banks.

The Backing of the Currency

For much of American history, the money supply was backed by precious metal, usually gold.[4] The money supply was decoupled from gold in two major steps, one domestic and the other international. Before 1933, the "gold clause" in many business contracts provided that payment should be

---

[4]   A bimetallic gold and silver standard was used during some periods in the nineteenth century.

made in gold or in currency backed by a designated quantity of gold. In that year, Congress abrogated the gold clause in public and private contracts.[5] Subsequently, under the postwar Bretton Woods agreement on a system of international monetary relations, the American dollar was the standard against which exchange rates were set, and the United States was committed to exchanging gold for foreign holdings of dollars at the rate of $35 per ounce. In 1971, President Nixon suspended that policy.

That first (1933) decision broke a restraint against a potentially inflationary expansion of the money supply. The second (1971) stemmed an outflow of gold that had resulted from such an expansion. The result is a complete uncoupling of the money supply from any commodity standard. The American currency is now "fiat money," legal tender that is produced and authorized by the government, wherein the government's capacity to print increasing quantities of money is not restrained by any commitment to convert money into any commodity in limited supply, such as gold or silver.

The elimination of commodity standards was no doubt related to the sustained increases in price levels since World War II, which were unprecedented in American history. That fact occasionally inspires arguments in favor of a return to the gold standard as a way to restore automatic discipline over monetary policy and to avoid the inflationary bias of fiat money. This book will not consider such proposals in depth, but two points should be made. First, a commodity standard did not prevent public officials from creating discretionary fluctuations in the money supply. Second, several prominent economic historians blame the rigidity of the gold standard for many of the mistakes in public policy during the Great Depression of the 1930s.[6]

The Existence of Central Banks

The other main institutional issue for monetary policy is the existence of central banks. There had been two instances of a "Bank of the United States" before the establishment of the Federal Reserve in 1913. The first bank, which was a part of Alexander Hamilton's plan to stabilize the credit standing of the United States, was chartered in 1791 and lasted until 1811.

---

[5] Friedman and Schwartz (1963, pp. 468–9).

[6] See Eichengreen (1992a) and Temin (1989). Fishback (2010) suggests that some of the mistaken monetary policies of the Depression era were related to efforts to maintain the gold standard. Ron Paul's quest for the 2012 Republican presidential nomination gave added publicity to a case for a gold standard. See Paul (2009).

It "was not intended to be a central bank; it was not to control the quantity of money. Nor was it to act as a centralized depository, an office of discount for commercial banks, or a lender of last resort" (Timberlake 1978, p. 4).

The same was true of the second Bank of the United States, which was chartered in 1816. However, under the leadership of Nicholas Biddle, the second bank took on some countercyclical activities (largely in response to foreign exchange disturbances) that went beyond the powers delegated to it. Timberlake pronounced Biddle's manipulations of the money stock as "mostly good," even though they went beyond the delegated authority (1993, ch.3, especially p. 33). The second bank's charter expired in 1836, when President Andrew Jackson vetoed its renewal. The experience with the second bank made it clear that even under rudimentary institutional arrangements, some discretionary control of the money supply was possible. That experience occurred in an era that predated by perhaps a full century any widespread awareness of the possibility of systematic monetary policy.

The United States had no formally constituted central bank from 1836 to 1913, when the Federal Reserve System, the current central bank, was established. The experience in the three-quarters of a century without a formal central bank is relevant for evaluating the arguments of two kinds of critics of the Federal Reserve: those who criticize discretionary monetary policy under a relatively independent central bank, and those who advocate a return to the gold standard as a rule-based way of imposing automatic discipline on monetary policy

During the 1836–1913 hiatus, several regimes were operative. The currency was backed by a bimetallic (gold and silver) standard until 1862, when the convertibility of paper money into specie (coin) was suspended by the U.S. (Union) government, which financed the Civil War in part by printing money. Accordingly, the period between 1862 and 1869, when specie payment was resumed, is called the "greenback era." Not surprisingly, that period saw substantial inflation. Because specie payment was resumed at the prewar standard, substantial deflation resulted.

The "golden age" of the gold standard as an international monetary system was between 1879 and 1914, when it collapsed with the outbreak of World War I. Kenneth Dam characterized as a myth the view that the gold standard was a rule-based, self-adjusting system that worked automatically to restore equilibrium after a disturbance. The system operated under discretionary changes in the "bank rate" or discount rate, which made the gold standard "far from automatic and self-adjusting" (1982, p. 17): "A further discretionary aspect of the pre-1914 gold standard had to do with what in the 1920s came to be known as 'the rules of the game' . . . But these *rules* of the gold standard game were strictly *discretionary*, and . . . central banks not only did not always abide by them but sometimes acted perversely" (Dam 1982, p. 18, emphasis added).

Dam acknowledged that the gold standard worked well for a number of decades, but he argued that it was a short-lived "incident in the history of international monetary organization" and that the common view of it confuses the gold standard as an international monetary system and as a domestic policy regime (1982, p. 19). As a domestic monetary regime, the gold standard in the United States was complex and varied substantially in the period between 1879 and 1914 (Dam 1982, pp. 28–9).[7]

If it had not been apparent earlier, the innovative policies of Leslie Shaw, secretary of the treasury from 1902 to 1907, showed that a central bank, as such, was not necessary for the government to be able to carry out discretionary monetary policy, nor did the presence of the gold standard preclude such policy. In Shaw's words,

If the Secretary of the Treasury were given $100 million to be deposited with the banks or withdrawn as he might deem expedient, and if in addition he were clothed with authority over the reserves of the several banks, with power to contract the national bank circulation at pleasure, in my judgment no panic as distinguished from industrial stagnation could threaten either the United States or Europe that he could not avert. (quoted in Friedman and Schwartz 1963, pp. 149–50)

The Treasury's powers of debt management were comparable to the open market operations that have become the most important of the Federal Reserve's monetary policy instruments.[8]

The banking panic that occurred in 1907 and the subsequent recession also illustrated that not everything was ideal in the golden age of the gold standard. Indeed, it was that experience that crystallized a broad recognition of a need for monetary reform. The emergence of the United States as a major world economic power had forced a recognition in the internationally oriented sector of the economy that changes were needed in America's monetary institutions. The panic of 1907 prompted many others to agree on the need for change.[9] In 1908, Congress provided for the creation of the

---

[7] See also Eichengreen (1985).
[8] See Friedman and Schwartz (1963, pp. 149–52, esp. note 24) and Timberlake (1993, pp. 186–95).
[9] See Broz (1997) for a thorough and insightful treatment of the founding of the Federal Reserve that emphasizes the role of internationally oriented groups.

National Monetary Commission, a bipartisan body "to inquire into and report to Congress ... what changes are necessary or desirable in the monetary system ... or in the laws relating to banking and currency" (quoted by Broz 1993, p. 353). Although Congress rejected the immediate recommendations of the commission, the plan that was accepted in 1913 bore considerable resemblance to the proposals of the commission.

A Lender of Last Resort Function

One function that has been associated with central banks since Walter Bagehot's classic treatise on central banking[10] is that of lender of last resort. In a financial crisis, a central bank can step in and make loans when private banks are not functioning. Bagehot's four principles are (1) "Lend, but at a penalty rate," (2) "Make it clear in advance the bank's readiness to lend freely," (3) "Accommodate anyone with good collateral," and (4) "Prevent illiquid but solvent banks from failing" (quoted in Bordo 1990, p. 20).

Allan Meltzer argues that allowing banks to fail is "*one* part of a policy toward financial firms. The other parts – represented by the four Bagehotian principles – work to separate the risk of individual financial failure from aggregate risk by establishing principles that prevent banks' liquidity problems from generating an epidemic of insolvency" (1986, pp. 84–5, emphasis in original).

Meltzer says that the Federal Reserve has never in its 100-year history had an announced policy regarding its role as lender of last resort (2003, p. 730). It stepped in on an ad hoc basis to bail out Continental Illinois in 1984 but did not bail out Lehman Brothers in 2008, leaving much uncertainty as to its motivations, goals, and policies. A publicly announced policy of the circumstances and terms under which the Federal Reserve will loan money to troubled banks would avoid, or at least minimize, the moral hazard that the nation experiences with so many ad hoc rescues.

The Independence and Decision Procedures of Central Banks

In comparative studies, the Federal Reserve is consistently counted among the world's most independent central banks. Independence is seen as a device to insulate monetary policy from inflationary pressures for expansionary activity, and several studies have found an association between

---

[10] Bagehot (1873/2012, ch, 2). See also McKinley (2011, pp. 27–8).

independence and low inflation.[11] It is not surprising, therefore, that the Federal Reserve is criticized for not being sufficiently expansionary and for obstructing economic growth.[12] These criticisms are sometimes associated with demands that the Federal Reserve be more accountable, implying a continuum between independence and accountability.

The Federal Reserve is also criticized for the opposite failing of being too responsive to inflationary pressures.[13] For critics who take this view, the existing degree of independence is not enough. For many of them, a major institutional alternative would be rules for monetary policy, as opposed to the discretionary choices that have characterized contemporary decisions.

Traditionally, the most commonly proposed rule is that the money supply should grow at a known, fixed rate, regardless of economic conditions. This proposal is a monetary counterpart to the balanced budget rule for fiscal policy to be discussed in Chapter 9. More recently, the rule that has been most discussed is the Taylor Rule, which targets the federal funds rate, the key short-term interest rate as a function of inflation and the deviation of output from its potential. The Taylor Rule recommendation for any given time is tracked in *Monetary Trends*, a monthly publication of the St. Louis branch of the Federal Reserve.[14] Inflation targeting is a current practice in many countries that embody rule-like behavior.

From one perspective or another, the Federal Reserve is regularly the subject of proposals for institutional reform.[15] The proposals that receive the most contemporary attention involve independence (versus accountability) or rules (versus discretion). Reform ideas regarding independence and accountability are common in both public and scholarly discourse. Reform ideas regarding rules and discretion are more subtle and far more common in the academic literature than in the public forum.

The status of the Federal Reserve as one of the world's most independent central banks is measured largely by formal legislated features that were defined in 1913 and 1935. However, the Federal Reserve did not become as independent as it now is until an informal agreement was reached in 1951, known as the "accord." This fact suggests that its independence may be as much a matter of norms, or informal patterns of behavior, as of intentional changes in formal institutions. Changes in formal institutional

---

[11] See Alesina and Summers (1993); Cukierman (1992, chs. 18–23); Grilli, Masciandaro, and Tabellini (1991).

[12] See Greider (1987) for a prominent example.

[13] See, for example, Havrilesky (1993).

[14] http://research.stlouisfed.org/publications/mt/20121001/mtpub.pdf

[15] See Havrilesky (1993) for a sampling. See also Woolley (1984, ch. 7) and Paul (2009).

arrangements may not have the consequences desired by their supporters unless they are accompanied by behavior patterns that cannot be created by legislative fiat.

Just as it may be difficult to legislate effective independence, it might be even more difficult to legislate adherence to rules for monetary policy making, such as a rule for a fixed rate of money growth or a Taylor-type rule that specifies a link between short-term interest rates and the conditions of the economy. Consider that independence involves insulation from accountability to elected officials, with a presumption that monetary authorities are more concerned about minimizing inflation than are elected officials. Such rules would be designed to limit the discretion of monetary authorities, and to make them even less responsive to the presumably inflationary pressures of the electoral process than they currently are under conditions of relative independence. As of this writing, the main threat to Fed independence is from the right, rather than the left, and is based on inflation aversion.

Originally, the case for rules ignored the problems of enforceability, because it was presumed that the rationale was so strong that the rules would be self-enforcing. However, more contemporary arguments recognize that enforceability is a serious problem. To whom would monetary authorities be accountable if they were to fail to follow a legislative rule? Elected official and the public are unlikely sources of enforcement, because the incentives of the electoral process are usually considered sources of inflationary pressures. If that is the case, the practical argument for rules becomes tenuous, even though it has generated some interesting scholarship.

Consideration of the enforceability of rules returns us to issues of accountability that are central to the democratic process, issues that began this book. Accountability has at least two important meanings in political life. The most common is that one is subject to removal from office because of inadequate performance. As we saw in Chapter 3, institutions designed to ensure this kind of accountability may have their own problems. An alternative meaning is that officials must explain, report, and justify. I argue that at the same time that independence makes the Federal Reserve less accountable in the removability sense, independence can be associated with meaningful accountability in the explanation sense.

The Motivations of Monetary Authorities

Although we can recognize that we have no reason to assume that the motivations of all monetary authorities need to be the same, it will be useful to identify some of the leading possibilities and their implications. The most careful effort to elaborate monetary policy goals in a general theoretical way is seen in the work of Alex Cukierman (1992), who identifies an employment motive and a revenue motive.[16] Although he gives inflation less explicit attention, Cukierman obviously considers it a comparably important motive. The goal of minimizing inflation is included in all of his objective functions, but the theme of his analysis is that the inclusion of other goals entails higher inflation.

The argument regarding the employment motive is the time-consistency argument first presented in Chapter 2. Recall that the key mechanism is that the monetary authorities have a target rate for unemployment that is below the natural rate, because of distortions in labor markets. (Equivalent arguments are easily made for growth targets above the natural rate.) Once labor contracts are signed, with a given level of expected inflation, the government has an incentive to create an inflationary surprise that will reduce unemployment or increase output. But according to this argument, labor contracts are signed with knowledge of the government's incentives. They anticipate the inflation, which is not a surprise. The results are no improvement regarding unemployment or output growth and a positive rate of inflation.

The argument regarding the revenue motive is also a time-consistency one, but it has different features. Government can gain purchasing power from the public by printing money. The amount of revenue it gains in this way will depend on the amount of cash the public chooses to hold. This amount is inversely related to the rate of inflation the public expects. The time-consistency problem takes the form that once the public has chosen the amount of money it will hold, the government can raise its revenues by printing more money and creating more inflation than was expected.

Cukierman's analysis of the motivations of monetary authorities is decidedly modern and reflects contemporary economic theory. For example, the time-consistency problem was not prominent in the economic literature before 1977, and we may wonder how motivations that were not recognized by economists may have affected the behavior of public officials.[17] This book itself is based on the presumption that politicians can have motivations other than maximizing the public interest, and as such it

---

[16] Cukierman also explains a balance of payments motive and a financial stability motive. Neither will be pursued in this book.

[17] It is, of course, possible that public officials can be motivated by goals that are not recognized by economists.

reflects a viewpoint and a systematic literature that scarcely existed in economics or political science as of 1975 or so. (Although I will not explore it here, there is also a possibility that the motivations of public officials could be affected by what political economists write and think.)

Cukierman's analysis of motivations, as reported here, treats the government as if it were a single entity, though he acknowledges that "there may be differences of emphasis on alternative policy objectives between central banks and political authorities," and that "the actual course of policy usually represents a compromise between alternative views" (1992, p. 16). Normally, we expect central bankers to be more inflation averse than elected officials. This is often true because of the values that are associated "by coincidence" with the professional background of monetary authorities.[18] But there are reasons to make this a matter of choice as well. Kenneth Rogoff (1985) explains how it may make sense for political authorities to appoint a central banker whose inflation aversion is greater than their own or that of the public.[19]

Neither the elected officials nor the central bankers themselves need be homogeneous. Just as in our discussion of political parties we recognized that not all politicians are alike, not all monetary authorities are alike. Chappell, Havrilesky, and McGregor (1993) have documented differences among central bankers according to their professional backgrounds and partisan affiliations. Chappell, McGregor, and Vermilyea (2005) estimate the diverse preferences of members of the Federal Open Market Committee (FOMC) from 1966 to 1996. Given these facts, we should recognize that the observed patterns of behavior might have been different if different people had been chosen.

The Targets of Monetary Policy

The money supply and interest rates are inversely related in the short run, in that the interest rate is the price of borrowing money. The greater the supply, the lower the price. The monetary authority can try to control the money supply, or it can try to control interest rates, but it cannot do both at the same time. If it controls the money supply, interest rates will fluctuate with changes in the public's demand for money. If it controls interest rates, the money supply will accommodate changes in money demand.

---

[18] See Woolley (1984, ch. 4).
[19] See Clark and Arel-Bundock (2013) for a related interpretation that hinges on party differences.

Whichever target the monetary authority chooses, the other will fluctuate as an "epiphenomenon," a secondary phenomenon that results from and accompanies another. In general, targeting the money supply is a more effective anti-inflationary strategy than targeting interest rates, because sustained increases in the money supply might be necessary to keep rates low. On the other hand, targeting the money supply may lead to interest rate fluctuations that create contractions in economic activity.

Usually, it is not at all easy to see what a monetary authority is doing, that is, which aggregates it is targeting, if any. One reason is that monetary policy is inherently technical and difficult to understand. However, monetary authorities can make use of this complexity for a variety of purposes, some of which may be more defensible than others. One possibility is that ambiguous monetary policy can mask the adverse consequences of fiscal redistribution (Havrilesky 1987). Another is that it can provide cover for elected politicians who do not wish to take the political heat for unpopular (but perhaps desirable) policies (Kane 1990).

THE FEDERAL RESERVE SYSTEM

The basic formal institution of contemporary American monetary policy is the Federal Reserve System ("the Fed"), established in 1913 specifically to deal with monetary issues. That specificity of institutional purpose distinguishes monetary policy from fiscal policy, whose formal institutions (Congress and the presidency) are among the most basic and general features of American government. Monetary institutions are therefore much more subject to reforms that are targeted to macroeconomic issues and not complicated by their consequences for other issues.

The Founding of the Fed

At its founding, the Fed bore some resemblance to the recommendations of the National Monetary Commission, which had been established in 1908 in the wake of the previous year's panic, under the leadership of Republican Senator Nelson Aldrich. Although the banking panic was a precipitating event, it had been apparent for some time that American monetary institutions were not well suited to handle the nation's increasingly prominent position in the world economy. The internationally oriented sector of the economy led a campaign to build support for the creation of a central bank. However, the commission's proposals were blocked in the Democratic

Congress elected in 1910, and it was left to the Wilson administration, with unified Democratic control, to create the new institution.

Congress's intentions in 1913 for the new central bank are not totally clear, and on many issues it is likely that there was no clear intent.[20] Congress represented Republicans and Democrats; nationalists and internationalists; creditors and debtors; and, therefore, many different interests in monetary policy. There does seem to have been a consensus that some reform was needed but considerable disagreement about the roles to be played by government, by the New York financial center, and by the rest of the banking industry. The result was a compromise that provided limited influence for each of those elements. Broz (1993, pp. 219, 422–3) has characterized previous American monetary history as a series of swings between easy money regimes and stable currency institutions. The newly established Fed had such diverse features that it was not easily characterized as a victory for any side.

The structure of the Fed reflected a compromise between those who feared the private power of Wall Street and those who feared the public power of Washington. A seven-member Federal Reserve Board in Washington reflected the desire for public control. Twelve privately controlled regional banks reflected the desire to limit political influence. The fact that the New York Fed was merely first among twelve equals reflected a desire to limit the power of Wall Street. Ten-year terms for the five congressionally appointed members of the Federal Reserve Board were meant to make them independent of elected officials. The secretary of the treasury and the comptroller general were originally ex officio members.

The structure, with something for almost everyone, can be seen as an improved way of dealing with both international and domestic monetary problems without having to take a definitive stand or express a definitive intent on a variety of issues. As we saw in Chapter 6, the officially legislated goals of the Fed were vaguely defined: to "furnish an elastic currency." In the context of the early twentieth century, that meant that the Fed should be able to respond to the seasonal fluctuations in the demand for money. That capacity implied that Congress did intend to give monetary authorities some kind of discretion to respond to changing conditions.[21]

---

[20] See Shepsle (1992).

[21] The United States had accumulated a massive gold stock in the preceding two decades, but under existing law, that stock did not provide the flexibility that gold stocks did for European countries with central banks. See Broz (1993).

But that discretion was understood to be structured and restrained by the gold standard and the real bills doctrine. The gold standard meant that the supply of money was limited by the requirement that currency be redeemable in gold. The real bills doctrine provided the standard by which credit was to be extended: for projects that produced "real" commodities. No one would argue that Congress in 1913 intended to create an institution whose chair would, at least occasionally, be seen as the second most influential person in the nation, after the president, nor an institution that would have the capacity to steer the economy.

The vagueness of the Fed's mandate and the decentralized character of its structure reflected the fact that the new reform institution was a response to a variety of needs, without a singular, easily definable purpose. Vagueness and decentralization were ways of resolving disagreement and avoiding conflict at the time of the legislation, but they would have consequences. The vagueness of the goals has given Fed officials substantial autonomy and reduced their accountability, as compared with a situation in which the goals are clearly defined.[22] Vagueness also facilitates adaption to changing circumstances, which can be a substantial advantage in the absence of a capacity to foresee how conditions, problems, and demands will change.

The development of institutions to control open market operations illustrates how the Fed and Congress adapted to newly discovered problems and possibilities. In particular, the decentralization that solved a political problem in 1913 was to have unanticipated consequences that would create a problem and lead to an adaptation.[23] The main instrument of monetary policy envisioned in the Federal Reserve Act was the discount rate, the rate at which reserve banks would lend to member banks. Control of that rate was meant to provide the elasticity of the currency that would adjust to shifting credit demands. The act did not anticipate the importance of open market operations, the buying and selling of government securities, which have become the most important of the instruments of monetary policy.

Originally open market operations were designed mainly to give the reserve banks "a portfolio of earning assets out of which to pay their expenses" (Eichengreen 1992b, p. 16). After it became apparent that such operations could have an effect on economic activity, it was recognized that there might be a need to coordinate the activities of the member banks. During the recession of 1920, member banks purchased large amounts of government securities to replenish their income. The Federal Reserve Board

[22] See Kane (1990), p. 290).
[23] This section draws on Eichengreen (1992b).

and the Treasury complained that the banks were bidding against one another and destabilizing the prices of government bonds. The result was the creation of an Open Market Investment Committee, later to be more broadly constituted as the Open Market Policy Conference (Eichengreen 1992b, pp. 17–20). That experience involved some tests of strength between the board and the reserve banks, resolved largely in favor of the banks, which dominated the coordinating body until the banking acts of 1933 and 1935 reconstituted the institutions of open market operations. In those acts, Congress established the FOMC, in which the reserve banks were clearly dominated by the government-appointed component, renamed the Board of Governors.

These developments illustrate some important points about monetary authority in the United States. Congress is the ultimate authority. However, it does not always specify exactly what it wants, surely in large part because it does not always know. Legislation creating monetary institutions is like an incomplete contract, allowing the Fed to adapt to changing conditions and unanticipated problems. The legislated institutions provide a structure in which tests of strength take place.

Even though the Fed was intentionally insulated from the influence of elected officials, it is still the agent of Congress, which is the principal in a principal-agent relationship.[24] Of course, as the principal, Congress has the power to abolish the Fed or to make any other change in the structure within which its agent operates. Although abolition is a most unlikely possibility, its potential is a fundamental fact that underlies the relationship between Congress and the Fed.[25]

Reforms of the 1930s

Congress passed significant amendments to the Federal Reserve Act in 1933 and 1935, after catastrophic economic performance. The Fed had failed to halt a banking panic that exceeded most previous panics in its severity, and that led to the Great Depression, the deepest in American history. Economic historians are still analyzing and debating the role of the Fed in the crash and the Depression, but regardless of the analysis, the central bank was seen to be in need of significant reform after those events.

---

[24] See Irwin Morris (2000) for a systematic treatment of the Fed as the agent of two principals, Congress and the president.

[25] Until his retirement at the end of the 112th Congress (2011–13), the chair of the House Financial Services Committee Subcommittee on Domestic Monetary Policy was Ron Paul, a longtime opponent of the Fed, whose recent book is entitled *End the Fed* (2009).

The changes of the 1930s shifted power from the regional banks to a reconstituted Board of Governors in Washington, and from private bankers to public officials. The Banking Act of 1935 extended the terms of the board members, now to be called "governors," to fourteen years.[26] The act also removed the secretary of the treasury and the comptroller of the currency from the board, making it more independent of the elected administration.[27] In addition to the power to set the discount rate, which had been granted in the 1913 act, the Banking Act of 1935 gave the Board of Governors the power to set reserve requirements, and it recognized the capacity to influence economic activity through open market operations, the buying and selling of government securities.

The new FOMC was created to carry out what has become the most important of the Fed's policy-making functions. The FOMC is composed of all seven members of the Board of Governors and the twelve presidents of the regional banks, but only five bank presidents have voting powers at any time. These changes made the Fed more "public" and better insulated from the power of the private banks, but they also made it more independent of administration influence.

Reforms of the 1970s

Until the late 1960s, the Fed defined the terms of its own accountability by what it chose to put in its annual reports. But in the turbulent economic times of the 1970s, Congress became restive and demanded more structured accountability. It incorporated its demands in House concurrent Resolution 1233, passed in 1975; in the Federal Reserve Reform Act of 1977; and in the Humphrey-Hawkins Act of 1978.

The theme of those actions was to demand that the Fed become more systematically accountable to Congress on Congress's own terms. Members of Congress wanted the Fed to set specific targets for its actions. The proposals included targets for economic outcomes, such as unemployment rates, and intermediate targets, such as interest rates. The Fed, under the leadership of Chairman Arthur Burns, consistently resisted yielding to demands that it accept such targets, citing the need to retain flexibility and discretion to deal with changing conditions.

The compromise embodied in the three legislative acts mentioned earlier was that the Fed chair would report to the House and Senate banking

---

[26] The Banking Act of 1933 had extended the original ten-year terms to twelve years.
[27] See Kettl (1986) on how this was partly inadvertent.

committees twice each year and would set targets for money growth. Burns succeeded in avoiding specific targets. Instead, the Fed set target *ranges* for money growth, and it set such ranges for several definitions of the money supply. In that way, there was latitude for the Fed to defend itself by shifting the emphasis in its reports to Congress.

Those changes of the 1970s did not significantly change the Fed's powers. The somewhat combative maneuvering between the banking committees and Chairman Burns obscured the fundamental fact that the Fed was a legislative creation of Congress and could be abolished or changed by Congress. However, in those interchanges, it was not clear that Congress had the upper hand, because the stature and reputation of the Fed restricted the realistic latitude that Congress had.[28]

In spite of Burns's protests, I would argue that the changes did not significantly weaken the Fed's independence. They may even have strengthened it by structuring its accountability. A powerful body created by Congress is vulnerable to major change if people become dissatisfied with its performance and there is no effective accountability. The Fed is not effectively accountable in the sense of being subject to sanction for poor performance, but since the reforms of the 1970s, it is more effectively accountable in the sense of having a regular forum in which it must report, explain, and justify its actions. The Fed did retain its independence by influencing the standards for the targets it was asked to defend.

INFORMAL INSTITUTIONS: PATTERNS OF DISCRETIONARY MONETARY POLICY MAKING

The actual patterns of monetary policy making have varied over time, independently of formal legislative changes, just as in the case of fiscal policy. When there is a general change in the continuing government policy or strategy, we speak of a change in *regimes*.[29] This section describes three regime changes: "the accord" of 1951; the disinflationary regime of Fed chairman Paul Volcker of 1979 to 1982; and the "Great Moderation" of the subsequent twenty-five years, ending in the financial crisis that began in 1987.

---

[28] See Kettl (1986, ch. 6) for a thorough and insightful treatment of this episode. See also Abrams and Butkiewicz (2012).

[29] See Sargent (1986, p. 41).

The Accord

The most clear-cut example of such a change in monetary policy was the accord of 1951 between the Treasury and the Fed. During World War II, monetary policy was defined by the acquiescence of the Fed to the Treasury Department's goals of supporting the prices of government securities and keeping interest rates low, "the peg," to accommodate the government's wartime borrowing needs. In effect, the Treasury set monetary policy, and the Fed voluntarily cooperated. There was no question that the Fed had the legal authority to set monetary policy independently, regardless of Treasury preferences, but the central bank did not seek to move abruptly from its wartime position of voluntary subordination to independence. Instead, it made known its restiveness incrementally, in a series of moves culminating in the agreement designated the accord, in March 1951.[30]

The president and the Treasury Department resisted those moves, and the Fed acted with considerable caution. One reason was surely that its legal independence was based on legislation and could be revoked at any time by a new law. The position of Congress was in fact supportive of the Fed's efforts to free itself from its commitment to support the government bond market, as illustrated in hearings held by a subcommittee of the Joint Economic Committee. That group was chaired by Senator Paul Douglas of Illinois, himself a distinguished economist. After a series of meetings and several misunderstandings, the following statement was issued: "The Treasury and the Federal Reserve System have reached full accord with respect to debt-management and monetary policies to be pursued in furthering their common purpose to assure the successful financing of the Government's requirements and, at the same time, to minimize monetization of the public debt."[31] Although it was not immediately apparent, that agreement marked the beginning of the contemporary era of monetary policy, an era in which the Fed is consistently counted among the world's most independent central banks.[32]

The legal status of the Fed had not changed since 1935, but the Fed did not exert its independence during the ten-year period between 1941, when the policy of supporting the government bond market was adopted, and 1951. However, there was a significant change in the Fed's actual independence after the accord, even though some observers contend that the post-

---

[30] See Meltzer (2003, pp. 699–716).
[31] Quoted by Stein (1969, p. 277). This section draws heavily on Stein's analysis.
[32] See Alesina and Summers (1993); Cukierman (1992, chs. 19–24); Meltzer (2009, pp. 18–22 and passim).

accord Fed is still significantly influenced by the executive branch and that its independence is limited.[33]

The general orientation of the Fed after 1951 was to use its discretion in stabilizing the economy. According to William McChesney Martin Jr., appointed chairman of the Board of Governors soon after the accord, the tasks of the central bank are to "lean against the wind" and to follow a countercyclical monetary policy. However, it is often difficult to infer just what the Fed is doing. Its policy is normally cloaked in considerable ambiguity. This ambiguity enhances the Fed's independence and allows it to limit its accountability in either of the two senses we have mentioned (to be subject to removal for inadequate performance, and to explain and justify). However, in the modern framework of time-consistency problems and asymmetric information, such ambiguity can enhance the possibility that the Fed can serve genuinely public purposes. As Cukierman suggests, there is a "politically optimal level of ambiguity" (1992, pp. 213–15).

Volcker's Monetary Targeting

The most clear-cut shift in Fed policy since 1951 occurred during Paul Volcker's chairmanship, beginning in October 1979 and ending in late 1982. Described as a new set of operating procedures, that shift involved more targeting of the money supply than had characteristically been the case. As assessed by Alt (1991, pp. 45–8), this period involved substantially less volatility in the money supply (M2) than at any time before or since, as well as considerable increases in interest rates. That policy is often credited with creating the recession of 1982 and the disinflation that accompanied it. It would be a mistake to consider it an experiment with a Friedman-type rule for a fixed rate of money growth, because no public commitment was made, and the possibility of discretionary change was preserved.

The appointment of Paul Volcker as chair of the Federal Reserve in 1979 made an important difference in monetary policy, and in the level of inflation. Clarida, Galí, and Gertler (2000) document a difference in the monetary policy reaction functions for the periods before and after Paul Volcker took over as chairman. In the period beginning in 1960:1 through 1996:4, these authors find a clear difference between periods before and after 1979:3, which separates the chairmanships of William Martin, Arthur Burns, and William Miller from those of Volcker and Alan Greenspan. The early period was distinctly more accommodative of expected inflation,

[33] See, for example, Havrilesky (1993).

whereas the second period did a better job of insulating the economy from shocks and of controlling inflation. One of the possible explanations that they consider was improved understanding in the economics profession (Clarida et al. 2000, p. 178).[34]

That episode is not universally admired. Some critics simply think of it as the deepest recession since the Great Depression. Others see it as a necessary step toward the desirable goal of reducing the inflation of the 1970s. The episode is a leading example of how independence and ambiguity can allow a monetary authority to bring about disinflation, which could be a difficult move for fiscal authorities. If a recession is necessary to reduce inflation, it will be difficult, if not impossible, for elected officials to take steps that will involve immediate pain to achieve a future goal. The insulation of an independent body can make such a step easier, and the ambiguity of monetary procedures can provide further cover.

The Great Moderation

For more than a decade after the Volcker disinflation, many economists failed to notice a smoothing of the business cycle and a decline in the volatility of inflation and output. In the 38 years from the beginning of 1946 through 1983, the United States experienced eight recessions lasting a total of 84 months, leaving the nation in recession 18 percent of the time. Inflation averaged 4.7 percent. In the 23 years from 1984 through 2006, the United States experience two recessions totaling 18 months combined, leaving the country in recession only 6 percent of the time. Inflation averaged 3.1 percent. Inflation volatility was also substantially less in the later period. The later period has been called the "Great Moderation," and the contrast is described in Table 8.1.

This period has been a positive development that, to some extent at least, reflects an academic and political achievement. It shows macroeconomic theory, macroeconomic policy, and democratic institutions at their best, using scientific advances to achieve desirable economic outcomes. It helps explain why many of the examples of political manipulation in Chapters 3 and 4 occurred before the mid-1980s.

Olivier Blanchard and John Simon take note of "The Long and Large Decline in U.S. Output Volatility" (2001). Though they trace this back to the 1950s, they pay special attention to the 1980s and 1990s and say that the reduced volatility is responsible for the greater length of the economic

[34] See also Goodfriend (2007); Taylor (2010).

Table 8.1. *Average inflation, unemployment, and GDP growth,*
before and during the Great Moderation

	Average		Standard Deviation	
	1946–83	1984–2006	1946–83	1984–2006
Inflation	4.7	3.1	4.0	1.0
Unemployment	5.4	5.7	1.7	1.0
GDP growth	3.0	3.3	3.6	1.4

Source: Economic Report of the President, Bureau of Labor Statistics, Bureau
of Economic Analysis.

expansions since the early 1980s (2001, pp. 135, 142–5). They note reduced
inflation volatility in the 1980s and 1990s and consider the possibility that
this was due to improved monetary policy, along with improvements in
financial markets (2001, pp. 162–4).

Stock and Watson (2002) do a time series analysis that favors a discrete
break over a trend, and they place that break in 1983 to 1984. The causes they
consider are changes in the structure of the economy, including "innovations
in financial markets that facilitate intertemporal smoothing of consumption
and investment," improved monetary policy, and finally luck or the "reduction in variance of exogenous structural shocks" (2002, p. 162).

Although there is widespread agreement among macroeconomists about
the existence of a Great Moderation, there is less agreement about an
explanation. Galí and Gambetti suggest two groups of interpretations: one
emphasizing smaller shocks and good luck, and the other involving structure or policy. Their own interpretation is that the explanation is complex,
but they do give credit to stable monetary policy (see Clarida et al. 2000).
Another structural possibility is that the financial innovations associated
with the financial crisis were part of the cause of the Great Moderation (see
Dynan, Elmendorf, and Sichel 2006). John Taylor (2010) attributes the
change to improved monetary theory and understanding of appropriate
monetary policy, and specifically to the use of rules.

So a case can be made that the Great Moderation was a government
success, in the sense that stable, transparent monetary policy kept inflation
low and allowed the economy to flourish. But even if the Great Moderation
was not caused by good monetary policy, as opposed to luck in the form of
the absence of adverse shocks, and to smoothing of consumption made
possible by financial innovation, the least we can say about monetary policy
is that it did not interfere with these favorable events. That is, monetary
policy to stabilize the economy in the period from the mid-1980s through

the mid-2000s was, to say the least, not a government failure and quite possibly a great government success that spanned administrations of both Republicans and Democrats.

The Great Moderation reflected little if any political opportunism of the kind represented by the electoral cycle or partisan models reviewed in Chapters 2 and 3. The Great Moderation was not noticed in academic research for fifteen years, but it seemed to indicate that any costs of democracy in macroeconomic stabilization policy were minimal. But the Great Moderation was about to give way to a catastrophic experience that would identify a new cost of democracy.[35]

These three examples of informal changes in American monetary policy regimes (the accord, Volcker's monetary targeting, and the Great Moderation) are among the most visible and clearly identifiable. There doubtless have been other, less dramatic shifts in operating procedures that have occurred much more often. My purpose is not to catalog such shifts, but rather to establish two points. The first is that informal changes can be as important as formal, legal changes in monetary institutions. By legislated standards, the Fed was as independent before 1951 as after, but in reality its effective independence was not declared until that date. That experience should promote caution in efforts to measure independence by formal, legal criteria.

The second point is that within the context of the independence that has existed since 1951, important and desirable shifts in policy might not take place in the absence of a body that is insulated from electoral accountability. Fiscal and monetary authorities are not equally vulnerable to expansionary pressures. Fiscal authorities, who are accountable to electorates, find it easy to respond to demands for fiscal stimuli in the form of tax cuts or expenditure increases. They find it less easy to respond to a need for restraint or austerity, which may involve tax increases or expenditure cuts.

Monetary authorities, who are insulated from electorates, are in a better position to respond to a need for restraint. To do so, they will not have to increase taxes or reduce expenditures, which might be an electoral liability. Their independence of the electoral process gives them more freedom to introduce austerity when needed than might be the case otherwise. (Of

---

[35] There is reason to suggest that the Great Moderation lulled policy makers into complacency about the possibility of a traumatic event such as the financial crisis and ensuing Great Recession. See work by Ging Cee Ng and Andrea Tambalotti reported in the following blog:

http://libertystreeteconomics.newyorkfed.org/2012/05/the-great-moderation-forecast-uncertainty-and-the-great-recession.html accessed May 14, 2012.

course that independence also gives them the same freedom when austerity is not needed. The identification of need is a matter of discretionary judgment.[36])

INDEPENDENCE AND RULES

As the preceding sections make clear, discretionary monetary policy has been available and has been used by public officials for well over a century, with and without central banks. Yet concerns have always existed that such power over the management of money might not be used wisely, and some have argued that such discretion should be restrained, if not eliminated. The gold standard surely restrained the discretion of such officials to some degree when it was in effect, but it was not nearly so automatic as the entitlements and taxes to be discussed in Chapter 9. The gold standard has often been considered akin to a rule for monetary policy, but even if there had been a rigid and inflexible connection between the money supply and the stock of gold (and there was not), monetary policy could have fluctuated automatically (and arbitrarily) with the discovery of new sources of the precious metal, as in California, Alaska, and South Africa.

The main theoretical alternative to the use of discretion in monetary policy would be the use of rules that would specify in advance what public officials should do. As indicted earlier, rules could be contingent or non-contingent. Contingent rules could try to specify what public officials should do in all situations that could be anticipated, or they might link policy to one or two target variables. Noncontingent rules would specify what should be done in all cases, regardless of conditions.

The classic example of a noncontingent rule for monetary policy is that there be a fixed rate for growth of the money stock, associated with Milton Friedman, who presented it in *A Program for Monetary Stability* (1960).[37] His rationale is that there are severe limitations to our knowledge about the causes of business fluctuations and the lags between policy action and economic response. Under such conditions, discretionary action is more likely to destabilize than to stabilize. A publicly known rule for a fixed rate of

---

[36] According to the scapegoat hypothesis, an independent Fed helps elected officials act responsibly with minimal political cost, by permitting them to blame the Fed for actions they may approve, but which it would be impolitic to defend. See Kane (1990).

[37] That proposal differed from Friedman's first proposal, which was for an automatic dollar-for-dollar creation (retirement) of money to cover government deficits (surpluses) as a result of automatic stabilizers set in tax and transfer laws (Friedman 1953a).

money growth would have avoided policy mistakes that Friedman documents and would provide a clear-cut basis for accountability.

This is noncontingent in the sense that the rate is meant to be achieved regardless of fluctuations in economic conditions. An advantage of noncontingent rules for purposes of accountability is that the standards of performance are relatively unambiguous and clear – I say "relatively" because the money stock is measured in several ways, and for a rule to be unambiguous, one specific measure and standard would have to be chosen.

The use of contingent rules is at least a theoretical possibility that could avoid the inflexibility associated with noncontingent rules. A contingent rule would try to anticipate all the important conditions on which given actions might depend and specify what should be done under these conditions. There are several problems with this. One is that it would be difficult to anticipate all the conditions on which an action might depend. Another is that the more elaborate the conditions become, the more likely it becomes that discretion will be necessary to determine whether or not a given contingency obtains. At the extreme, contingent rules and discretion merge and become almost indistinguishable.

Monetary rules have two other rationales. One is similar to the rationale for a balanced budget amendment, to be discussed in Chapter 9, which I designate the public choice rationale. The idea is that the central bank cannot be trusted to resist inappropriate pressures from elected officials. Thomas Havrilesky (1987, 1993) has the most elaborate theory for why such pressures are inappropriate. He argues that elected officials appeal for votes by enacting redistributive tax and transfer schemes that create costly inefficiencies in the economy. To disguise the slowdown in growth and productivity caused by such programs, presidents (and, to a lesser extent, Congress) pressure the Fed to expand the money supply, with inflationary consequences.

Another rationale for rules is the time-consistency argument. In this argument, inefficiencies in the economy are due to distortionary taxes, labor unions, or laws affecting the labor market (e.g., minimum wages and unemployment compensation). Such features are said to result in a rate of economic growth below the potential of the natural rate, or unemployment rates above the natural rate. Monetary authorities operating in a rational expectations framework try to improve output to its natural rate, even though they know that they can do that only by surprising the public with an inflationary increase in the money supply. But the public knows that they will do that and expects the increase. The result is that output does not increase, but inflation does. It is said that a rule would help politicians resist the temptation to carry out such policy.[38]

The time-consistency rationale differs from Friedman's lack-of-knowledge rationale in that it is based on the strong presumption that both the public and the monetary authority understand how the economy works and understand each other's goals and strategies. The time-consistency rationale differs from the public choice rationale in that there is no misunderstanding or effort to mislead, though asymmetric information is likely.

In some respects, the two arguments are similar but use differing language. The time-consistency argument is presented in the language of rational choice and enlightened self-interest, whereas the public choice argument uses language that emphasizes the venal or self-serving motivations of public officials and the failure of the public to understand the consequences of the policies it supports.

The Taylor Rule

John Taylor, of Stanford University, developed a rule of thumb in the early 1990s that has become widely used as a guide for good monetary policy and a diagnostic for poor monetary policy. The rule is that a controllable interest rate be a function of deviations of inflation from targeted inflation and of output from potential output:

$$ff = a + b(\pi - \pi^*) + c(y - y^*)$$

where ff is the federal funds rate; π is the inflation rate; π^* is the target inflation rate; y is output; y^* is potential output; and a, b, and c are weights that can reflect the goals and preferences of policy makers.

Estimations of the Taylor Rule for the inflationary period of the 1970s suggest that the actual federal funds rate was consistently lower than would have been recommended by the Taylor Rule (Granato and Wong 2006, pp. 92–100). After the Volcker disinflation, the Taylor Rule was followed for most of the Great Moderation, from 1984 until early 2002, when interest rates were held below what the Taylor Rule would have recommended, until 2006 (Taylor 2009, p. 3) In this way, the Taylor Rule explains the poor inflationary performance of the 1970s and the good performance of the

---

[38] See Kydland and Prescott (1977) for the seminal formulation. See also Barro and Gordon (1983). As several people have observed, a superior solution to this problem would be to eliminate the distortions.

Great Moderation. Deviation from it contributed to the financial crisis, though, of course, these low interest rates were not the sole cause.

Accountability

Friedman pointed out that a rule for monetary policy would provide a clear-cut basis for accountability, which is a concept that is widely used as if it needed no definition, but it is, in fact, used in different ways. As we have seen, one meaning is that officials be subject to sanction for inadequate performance, such as by removal from office through defeat in election or through impeachment. The other is to be subject to the need to give account (i.e., to explain, report, or justify), such as through a state of the union message or through a judicial opinion that embeds a court decision in the law. Like federal judges in the United States, central bankers have been intentionally shielded from the first kind of accountability by their long terms (Keech and Morris 1997). (The current term for governors of the Fed is fourteen years.) For much of the twentieth century, the Fed was in a position to use its own discretion to define its own standards for explaining, reporting, and justifying its actions in its annual reports.

In the absence of independent, authoritative standards for evaluating the performance of monetary authorities, that discretion to define the standards for its performance provided considerable latitude to Fed officials. For all three of the rationales for rules, a clearly defined standard is meant to provide a basis for knowing when the monetary authority has deviated from proper performance.

In my view, monetary policy has been most successful in the period of the Great Moderation, when the Federal Reserve acted as if it were following a Taylor Rule. If it had continued to follow such a rule after 2002, the housing crisis might have been less severe. There is much to be said for transparency and precommitment to a widely known and easily understandable rule.

9

Rules, Discretion, and Accountability in the Fiscal Policy Process

The United States faces an easily predictable fiscal crisis of unprecedented proportions, but democratic institutions and processes are standing in the way of confronting painful choices and making responsible fiscal policy. Fiscal policy is the biggest failure of democracy in the United States since the first edition of this book appeared. A single sentence goes a long way toward explaining the problem: "The country faces a fundamental disconnect between the services the people expect the government to provide, particularly in the form of benefits for older Americans, and the tax revenues that people are willing to send to the government to finance these services."[1]

It is surely not new for people to want more services than they are willing to pay for. Among what is new is the size of the present and future gap between revenues and expenditures. Also, both revenues and expenditures are largely on autopilot and would take painful action to correct. There was a time, before the 1960s, when belief in the balanced budget norm was strong enough and pervasive enough to make reconnecting revenues and expenditures politically feasible, but that time is long past. The formal institutions of fiscal policy have not changed much, but the informal, unwritten institutions have changed since the 1960s.[2]

Because of the changes in the informal institutions, the two most fundamental institutions of democracy are standing in the way of a fiscal plan that would avert a crisis and ensure a sound fiscal future. These institutions are popular elections and checks and balances as a limitation on government. Popular elections keep candidates from proposing to cut popular spending

---

[1] Douglas Elmendorf, director of the Congressional Budget Office, quoted in Wessel (2012, p. 158).

[2] Several sources suggest that the 1960s are the turning point: Buchanan and Wagner (1977); Wagner (2012); Ippolito (2012); Hoover and Sheffrin (1992); Hoover and Siegler (2000).

programs or from proposing to raise taxes. Checks and balances under conditions of partisan polarization keep any party from proposing or implementing a viable plan. The fact that taxes and entitlement spending are automatic means that the default in case of gridlock is low revenues, high expenditures, and deficits projected to increase unsustainably.

In general, fiscal policy consists of public decisions about government expenditures and revenues. Spending policy and taxing policy have always been of interest in their own right, but at least since the 1930s, spending and taxing and the balance between them have been seen by at least some economists as having controllable consequences for the overall performance of the macroeconomy. For example, Keynesians have advocated active discretionary manipulation of the size of the budget deficit (or surplus) to stabilize the economy, to reduce unemployment, and to shift the path of economic growth. The Kennedy-Johnson tax cut of 1964 is seen by Keynesians as a successful example of how fiscal policy can increase prosperity by increasing aggregate demand. Supply side economists have acknowledged the success of that tax cut, but explain its success in terms of increasing aggregate supply, rather than demand. They would defend President Reagan's Economic Recovery Tax Act of 1981 and President Bush's tax cuts of 2001 and 2003 on the same, supply-oriented grounds.[3]

Causality goes in the other direction as well. That is, the performance of the economy has an effect on the size of the government's deficit (or surplus). Specifically, when the economy expands, revenues may rise faster than expenditures, thus reducing a deficit. And when the economy goes into a recession, expenditures may rise (e.g., because of increased unemployment compensation claims), whereas revenues fall because of declining incomes and reduced economic activity. Both these effects are *countercyclical*, which means that a system of expenditure and taxation programs can automatically stabilize economic fluctuations. This would not have always been the case, but with a sizeable public sector based in part on a system of transfer payments and progressive income taxation, it has been so for the United States for nearly three-quarters of a century.[4]

Even if the federal budget is set to be balanced at potential output or "full" employment at its natural rate, there will be automatic deficits when the economy goes into a recession or suffers a negative shock. As Taylor (1993)

---

[3] A leading alternative hypothesis about fiscal policy is that the government plans for equal marginal tax rates over time to minimize the distortionary effects of taxation on private efforts to work, invest, and consume. In this view, deficits are, and should be, passive adjustments to economic shocks (Barro 1979, 1986).

[4] See Stein (1969, 1996).

points out, this is akin to a rule for policy, but it does not demand rule-based policy action. A passive response is all that is required. Because tax revenues will drop automatically, and safety net expenditures such as unemployment compensation will increase automatically, there is a constructive, built-in response to a downturn. This desirable response would be prohibited by a rule that insisted that budgets be balanced at all times. I am confident that the economic forces would overwhelm such a rule, even if the rule were incorporated into the Constitution as a balanced budget amendment.

Even the defenders of fiscal stabilization policy now claim only a secondary role for fiscal relative to monetary stabilization policy. Alan Blinder introduces a defense of fiscal policy saying that he has no intention "of challenging the now-standard view that the central bank *should* and *does* have a dominant role in stabilization policy" (2006, p. 26, emphasis in original). In their "exploration of optimal stabilization policy," Mankiw and Weinzierl say that "conventional fiscal policy is the demand management tool of last resort" if the conditions for the three preferable strategies are absent (2011, p. 31).

THE FISCAL CRISIS

In my judgment, U.S. fiscal policy has become increasingly irresponsible since the original publication of this book. Moreover, the incentives of democratic politics have contributed to dysfunctional fiscal policy. According to the National Commission on Fiscal Responsibility and Reform (the Bowles-Simpson Commission),

Our nation is on an unsustainable fiscal path. Spending is rising and revenues are falling short, requiring the government to borrow huge sums each year to make up the difference. We face staggering deficits. In 2010, federal spending was nearly 24 percent of Gross Domestic Product ... Only during World War II was federal spending a larger part of the economy. Tax revenues stood at 15 percent of GDP this year, the lowest level since 1950. The gap between spending and revenue – the budget deficit – was just under 9 percent of GDP.

Since the last time our budget was balanced in 2001, the federal debt has increased dramatically, rising from 33 percent of GDP to 62 percent of GDP in 2010. The escalation was driven in large part by two wars and a slew of fiscally irresponsible policies, along with a deep economic downturn. We have arrived at the moment of truth, and neither political party is without blame. (2010, p. 6)

The situation is even worse, when we consider that the figure for federal debt is "debt held by the public" and excludes borrowing from government trust funds, such as Social Security. These are obligations that must be repaid. The Congressional Budget Office (CBO) gives extended forecasts of budgetary matters each year, and it projects debt as a percentage of GDP into the future. Since the American Taxpayer Relief Act of 2012 made the Bush tax cuts permanent for all but the wealthiest of taxpayers, federal debt as a fraction of GDP will stay at levels that have not been seen since 1950.

Such policies are not sustainable. The United States has gotten to where it is with a combination of discretion and automatic policy, and with a deterioration in informal rules or institutions.

DISCRETION, AUTOMATIC POLICY, AND RULES IN THE POLICY PROCESS

The distinction between discretionary fiscal policy and automatic fiscal policy picks up an issue that will occupy us in this chapter. "Discretion" involves the capacity to act on one's own, using one's own judgment. At best, this implies the judgment of the benevolent dictator, or guardian, who by definition knows the best thing to do. At worst, it implies the judgment of the opportunistic public official who makes improperly expedient decisions. In terms of the time-consistency problem, discretion may mean doing the best thing at the time, rather than following an optimal plan.

Discretionary decisions could be improper by a variety of standards, such as favoring narrow interests at the expense of broad interests, or inappropriately favoring the present at the expense of the future, not to speak of being venal or corrupt. Democratic institutions are designed to ensure that there will be accountability for officials who are empowered to exercise discretion, but as we have seen in the analysis of electoral cycles, the very institutions of accountability may have perverse incentives if policy makers try to exploit the inattention of the voters or the asymmetries of information between themselves and the electorate.

Discretionary policy making has two alternatives. One is *automatic policy*, such as the automatic stabilizers described earlier. Here, the institutions of progressive taxation and of entitlement-based transfer payments ensure that there will be an appropriately countercyclical response to economic fluctuations, even without discretionary intervention. Automatic policies do not deny the possibility of discretionary decisions to supplement or even to counteract them. They simply ensure that certain actions will be taken without any conscious decision to take new action.

Automatic policies are not necessarily desirable, though I think automatic stabilizers, as described earlier, are very desirable.

The second alternative to discretion is *rule-based policy*. Like automatic policy, rules do not involve discretion, but unlike automatic policy, they are meant to exclude discretion in favor of a presumably superior standard that decision makers will follow. The most commonly advocated rule for fiscal policy is a constitutional amendment prohibiting deficit spending under most circumstances. Another rule, known as "tax smoothing," is less a prohibition than a guideline for policy. It implies that taxes be fixed at a level designed to cover expected government expenditures over the long term and that deficits be allowed to fluctuate secondarily (and automatically) in response to unplanned events such as wars and economic shocks. In monetary policy, Milton Friedman's proposal for a fixed rate of money growth has been displaced by the Taylor Rule.[5]

Various rationales have been provided to support specific rules and rules in general. One is that the limitations of knowledge and information are likely to make discretionary policy worse than policy that follows a simple rule, even without raising questions about the motives of public officials. This is the basis for Milton Friedman's case for a fixed rate of money growth (1960). A second rationale is that the discretionary behavior of politicians in an electoral process is not to be trusted, and the institutions of electoral accountability do not adequately restrain irresponsible and shortsighted policy making. This is the basis for most arguments in favor of a constitutional amendment to require a balanced budget.[6] A third rationale that is common in contemporary economics concerns the time-consistency problem, wherein the best policy for all times, ex ante, may not be the best policy for a given time, ex post. This, too, has been a basis for proposals for a fixed rate of money growth.[7]

Regardless of the rationale, rules may be contingent or noncontingent. A noncontingent rule is one that would prescribe policy regardless of conditions, and without feedback from performance. For example, as discussed in Chapter 8, a fixed rate of money growth is generally prescribed as a noncontingent rule. A fiscal example of a contingent rule is provided by the proposals for a balanced budget amendment that specify that the rule can be relaxed in wartime or by a two-thirds vote of Congress.

---

[5] See Chapter 8.
[6] See Buchanan and Wagner (1977).
[7] See Kydland and Prescott (1977); Barro and Gordon (1983).

The more a rule is contingent on conditions, the more similar it becomes to discretion. In the extreme, a state-contingent rule could aspire to specify exactly what a benevolent dictator or guardian would do under whatever circumstances might arise. There are two problems with this. First, as we have seen, it is not easy to define what a benevolent dictator should do. Almost all decisions about macroeconomic policy inevitably involve choices that are inherently contestable, and hence political. Second, the more contingencies a rule has, the more difficult it is to know whether or not it has been followed – it becomes more complicated and difficult to see whether or not the decisions appropriately matched the contingencies specified in the rule. Problems of accountability and enforcement become more severe if rules are contingent. The information asymmetries between the public and the policy maker become more and more significant, and they imply larger costs of democracy because of principal-agent issues.

Procedural "Justice" and Legitimation by Process

In American national politics, few noncontingent rules specify the desired outcomes of the policy-making process, though there are numerous ways in which laws make fiscal outcomes automatic. Not all of these are desirable. In general terms, authoritative decisions about fiscal goals and policies are made through a political process. Even if the goals and policies cannot be defined as authoritative in their own right, they gain authority and legitimacy through a political process grounded in constitutionally defined public institutions. Elected governments make authoritative policy that may work well or not so well. They are accountable for their performance at the next election. This process is continuing and iterative, so that most choices are subject to revision in the light of experience. New elections can select new public officials to set new directions.[8]

This description of the political process echoes John Rawls's conception of pure procedural justice, wherein a perfect process transmits desirability and moral force to an outcome (1971, pp. 83–90). But the institutions through which the political process takes place are themselves not perfect. They are subject to criticism and revision. Institutions and procedures are themselves matters of political choice. Procedural institutions can be revised when they are seen as needing improvement, from a variety of perspectives, which might range from changing the standards of political legitimacy to

---

[8] This conception of the political process echoes Simon (1978) on procedural as opposed to substantive rationality.

specifically macroeconomic issues. Given an existing set of institutions, we may think of the political process as one of procedural legitimization rather than procedural justice.

Can the Means Justify the Ends?

The institutions through which American fiscal policy is made include the most fundamental in the polity. These are Articles I and II of the Constitution, which define the roles of Congress and the president in taxing and spending policy. Fiscal institutions also include legislated procedures, such as those prescribed in the Budget and Impoundment Control Act of 1974. These procedural institutions are not perfect in any non-contestable sense, but because they are official, they transmit legitimacy and authority to the policy choices that are made through them. They are the "means" that at least provisionally justify the policy choices, or the "ends" that emerge.

The rules of sport provide an analogy. A game, such as a basketball game, is a procedure designed to determine a winner between two teams, each of which has its own supporters. A game can be seen as a procedure designed to determine which is the better team. No one doubts that inferior teams occasionally upset superior ones. Otherwise, there would be much less interest in sport. However, regardless of other considerations, a victory is an authoritative determination of superiority in that game, and an operational definition of which was the better team at the time of play. The official procedure defines and legitimizes the result.

Similarly, constitutional and legislative institutions are authoritative ways of determining which policy should prevail among alternatives, each of which has its own supporters. The alternative that prevails is not necessarily superior in a normative sense, but it is official and legitimate if it emerges from the mutually agreed procedure. Just as different teams may win on different days, different policies may emerge under different circumstances, even though the rules do not change.

But the rules may change. For example, in both professional and college basketball, originally all field goals were worth two points, regardless of the length of the shot. Countless games were won and lost under that rule. Some time ago, that rule was changed to add interest to the game. Now field goals shot from behind a semicircular line count three points, and all others count two, as before. Not everyone favored the new rule, but once it was adopted, it was accepted as an authoritative way of scoring goals and determining the winner of the game. Many outcomes would be the same under both the old and the new rules, but others would surely be different. The new rule would affect the outcomes of some games if they were played exactly the same way. But, of course, the new rule affects the strategy and the play of the game, so differences in outcomes are likely to be fewer than they would be without adjustments in strategy. The point for our purposes is that the outcomes are authoritative and legitimate, given the rules in place at the time of play, and regardless of the fact that the rules are not necessarily the best possible rules. And the best possible rules in a democracy are not definable.

Public institutions and public policy are, of course, far more consequential than sport. Moreover, the relative merits of alternative institutions and policies have received meaningful, serious analysis. But such analysis is usually contestable, and the resolution takes place within the existing procedural institutions, which can themselves be changed. These institutions are changed from time to time, usually with the expectation that the change will improve outcomes either for the public as a whole or for the winning coalition. The point of my analogy is that there is a reciprocal and provisional quality to the interaction between procedures and policy. Neither provides normative bedrock from which all else can be evaluated.

This chapter analyzes the institutions in which fiscal policy is made. The next two sections deal with formal institutions: the relevant parts of the Constitution and the relevant legislated institutions. But institutions are not necessarily legislated or formal; they can be informal patterns of behavior, or norms, and these are analyzed as well. For each, we consider whether or not the institution is neutral with regard to fiscal policy issues and how decision makers are accountable under it.

CONSTITUTIONAL INSTITUTIONS OF FISCAL POLICY

The fundamental constitutional institutions of fiscal policy are the basic institutions of American national government: the separated powers and checks and balances between the legislative and executive branches as defined in the Constitution. Congress has the constitutionally defined power to "lay and collect taxes" and "to borrow money on the credit of the United States," as well as to spend money for various purposes (Article I, section 8), subject to presidential veto and congressional override of such vetoes.

The Separation of Powers and Countercyclical Fiscal Programs

The institutions of separated powers apparently were neutral regarding taxing and spending in the pre-Keynesian era, before intentional deficits were considered (by some) to be appropriate, because nothing in the separation of powers inherently obstructed the achievement of balanced budgets under most circumstances. Between 1787 and 1929, the government budget was in surplus about two-thirds of the time, with most exceptions resulting from wars and recessions.[9] From 1930 through 1946, there was only one surplus (1930), but from 1947 through 1960, there were seven surpluses and seven deficits. Since 1960, there have been only four years of surplus. I argue later that Keynesian and supply side economics broke a norm, an informal institution that had not been written down, that demanded that revenues and expenditures be more or less in line with each other.

This experience suggests the possibility of different behavioral regimes for dealing with deficits within constant constitutional institutions. However, Barro (1986) has demonstrated that in the period from 1916 through 1982, which includes each of the periods mentioned earlier, a single model derived from the tax-smoothing hypothesis can explain the entire range of deficits in terms of temporary bursts in public expenditures, such as those associated with wars. Nonetheless, I argue later that different patterns of fiscal policy making exist in different periods.

In a Keynesian world where activist discretionary fiscal stabilization policy is appropriate, the separation of powers may become a problem. This separation reduces the speed with which the government can respond to economic conditions, because agreement must be reached between the two houses of Congress and (short of veto-proof majorities) between the president and Congress. This feature distributes blocking and delaying powers, and it stands in the way of immediate action.

At a minimum, the separation of powers adds to the length of the "long and variable lags" that Milton Friedman has identified in stabilization policy (1953a, pp. 144–8). These lags are divided into the "inside lag," between recognition of a problem and policy action, and the "outside lag," between action and result. The structure of American government lengthens the inside lag of fiscal policy. This fact derives from the rationales for the separation of powers. James Madison observed in *The Federalist* 62 and 63 that if bodies chosen in dissimilar ways can agree at all, they are more likely to agree on something good. Alexander Hamilton had a more negative way of putting a similar point, observing in *The Federalist* 73 that the advantage of defeating a bad law is worth the risk of defeating a few good ones.

---

[9] "From 1789 to 1930, deficits were routinely incurred during wars and financial upheavals, but nearly 70 percent of annual budgets were in surplus. The Great Depression and World War II produced a long series of consecutive deficits, but the balanced budget standard was revived in the late 1940s and 1950s" (Ippolito 2012, p. 244). See Stein (1978).

In the eighteenth-century environment in which Madison and Hamilton wrote, inside and outside lags were far from anyone's imagination. We can assess the contemporary fiscal consequences of these institutions of separated powers for Keynesian stabilization by reviewing the history of fiscal action in the postwar era. In general, all such actions were taken after recovery had begun except for the American Recovery and Reinvestment Act of 2009. Bruce Bartlett has identified the dates of passage for all of the postwar countercyclical programs up to the 1990s. None of them was finally enacted before the date the preceding recession ended, according to subsequent "official" dating by the National Bureau of Economic Research. Specifically, for the recession beginning in November 1948 and ending in October 1949, President Truman proposed an eleven-point program on July 11, 1949. Only one of the points was enacted, an Advance Planning for Public Works Act, signed in October, the month the recession ended. No fiscal action was taken to stem the recession of July 1953 to May 1954.

Congressional Democrats passed three countercyclical bills to deal with the 1957–8 recession, and President Eisenhower signed them. A highway bill was signed in April 1958, the month the recession ended, and unemployment compensation and rivers-and-harbors bills were passed later that summer. The brief recession of April 1960 to February 1961 spanned two administrations. President Kennedy proposed several measures in February 1961, the month the recession ended, and an unemployment compensation bill was passed in March. The Area Redevelopment Act was passed in May, and a Social Security bill was passed in June, all after the recession was over.

The recession of December 1969 to November 1970 led to one major legislative act, the Public Works Impact Program, enacted in August 1971, almost a year after the recession had ended. The recession of November 1973 to March 1975 prompted several pieces of legislation, the first of which passed in the month the recession ended. That law included tax rebates and extended unemployment benefits, along with some tax changes.

No action was taken regarding the January-July 1980 recession other than to remove credit controls. However, the Reagan administration did adopt two countercyclically oriented programs for its recession. The Surface Transportation Assistance Act was enacted in January 1983, and the Emergency Jobs Appropriations Act was also passed in the year after the recession had ended.[10] The recession of 1990–91 prompted a Democratic

---

[10] This material is drawn from "If It Ain't Broke, Don't Fix It," a *Wall Street Journal* op-ed article by Bruce Bartlett, December 2, 1992, and from a memorandum he prepared in the Treasury Department, dated December 7, 1991.

proposal, which President Bush vetoed. President Clinton's stimulus program, which was submitted after the recession was officially over, was defeated in Congress.[11]

This history is a powerful demonstration of the inside lag in stabilization policy following the occurrence of a downturn and preceding the recognition of the problem and countercyclical action. Until 2009, there is no example of a program that was passed before the final month of the recession it was designed to correct. Although the fact that the government was divided between the parties was relevant in most of the recessions, it is not clear that unified partisan government helped a great deal in speeding a response (as in the recessions of 1948–49, 1953–54, and 1980). Although it is not clear that parliamentary governments would act faster, the need to secure agreement among the two houses of Congress and the president surely adds to the inside lag.

For supporters of timely, discretionary fiscal stimulus to deal with recessions, this experience is surely discouraging. However, those advocates might defend such programs as enhancing the nascent recovery. For the 2007–9 crisis, the recession was over before unemployment recovered, and a stimulus could be considered appropriate to deal with the latter problem. For those, such as monetarists and new classicals, who would argue that the countercyclical programs are misguided, a blocking capacity is likely to seem desirable, echoing the rationale of Alexander Hamilton about the desirability of defeating bad laws. However, if those were bad laws, they were not all defeated. Several were merely delayed, and that delay may have made them even less desirable.

For a time, when economists had more confidence in the power of fiscal policy, there were suggestions for institutional change designed to reduce the inside lag without changing the basic structure of American government.[12] Some of these proposals would have given the president the power to make small proportional changes in tax rates at his discretion, and subject to a congressional veto. But as two leading economists observed more than three decades ago, "no such proposal has ever seemed close to enactment" (Blinder and Solow 1974, p. 45). At present, it is difficult to imagine such a thing even being proposed. There is considerable distrust between the two branches in this era that has seen more government that is divided than unified by party, and the parties have become considerably more polarized. Also, there is a lack of interest and confidence in fiscal policy, because of the

---

[11] Note that the ends of all of these recessions were identified in hindsight.

[12] See Portney (1976) for an example.

sizes of the deficits and the public debt, and because of developments in macroeconomic theory.[13]

In spite of all of these cautions, there seems to be powerful public pressure during a recession to "do something," if only to show evidence of government concern for the suffering associated with economic downturns. Stimulus programs, such as those of presidents Kennedy and Clinton, are sometimes proposed after a recovery has begun, with the goal of speeding or improving the recovery. A recession may provide a convenient pretext to do something a government wishes to do anyway. In any case, the separation of powers seems to slow the timing. For those who argue that fiscal stimuli are misguided, too little too late may ironically be better than speedy and decisive action.

Divided Government and Deficits

The period since 1952 has seen more divided partisan control of the national government than any other previous period of comparable length in American history (Fiorina 1992, pp. 6–10). It has also seen the largest sustained peacetime deficits of any previous period. Mathew McCubbins (1991) has developed a theoretical model to show that divided government causes deficits. The basic idea is that the two parties have sharply different spending priorities, with the Democrats favoring domestic programs and Republicans favoring defense. According to McCubbins, each party is able to block increases in the other party's favored programs, but each party would prefer to let both parties' programs grow over having both restricted to current levels. With Republicans able to block tax increases, the default was growth in both defense and nondefense spending, without accompanying tax increases.

McCubbins (1991) provided evidence to support his interpretation,[14] but Alt and Stewart (1990) applied that hypothesis to the entire history of American government and found that it fit poorly with previous experiences of divided government, such as those in the nineteenth century. It seems, provisionally, that divided government may be causally associated with deficits, but the association is at best conditional rather than inevitable.[15]

---

[13] See Mankiw and Weinzierl (2011); Auerbach, Gale, and Harris (2010).

[14] Barro provides a sardonic critique as a commentary, included in McCubbins (1991).

[15] See Roubini and Sachs (1989a) and Grilli, Masciandara, and Tabellini (1991) for a cross-national perspective. See Alt and Lowry (1994) and Poterba (1994) for analyses regarding American states.

If divided government contributes to deficits under some circumstances, there is reason to believe that it can play a constructive role in resolving deficit crises. Two of the most significant recent agreements that involved cutting expenditures and raising taxes were the Greenspan commission of 1983 and the budget agreement of 1990, both of which occurred under divided government.

The Constitutional Status of the Income Tax

Article I says that representatives and direct taxes shall be apportioned according to population, which would seem to rule out income taxes. Such taxes were used to fight the Civil War, but the Supreme Court subsequently declared them unconstitutional in *Pollock v. Farmers Loan* (1895). Therefore, it took the Sixteenth Amendment to the Constitution, ratified in 1913, to begin modern government's heavy reliance on income taxes. Because the income tax is a visible tax, this may have something to do with the increasing number of deficit years in the twentieth century. In the nineteenth century, the tariff, an invisible tax, was the main source of government revenue, and raising revenue through tariffs was not nearly as risky politically as raising taxes through an income tax.

Discretion, Rules, and Accountability

Countercyclical stimulus programs such as those reviewed earlier are classic examples of discretionary policy. Their desirability is highly contestable. For those who like them, the blocking and delaying that American constitutional institutions facilitate are impediments. For those who oppose them, these institutions are useful. When overall performance is deemed unsatisfactory, however, these institutions do not facilitate accountability. None of the responsible agents was pleased with the deficits that began to emerge in the 1980s, but none was effectively held accountable. Republicans and Democrats blamed each other, and the president and Congress blamed each other. But it would be difficult to argue that any of the responsible officials were punished for the deficits.[16] The American system of separated powers and of checks and balances obstructs accountability. This fact has been recognized at least since Woodrow Wilson's time and has prompted many proposals for general constitutional reform.

---

[16] Bratton (1994).

The United States has had little direct experience with rules as alternatives to discretion. However, the original constitutional requirement about direct taxes could be considered a rule against income taxes. This rule was effectively followed for most of the period before the Sixteenth Amendment was ratified in 1913, but it was ignored during the Civil War and after. The institution that enforced the rule was the Supreme Court, in the *Pollock* case, though it had looked the other way during the Civil War. That experience may be relevant to the prospects of enforcing a balanced budget requirement as a constitutional amendment.

Constitutional Budget Rules

A constitutional amendment to require a balanced budget has been proposed many times over a very long period of American history (Savage 1988). This proposal has a superficial and simplistic appeal that belies incentives and enforcement problems. Just because something is in the Constitution does not mean that it will be obeyed. This point is illustrated by the Fifteenth Amendment, which provided in 1870 that "The right of citizens of the United States to vote shall not be denied or abridged by the United States or by any State on account of race, color, or previous condition of servitude." This amendment was ignored and violated for ninety-five years until the passage of the Voting Rights Act of 1965, which had enforcement mechanisms.[17]

All but one (Vermont) of the fifty American states has some sort of constitutional requirement for a balanced budget, and this fact is often mentioned as a reason to have a balanced budget amendment to the U.S. Constitution. According to David Primo (2007), these rules vary considerably in their effectiveness. The weakest are those that simply demand that a *proposed* budget be balanced, without a penalty for failing to deliver on that proposal at the end of the fiscal year. The strongest are those that prohibit a carryover of a debt to the next fiscal year or biennium period and demand that the shortfall be made up with spending cuts or tax increases in the current fiscal period. This effect of carryover prohibition is greatest when the state high courts are elected rather than appointed. Primo suggests that the surprising strength of the state constitutional requirements is due to the fact that most of them were enacted in the distant past, when budgets were smaller and the stakes were lower. He suggests that such rules would be less effective if they were to be designed by contemporary legislatures, which

---

[17] See Keyssar (2000) for a history of suffrage in the United States.

would have incentives to build in features that would undermine their effectiveness (Primo 2007, ch. 5).

Constitutional amendments to require a balanced federal budget have been proposed many times. - Primo, whose explanation of the success of such provisions in state constitutions we just reviewed, argues that

> a constitutional amendment is unlikely to be effective in eliminating the [federal] deficit for two reasons. First, the amendment would be the product of political compromise and, as such, would contain loopholes rendering it ineffective. Second, these loopholes would render impotent the special type of enforcement implied by a constitutional amendment, leaving only the constituency costs for violating the spirit of the amendment to provide for enforcement. (2007, p. 115)

Primo explains this with respect to the 1995 version of a balanced budget amendment (BBA), which came within one Senate vote of going to the states for ratification. For example, the requirement that total outlays not exceed total receipts could be overridden by a two-thirds majority of both houses. Getting to that majority could involve more spending rather than less. The requirement could (and surely would) be waived in time of declared war or military action. The amendment provides that "Congress shall enforce and implement this article by appropriate legislation, which may rely on estimates of outlays and receipts" (Primo 2007, p. 117). Nothing indicates how deficits at the end of the fiscal year must be made up.

I regard a constitutional balanced budget amendment as dangerous symbolic politics. This is not because I do not prefer that the federal budget be balanced, but because I regard such an amendment as unenforceable. I anticipate the likelihood of a BBA coexisting with more deficits, and creating even more cynicism about the American political system. Moreover, even if it did work, its rigidity would override the automatic stabilizers, which would otherwise work countercyclically to smooth out the fluctuations of the business cycle.

LEGISLATED INSTITUTIONS OF FISCAL POLICY

Legislated institutions of fiscal policy define the procedures by which fiscal policy is made in greater detail than Articles I and II specify. These procedures are often defended as neutral or as designed to achieve general public purposes. They sometimes reflect the efforts of winning coalitions to extend the reach of their legislative victories beyond their time in office, either by "stacking the deck" in some way or by making certain desired outcomes automatic.[18]

---

[18] See Stewart (1989) for such an argument.

Institutions of Centralization and Coordination

Although the separation of powers may have consequences for fiscal policy, it was chosen for far broader purposes than fiscal policy as we know it. Ancillary institutions may be created or amended through legislation in response to the problems of the day. From time to time, "reform" movements have gained strength and prompted major innovations in the procedures by which fiscal policy is made. Such movements achieved success in 1921 and 1974. The basic issue was the coordination between spending and revenues. For most of American history before 1921, spending and taxing decisions were quite independent, at least formally. The substantive committees and the appropriations committees made the spending decisions. The revenue committees made the taxing decisions, usually by setting tariffs. Other than what took place in the minds of the members and on the floor of Congress, there often was no institutional coordination of these decisions.[19]

The Budget and Accounting Act of 1921 changed that situation. That act was the culmination of a desire by reformers to impose a more centralized and hierarchical process on federal taxing and spending. The act was a reflection of dissatisfaction with the results of the more decentralized process that had characterized budget policy before that time. It reflected a concern with deficits that had begun to mount even before World War I and that had become far larger as a result of the war. It reflected an intellectual climate associated with the Progressive movement, which preferred government structures that were "centralized, rational, and streamlined" (Stewart 1989, p. 215). The act created an executive agency, the Bureau of the Budget, which would assemble government agencies' requests for appropriations and adjust and coordinate them with one another and with projected revenues before sending the entire package to Congress as the president's budget. Congress would then act on that proposed budget, which theoretically had been derived from a synoptic approach designed to take into account all relevant considerations and package them in a coherent manner.

That act sounds like a neutral, public interest, good government-oriented innovation, and it was presented that way. However, Stewart (1989) has seen it (along with other innovations that preceded it in the nineteenth century) as a procedural device by which a contemporary majority tries to impose its wishes on its successors. In this case, the majority was interested

---

[19] But see Fisher (1975, ch. 1) and Stewart (1989, pp. 16, 32).

in restricting government spending, and the institutional device was one that ensured that a complete set of programs would be considered together as a package. Stewart has presented a compelling defense of his hypothesis, though it remains possible that some of the support for the Budget and Accounting Act was, in fact, genuinely based on more neutral, good government rationales.[20]

Regardless of the interpretation of the motives of those who passed the Budget and Accounting Act of 1921, Stewart raises a general question about the nature of institutional choice, to which there is likely to be no single answer. Surely, it is sometimes true that changes in institutions are, as he suggests, efforts of contemporary majorities to impose their views on those who will come after. But, surely, it is also sometimes true that institutions are efforts to achieve more generally beneficial solutions to problems of collective action. Stewart's view is one that gives considerable credit to the winning majorities for an understanding of the consequences of institutions. Still another possibility is that the consequences of institutional change cannot always be readily anticipated. Some reformers have surely been surprised and disappointed at the unanticipated consequences of their activity.[21]

The Budget and Impoundment Control Act of 1974 was a similar innovation. That act reflected dissatisfaction with the way the procedures set up by the Budget and Accounting Act of 1921 were working, as well as the fact that deficits seemed to be out of control. Most importantly, it was a reflection of divided control of the government and of the conflict between the Democratic Congress and the Republican president, Richard Nixon. Nixon had been using the executive power to override spending decisions made by Congress, by impounding, or refusing to spend, some of the money that Congress had appropriated. The president had also criticized Congress for lacking fiscal discipline.

The 1974 act responded to that situation by placing restrictions on the authority of the president to impound funds appropriated by Congress. More to our point, the act created a legislative counterpart to the Office of Management and Budget, into which the Bureau of the Budget had evolved. That new Congressional Budget Office was designed to make Congress less dependent on the executive branch for information about fiscal policy. It also set up a new budget calendar, new committees, and a new set of

---

[20] See Brady and Morgan (1987) for another relevant case.

[21] For example, it is unlikely that those who passed the Campaign Finance Reform Act of 1974 anticipated the proliferation of political action committees.

procedures that were designed to facilitate congressional control over taxing and spending.

Some of the purposes of the 1974 act had been to ensure that Congress could take an overall, top-down perspective on taxing and spending and to reduce federal deficits, which had become a topic of increasing concern. As Gilmour put it,

The budget reforms adopted since 1974 have increased the power of congressional majorities: helping overcome a lack of coordination in budgeting that weakened Congress vis-à-vis the executive; providing Congress with procedures that permit adopting a far more coherent budget policy than previously possible; and enabling Congress to exercise more deliberative control over the budget and deficit. Now what majorities want to accomplish with the deficit, they can. (Gilmour 1990, p. 224)

Yet almost nobody professes to be satisfied with the results of the budget process: "Judged by nearly any conceivable output criteria, the budget process has not solved the budget problem" (Gilmour 1990, p. 225). This statement remains as true now as it was when it was first stated.

The key to understanding this puzzle is in the relationship between the preferences reflected in the desire to solve the budget problem, known as a top-down perspective, and those that are reflected in specific spending and taxing decisions, known as a bottom-up perspective. A member of Congress (or a citizen, for that matter) may wish to spend more on needed programs but at the same time wish to have the overall level of spending curtailed. The Congress may well have a majority of such individuals. A majority that wishes to curtail spending may well be an ambivalent majority when it faces the consequences of overall cuts for specific programs. Both as individual members and as an institution, Congress reflects ambivalence about the incompatibility of preferences regarding taxes, spending, and deficits.

Since the 1974 Budget and Impoundment Control Act, presidents have continued to present unbalanced budgets to the Congress, even as some of them have advocated balanced budget amendments to the Constitution. And Congress has continued to pass unbalanced budgets, even given the presence of the institutions that force top-down consideration of the overall consequences of the sum of spending and taxing decisions. A likely explanation for this is that these decision makers prefer the budgets they pass to budgets that would reduce spending or increase taxes.

The implication for the choice of procedural institutions is as follows: forcing the decision makers to confront the long-term or overall consequences of the sum of their specific decisions does not ensure that the general considerations will prevail over the specific considerations. David

Stockman has argued that Congress and the people are getting what they really want when they pass the expenditure programs (and deficits) that have been emerging from the congressional process (Stockman 1986, pp. 376–94). In effect, the use of discretion in the procedures set up by the Constitution and the acts of 1921 and 1974 may not lead to patterns of outcomes that are satisfactory by any standard, including perhaps even some of the standards used by the decision makers in question.

The problem may be due to a conflict between individual or district preferences and the public good, as in a collective action problem or prisoners' dilemma. Several theoretical models have developed rationales for why the public sector might be too "large." Most of them emphasize distributive politics. In these models, committees composed of members who have a high demand for public projects control the legislative agenda, producing concentrated benefits for their constituents, but distributing the costs over the whole population. Because majority rule permits those who enjoy the benefits of public programs to share the burden with those who do not, it is possible that the political process will choose inefficient programs whose benefits are less than their costs.[22] Because most of these models implicitly or explicitly assume that taxes cover the benefits, they do not directly address the incentives for budget deficits.[23]

In any case, there is an apparent disjuncture between the individual taxing and spending decisions that members of Congress make and their satisfaction with the aggregated results of those decisions. The dissatisfaction with such results is not effectively redressed by periodic elections as a system to hold accountable the public officials who make fiscal policy. These processes may not be effective for ensuring that policy is congruent with reasonable overall or long-term views of what is appropriate and desirable. This dissatisfaction has led to proposals for rules that would limit discretion and ensure achievement of a desired goal. We consider these later in the section on precommitment institutions. But before doing that, we consider another set of legislated institutions.

Entitlements and Indexation

Traditionally, government expenditures have had to go through two processes: authorization and appropriation. A subject-matter committee, such

[22] See, for example, Shepsle and Weingast (1981, 1984); Weingast and Marshall (1988); Baron (1991).
[23] For rational choice models of deficits, see Alesina and Tabellini (1990); Tabellini and Alesina (1990).

as a public works committee, might recommend authorization for a project that would cost money (e.g., authorizing a flood control project), whereupon it could be passed by Congress and become law. But the passage of that law would not bring action until another process appropriated funds to pay for it. The appropriations committees traditionally did that according to "roles," by which the House Appropriations Committee served as a tight-fisted "guardian" of the public purse, and the Senate Appropriations Committee was an "appeals court" for those who felt unjustly denied in the other committee.[24]

Such decisions are discretionary rather than automatic. They may be operative for one year or several years, but they are not permanent. The advocates for certain programs who wanted to impose a more lasting quality on the programs they legislated developed a practice called "entitlements." This is legislation that authorizes expenditures to eligible recipients permanently, or at least until the law is changed. The unemployment benefits described earlier as part of the system of automatic stabilizers provide an example.

The Social Security Act of 1935 authorized a program of unemployment compensation and provided that persons whom the law defined as eligible could automatically receive benefits for a specified period. The terms of eligibility have changed from time to time and the levels of benefits have changed, but the basic structure of the law has remained. The amount of expenditure in any given year is not defined in Congress by the appropriations process but is determined by the number of individuals who are eligible and report to the government to demand their benefits. Social Security retirement benefits, veterans' benefits, and Medicare and Medicaid benefits are structured as entitlements.

Entitlements provide a way for the winning majorities who establish such programs to ensure that the programs will outlive the (possibly) temporary tenure of those majorities. They ensure that money will be expended without regard to the availability of revenue. They put a heavy burden of initiative on those who would change the existing programs. Entitlements are pro-expenditure institutions, as compared with arrangements in which either the authorization or the appropriation is structured to expire after a given period.

Inflation may erode the real value of the legislated entitlement amounts, in which case the real worth of such a program can decline. One way for a legislature to deal with eroding real values of a program is to have regular

---

[24] See Fenno (1966) and Wildavsky (1964) for the classic descriptions of this system.

increases in the nominal value. Some of the most dramatic early evidence of an electoral cycle was seen in the increases in Social Security and veterans' benefits in election years (Tufte 1978, ch. 2). Members of Congress were able to take credit for maintaining or even increasing the real value of the benefits.

Indexation is an alternative mechanism to deal with the same problem. If benefits are indexed to inflation, their real value will automatically stay constant, also without regard to the availability of funds (Weaver 1988). As such, indexation is neutral, given the existence of a program. Relative to regular increases in the real value of benefits (as seemed to be the congressional practice in the 1960s and 1970s), indexation is conservative and is a limitation on the growth of expenditures. But relative to the erosion of real value resulting from inflation, indexation is a pro-expenditure institution.

Entitlements, indexed and otherwise, are automatic devices to keep certain expenditures from decreasing. There had been, until recently, a counterpart on the revenue side. Tax laws are almost always permanent in the same way as entitlements. They are usually structured to last until they are changed. The default is their continuation. The income tax passed in 1916 was progressive in that it provided for increasing rates of taxation for higher levels of income. Progressive income taxes without indexation will produce automatic increases in revenue under conditions of inflation. When the nominal value of income rises with inflation without increasing its real value, the recipient may rise into a higher tax bracket and, therefore, pay a higher rate of tax on effectively the same income. With inflation and without indexation, a progressive income tax provides for automatic revenue increases.

The anti-tax Reagan administration, of course, realized that and successfully proposed the indexation of tax brackets in the 1986 Tax Reform Act. On the revenue side, indexation has an effect that is opposite to its effect on the expenditure side. Indexation of tax brackets keeps tax rates down by keeping them from automatically rising with inflation, whereas indexation of benefit programs keeps benefits up by preventing their real value from eroding with inflation. Without indexation, inflation increases the value of revenue from progressive taxes, while eroding the value of expenditures.

Institutions of Precommitment

When the processes of fiscal policy are seen as producing an undesirable pattern of outcomes, we may hear suggestions for rules that will predetermine the outcomes of the process. The leading example of such a rule is the proposal for an amendment to the Constitution to require a balanced federal budget discussed earlier in this chapter. Other examples are the Gramm-Rudman-Hollings (GRH) law discussed in Chapter 6, and the Budget Enforcement Act of 1990, to be discussed here.

We may view a member of the public or of Congress as having multiple, incompatible preferences. The preference for a small public sector and a balanced budget may be incompatible with preferences for expenditures on a variety of programs. The history of passing budgets that emerge from piecemeal decisions about individual programs seems to reveal a collective congressional preference for these programs, even if the institutions force a confrontation of preferences that are incompatible.

Those who wish to go further in the direction of imposing top-down perspectives on the budget process have supported rules for outcomes that may be seen as institutions of precommitment, such as the GRH law and the Budget Enforcement Act of 1990. The GRH law defined specific deficit targets that would decline to zero, and it identified specific automatic procedures to ensure spending cuts in case Congress lacked the will. Those procedures were full of loopholes, and GRH did not come close to achieving its goals.

Yet Robert Reischauer, formerly director of the Congressional Budget Office, doubts that other processes could have done as well:

GRH may not have brought the deficit cows back into the barn, but it has kept them from stampeding over the cliff. It may have encouraged budget makers to resort to optimistic economic assumptions and other sleight of hand, but it has also focused public attention on their expediencies and made them somewhat uncomfortable.

The lesson of the last five years is that process reform, by itself cannot guarantee that significant deficit reduction takes place. *No budget process can force those engaged in it to commit what they regard to be political suicide.* The nation, therefore, will probably have larger than desired deficits until the political costs of continued large deficits are perceived to exceed those of spending cuts and tax increases. (Reischauer 1990, p. 232, emphasis added)

The problem was that those provisions were not "incentive compatible." They were at odds with the day-to-day political incentives of the policy makers, especially those in Congress. Moreover, they were not readily enforceable. The deficit targets were targets in the projections for planned spending, not for final, actual expenditures. That made the law vulnerable to overly optimistic projections.

The Budget Enforcement Act of 1990 (BEA) was also not admired, but there is more reason to believe that it has limited spending. The BEA was passed along with the Omnibus Budget Reconciliation Act of 1990 (OBRA), renewed several times, and allowed to expire in 2002. It set up pay-as-you-go (PAYGO) procedures for increases in domestic expenditures (favored by many Democrats) and for military expenditures (favored by many Republicans). By blocking the switching of funds across that divide, and by otherwise providing that new expenditures would be covered by reduction of existing expenditures or increased taxes, the BEA imposes fiscal discipline on the congressional advocates of both domestic and military expenditures. The BEA worked to prevent the savings in the military budget from being shifted to domestic programs, and Congress defeated proposals to break the agreement and shift those expenditures. Still, the BEA did not succeed in reducing deficits. In fact, they increased after its passage, largely because of the automatic stabilizers and a weak economy. Without the BEA, it is likely that the deficits would have increased even more.

The experience with these institutions of precommitment demonstrates that there are problems of accountability with them as well as without them. No evidence indicates that anyone has been punished for failure to comply with GRH targets, but conventional wisdom suggests that plenty of punishment might result for raising taxes or cutting entitlements. The closest approximation to an electoral punishment regarding contemporary fiscal policy was the defeat of President George H. W. Bush. The cumulative real income growth under the first Bush administration was below the figures for all administrations since 1948 except those of Carter and Eisenhower (II), and no administration has been reelected with such performance (Hibbs 2012b). However, the breaking of his pledge ("Read my lips: No new taxes") doubtless worked against him as well, but it would be too simple to argue that he was punished simply because he went along with increased taxes.

In my judgment, the fact that the first President Bush went along with a budget deal that included some tax increases was less significant than the fact that doing so was at odds with what was probably the most visible and unambiguous promise a winning presidential candidate has made in recent memory. President Bush allowed his behavior to undermine his credibility. If the budget agreement is considered to have been a reasonable way to limit spending, the mistake was to have made the pledge in the first place. He may have believed that he had to make that pledge to be elected, in view of the fact that he has acknowledged publicly that he did what he had to do to be elected.

The experience with GRH makes it clear that changing the formal institutions of fiscal policy making by passing a rule cannot prohibit public officials from following the incentives of electoral politics when such incentives are at odds with the general goals of reducing annual deficits and slowing the growth of the national debt. The problem was not that GRH was not in the Constitution. The problem was that it was not enforceable. In Reischauer's words, these formal institutions cannot force politicians to commit political suicide. But the definition of political suicide depends on the expectations and preferences of voters, which will vary over time, as the next section suggests.

Auerbach (2008) asks whether these acts had any real impact on budgetary outcomes, as opposed to codifying congressional intentions for what would have been done anyway. After a careful analysis, he concludes that each one did have some impact on budget policy. Sometimes, negative side effects occurred, such as a pro-cyclical impact of GRH. Their impact was never large, and, except for the Congressional Budget Act and the institutions it set up, they have all expired.

INFORMAL INSTITUTIONS: PATTERNS OF DISCRETIONARY FISCAL POLICY MAKING

Normally, the level and composition of public expenditures are determined in a political process that reflects popular preferences for the size and composition of government programs. A government has three possible ways to pay for these expenditures: taxation, borrowing, and printing money. The "government budget constraint" defines this relationship:

$$G \equiv T + dB + S$$

where G is government spending; T is taxes; dB is borrowing (wherein d refers to change, and B refers to bonds); and S is the seignorage, the possibility of raising revenue by expanding the money supply (e.g., paying the government's bills with money the government simply prints).

Note that each of these four variables is subject to government control, but they vary in their salience and visibility and in their logical and causal primacy. The expenditures are the benefit and presumably are of primary political importance. Milton Friedman, for example, proposed that the volume of government expenditures be determined "entirely on the basis of the community's desire, need, and willingness to pay for public services" (1953a, p. 136). As previous parts of this book have suggested, it is not a simple and unambiguous task to identify the proper volume of spending. There seems to be a gap between the political community's desire and need for public goods and its willingness to pay for them. Barro (1986) suggested that government expenditures are exogenous and, therefore, are causally prior to items on the right-hand side of the foregoing identity, but later we consider the possibility that spending is affected by the availability of the resource variables on the right-hand side.

Among those variables, taxes are likely to be visible and politically painful. Borrowing may be a way of covering expenditures that is less painful in the short run. However, it is still visible and easy to measure in nominal terms. Seignorage is even less visible, and not at all easy to measure.[25]

Expenditures and revenues are determined by popularly elected legislatures in representative democracies. With qualifications for the automatic character of some spending and revenue policies mentioned earlier, they are more or less actively chosen. Debt and seignorage, in contrast, may be relatively passive responses to the failure of governments to cover expenditures with taxes.[26] If there is a shortfall of revenues, the government may be able to borrow the difference by selling bonds. Alternatively, a compliant central bank can expand the money supply.

The distinction between active and passive is a matter of degree, not a simple binary choice. The question is the difficulty the government has with each source of revenue. Elected officials may be reluctant providers of revenue because of the political costs to them of raising taxes. So long as investors are willing to lend money to the government, borrowing may be a relatively passive option. For some time for the U.S. government, it seems to be much easier to borrow money than to raise taxes, hence a more passive choice.[27]

Whereas a compliant central bank may readily issue credits to a government, an independent central bank may resist such demands. In the United States, with a relatively independent central bank, borrowing is a more passive option than is seignorage. Insofar as it is easier to raise money through debt and seignorage than with taxes, these alternatives are likely to be passive responses to the failure of governments to match expenditures with taxes. However, as we saw in Chapter 4, debt might also be chosen as a strategic variable to limit the spending choices of the next government.

If the desired level of expenditures is taken as a given, the government may choose how to allocate the cost among taxes, borrowing, and seignorage. However, there are other alternatives. The government may consider revenues as given and adjust spending to the available revenues. And, of

---

[25] See Klein and Neumann (1990).
[26] See Andrabi (1993) for an elaboration of the difference between active and passive.
[27] The debt limit showdown of 2011 may have identified a limit on this.

course, revenues and expenditures may be jointly determined. There is reason to expect that these phenomena do not always follow a single pattern.

Historically Defined Regimes

Several patterns of fiscal policy making have been observed in American history, but one overall phenomenon explains a great deal. Until the current era, the main reason for public borrowing by the federal government had been military. The United States incurred large debts in fighting each of its wars. After each war, the debt/GDP ratio declined steadily. That pattern is predicted by the tax-smoothing hypothesis presented by Barro (1986).

However, some variation is not predicted by the tax-smoothing hypothesis. According to Cary Brown, until World War II, the avowed policy was to repay or liquidate public debt, which he calls a creditor-dominated policy. Since that war, inflation and economic growth, rather than debt retirement, have brought the debt/GDP ratio down, which he calls a debtor-dominated policy (Brown 1990, pp. 230–3).

Moreover, there were other patterns within the period before World War II. For much of American history, government revenues were not defined by the need to cover expenditures. They were determined by a protectionist trade policy, which produced large revenues from the tariffs imposed on important goods. In the early years of the nation, before the Civil War, the dominant Democratic Party opposed public expenditures at the federal level; tariff revenues were used to pay down war debts, and sometimes large amounts were turned over to the states (Brown 1990, pp. 230–3).

For most of the period between the Civil War and the Great Depression, the Republicans dominated national politics and pursued a program of public expenditures for internal improvements. Even so, revenues often outpaced expenditures, leaving large surpluses in many years. Those revenues, which were secondary consequences of protectionist policy, created "problems" for the mostly Republican administrations. Nineteenth-century Republicans did not have the aversion to public spending by the federal government that had characterized the Democrats in the early part of that century, and revenues were used for internal improvements and veterans' pensions, as well as for paying down the Civil War debt. According to one nineteenth-century observer, Henry C. Adams,

the Arrearage Pension Acts, by which the treasury was relieved of its plethora of funds, find their true explanation in the desire of Congress to maintain inviolate the system of protective duties. This could not be done in the face of an ever increasing surplus, and protectionist politicians did not dare to advocate the abolition of the whisky tax; it only remained for them to spend the money. (Brown 1990, p. 236)

This case shows that it is at least possible for revenues to be causally prior to expenditures, and in certain circumstances spending can rise to meet the available revenues.

After passage of the income tax amendment in 1913, revenue raising became more visible, and there was no longer a problem of revenues outpacing expenditures. More obviously in the case of the two world wars, expenditure needs drove, or causally influenced, increases in both taxes and deficits.

Characterizing Fiscal Policy since the New Deal

Nominally, the United States has almost always followed a publicly avowed policy of balancing the federal budget. That was the policy of Franklin Roosevelt, in spite of the fact that there was not one balanced federal budget during his presidency. (Cary Brown has observed that Keynesian deficit spending did not fail during the prewar portion of the New Deal; "it was not tried" [1956].) That was the policy of the Truman and Eisenhower administrations, during each of which the deficit years were roughly balanced by surplus years. Although President Kennedy paid lip service to the concept of balanced budgets, his was the first administration to run up an intentional deficit in peacetime for the avowedly Keynesian goal of stimulating economic growth.

Economists had long struggled with standards for budget balance that would recognize the importance of automatic stabilizers and of intentional deficits when the economy was below full employment. Instead of annual balance, they proposed balance over the business cycle, and balance at full employment. But none of these standards had the clarity and simplicity of balance between nominal revenues and expenditures. Even though the public rhetoric regarding deficits did not change much, a shift seems to have occurred after 1960. James Buchanan and Richard Wagner (1977) identified the Kennedy administration as the turning point after which Keynesian economics was self-consciously applied, and after which the balanced budget norm was effectively broken. Once politicians accepted the idea that deficits were occasionally to be desired, that new idea gave them an opportunity to justify politically popular endeavors that would have earlier been considered too expensive.

In the absence of a clear-cut standard for when the economy was sufficiently healthy that intentional deficits were not needed, zero deficit as a simple standard for self-discipline was lost. Not only did Keynesian theory provide a justification for intentional deficits, it also provided a warning that increases in taxes or reduction in expenditures could pose significant risks for economic performance. Accordingly, there have been only five years of surplus in the four decades since the end of the Eisenhower administration. For the period between 1961 and 1981, the pattern probably reflected the asymmetric incentives of Keynesian economic policy as identified by Buchanan and Wagner.

The Reagan-Bush years evidenced a substantial change in fiscal policy.[28] In the Reagan administration, deficits grew dramatically in nominal size, and somewhat less dramatically as a fraction of GDP. Total federal debt as a fraction of GDP, however, doubled from 33.5 percent in 1981 to 68.2 percent in 1992, after a more or less steady decline subsequent to World War II. The increase resulted from large tax cuts during the Reagan administration; repeated automatic increases in entitlement spending; and a shift in the stance of the Republican Party regarding taxes, the new stance being that the commitment to low taxes could override the party's commitment to balanced budgets.

Part of that change in Republican fiscal ideology seems to reflect a belief that taxes cause spending, that increases in tax revenues will not be used to reduce deficits, given the contemporary political climate, but only to increase spending. This is sometimes known as the "starve the beast hypothesis."

Econometric Studies of Budgeting Regimes

Kevin Hoover and two of his colleagues have investigated what might be considered regimes of causality between taxes and spending. Hoover and Siegler (2000) argue that for most of American history, taxes have caused spending, with one short interlude (1829–47) in which spending caused taxes. One major underlying point of their analysis is that there was consistently a causal relationship between taxing and spending, at least up to the 1960s or 1970s. Whichever was causally dominant in any given period, revenues and expenditures were systematically related, and unlikely to get too far from each other. This is consistent with budgets never getting too far out of balance until recently in the broad sweep of American history.

Hoover and Sheffrin (1992) show that the causal interdependence between taxes and spending broke down about 1970. After this shift,

---

[28] See White and Wildavsky (1989).

revenues and expenditures became causally independent. If the spending and revenue sides are each operating independently of the other, this removes the possibility of controlling one with the other, which seriously undermines the starve the beast rationale for cutting taxes. This hypothesis has been discredited by scholars as diverse as William Niskanen (2008) and Christina Romer and David Romer (2007).[29]

Two major developments undermined the mutual causality of spending and expenditures, one from the left and one from the right. One is the emergence of Keynesian economics in the 1930s and 1940s, which gave a demand side economic rationale to deficit spending under some circumstances. The other is the emergence of supply side economics, which gave a growth and productivity rationale for cutting revenues before balancing the budget. In both cases, an intellectually respectable argument has been caricatured in popular discourse.

John Maynard Keynes explained the Great Depression in terms of inadequate aggregate demand for goods and services. He suggested that government might use its taxing and spending powers to run intentional deficits to stimulate aggregate demand. Keynes himself said little about fiscal policy, but his followers developed theories of intentional deficits to stimulate the economy. Although Keynesian ideas were the initial inspiration for the Employment Act of 1946, the first policy proposal with explicitly Keynesian roots was the cut in taxes initially proposed by President Kennedy in 1961 and enacted in 1964.

The economic success of these tax cuts was later claimed by a group of economists and policy advisors who called themselves "supply siders." Supply side economics was driven by two ideas. One was that economic agents responded to higher taxes by working less. Therefore, beyond a certain point, higher tax rates would bring in less revenue, rather than more. From this, it was a short step to arguing that lower taxes could, and would, increase revenue.

The second idea was that low taxes would be a mechanism to starve the beast of big government. This idea, of course, was based on the argument that taxes cause spending. As we have seen from the work of Kevin Hoover and his colleagues, there have been times in U.S. history when this might have worked, but since the late 1960s (and before the political emergence of supply side economics) that causal connection had become broken.

---

[29] These inferences by Hoover et al. are congruent with those of other observers of the budgetary process from political science as well as economics (see Hoover 2001, pp. 246–8.)

A third idea is that higher taxes hinder economic growth. There is something to this, but a specific level or target for taxes above zero is rarely articulated or defended. Nor is it widely acknowledged by tax opponents that government can and does provide public goods such as transportation infrastructure, education, and research that enhance economic growth, or that large public debt also hinders economic growth (Elmendorf and Mankiw 1999).

So in very different ways, both Keynesian and supply side economics gave substantive economic rationales to raise government expenditures or to lower the level of taxes (respectively) that were independent of basic fiscal balance. For the Keynesians, it might not be time to balance the budget because the economy is not yet at full employment. For the supply siders, there was always a rationale to cut taxes regardless of expenditures to improve incentives to work and invest. James Buchanan and Richard Wagner wrote a book-length essay about how, regardless of the quality of the intellectual rationale, Keynesian economics gave a political rationale for deficit spending (1977). Supply side thinking about taxes has suffused political discourse to the extent that almost no serious politician now speaks of raising taxes on anybody but "the rich." As a result, there is little recourse for revenue increases that are not vulnerable to cries of "class warfare."

ACCOUNTABILITY, RULES, DISCRETION, AND THE POLITICAL PROCESS

We have identified numerous situations in which, intentionally or otherwise, decisions have had consequences that have outlasted the office tenure of those who created them, such as indebtedness and the creation of a pay-as-you-go Social Security system. Under such circumstances, elections do not provide an effective means of holding public officials accountable. Even when the dimensions of the consequences of decisions are visible, as in the savings and loan crisis, the separation of powers precludes any clear process for holding incumbents accountable, unless it is to throw all of the rascals out. But when much of the responsibility lies with former presidents and with members of Congress who have been out of office for years, wholesale punishment of those currently in office makes less sense.

Efforts to change the rules and procedures of the political process are usually efforts to change outcomes. Charles Stewart has shown that efforts to centralize control of the spending process, such as the Budget and Accounting Act of 1921, may have been victories for the effort to limit expenditures. A coalition that succeeds in doing that can not only enjoy its victory at the time the change is passed, but it can also enjoy an extension of that victory over time, for the rules it creates will constrain and guide future majorities that have different preferences. However, rules can merely guide the aggregation of preferences; they may not prevail over new majorities that are determined to go in a different direction, such as to cut taxes or to spend more generously. This is apparent in the failure of the 1974 Budget and Impoundment Control Act to eliminate the deficits.

Recalling Plott's fundamental equation of social choice, we see that the institutions process preferences into outcomes:

$$\text{preferences} \times \text{institutions} \rightarrow \text{outcomes}$$

Advocates of procedural change hope that a new procedure will process the preferences into outcomes that they prefer. However, certain preferences may not be translatable into certain outcomes by any procedure, and so long as we consider the preferences as fixed and given (i.e., exogenous), there may be little that can be done to improve outcomes. Preferences for keeping entitlements up and taxes down cannot be translated through any existing institution into balanced budgets when automatic policy keeps expenditures rising and taxes constant.

Yet, as I have argued in Chapter 7, voter preferences are not always fixed, and voters may adapt their preferences to what they think is possible, or even to what they think is inevitable. Indeed, most people have a variety of opinions, some of which may be incompatible with one another, and this is not necessarily evidence of irrationality. A good example concerns preferences for spending, wherein individuals want, simultaneously, low taxes, high expenditures, and balanced budgets – incompatible combinations. As David Stockman has shown with the "budget quiz" he gave to Ronald Reagan, even presidents are not immune to such inconsistency (1986, pp. 356–7). It may be useful to consider individuals as composed of multiple "selves" with multiple, and not necessarily compatible, desires.

Efforts to impose rules for outcomes, such as the GRH law, are efforts to elevate one "self" and one set of preferences above others. This effort seems to have failed on the federal level, but this kind of provision seems to have worked on the state level. As Poterba (1994) has shown, there are a great variety of provisions for budgetary restraint among the states, and many of them seem to work. One difference between the state and federal experiences is that most state rules have been in place throughout the contemporary era and have been operating to avoid massive buildup of debt. It is not clear that they would have worked as well as they have if they had been imposed after the creation of large debts.[30] In any case, the states and their experience can provide a valuable laboratory for investigating the kinds of fiscal rules that may be more effective than those that have been tried on the federal level.

The political process in a democracy aggregates fluid preferences into collective decisions through institutional processes that are themselves subject to change and manipulation. The outcomes that result are functions of the collective decisions interacting with the constraints of a world that is imperfectly understood. There is in all this interaction no Archimedean point, no firm bedrock for analysis and evaluation. The process legitimizes the outcomes, and when the outcomes are viewed as unsatisfactory, the process or the preferences may be changed.

We are able to learn about democratic processes by creating models in which certain features, such as preferences, are artificially held as fixed. In the real world, some things are more changeable than others, but little is truly fixed. Democratic processes provide for continuous feedback from outcomes to preferences and procedures. We have seen ways in which this feedback process can produce pathological outcomes, as with electoral cycles or with budget deficits. The shift to pathological outcomes is not inevitable, and broader experience shows that it is not irreversible.

Still, it appears that the formal institutions and the informal norms of fiscal policy have not provided adequate restraints against the temptation to let expenditures outpace revenues, or against the unprecedented peacetime expansion of debt as a fraction of GDP. The institutions of electoral accountability, which are fundamentally the institutions of restraint against governmental arbitrariness or tyranny, have not been notably effective in curbing the temptations to permit expenditures to outpace revenues and to allow short-term perspectives to override the long view.

---

[30] Actually, Brown (1990) suggested that the rules were created in the 1830s after massive deficits had been built up in the states.

PART FIVE

CONCLUSION

The first edition of this book spoke of a "deep and fundamental faith in democratic institutions," based largely on an analysis of political and economic practice in the United States. Recent experience has shaken that faith. I have learned more about democracy in the years since the first edition. It was not previously apparent to me how much the good economic performance of democracy in the United States was contingent on practices that are not part of the definition of democracy.

Since that first edition, the United States has experienced soaring government indebtedness, unintended adverse consequences of an effort to make housing more affordable, and massive moral hazard and time-consistency problems in the financial system. Each of these was permitted or encouraged by the incentives of electoral politics and by limitations on government, the two essential features of democratic institutions. To paraphrase Winston Churchill, American democracy may ultimately do the right things, but it is trying many alternatives before getting to them. And by the time it does them, it may have reduced its own standard of living and position of leadership in the world.

10

The Costs and Risks of Democracy

The world's richest and freest countries are democracies. More than any other political system, democracies have the capacity to correct themselves. Democracy is basically about procedures, in contrast to political systems defined by eligible rulers, such as monarchs, military dictators, or other types of authoritarian rulers. The central procedural feature of modern democracy is elections, which provide the opportunity to replace the incumbents with alternatives. This is Riker's (1982) minimalist liberal democracy, the opportunity to throw the rascals out, with no claims made about who or what will replace a rejected government.

Democracies can perform well or badly, The first edition of this book suggested that democracy in the United States was doing rather well when measured by its macroeconomic performance, even though the book was guided and informed by models and theories that emphasized that politicians might be motivated by careerist and opportunistic goals, rather than by a desire to deliver good policy and good performance for its own sake. The previous version found little evidence of policy or performance that was systematically inferior because of opportunistic behavior.

This version has emphasized different problems: unintended consequences, moral hazard, and time-consistency. It has emphasized suspicion and distrust between the major parties. The first edition interpreted voting behavior in the United States as not systematically demanding inferior or suboptimal policy. This may still be true, but the context has changed so that elections may no longer be as constructive or even as neutral as they were. Something in the options being offered to voters makes elections more risky than they were. And something in the implementation of checks and balances and of limitations on government is also not constructive.

The institutions of macroeconomic policy making are no longer working as well as they did. Monetary institutions and practices had actually improved since 1979, and the Great Moderation was a distinct improvement in monetary policy making. But monetary institutions were not blameless in bringing on the financial crisis. Once it was here, a case can be made that the Federal Reserve has acted in a constructive way. An alternative case can also be made, of course, and I have tried to be agnostic in the chapter on monetary policy and institutions.

Fiscal institutions and policy making are another matter. The United States has no coherent fiscal policy. The capacity of the United States to pay its bills and honor its obligations is not questionable, but its willingness do so was brought into considerable doubt with the debt limit fiasco of 2011. The cause of the deadlock was unwillingness to compromise. In my view, even though this unwillingness was shared by both parties, the Republican Party has become more rigid and uncompromising. The Grover Norquist pledge not to raise taxes under any circumstances, signed by most Republicans and a few Democrats, has become a major obstacle to sensible fiscal policy.

This statement may reflect a value judgment, so let me step back from the political agnosticism that I mean to characterize this book. The value that drives this judgment is a moral obligation for a country to pay its bills. I take seriously the idea that appropriate government actions should be linked to the list of powers of Congress in Article I, section 8, of the Constitution, and I welcome the Republican-inspired move to demand that all legislative proposals be linked to specific provisions of the Constitution. I would welcome a serious reevaluation of government programs to ensure that they pass constitutional muster. Just as the federal tax code includes many loopholes and preferences that cry out for tax reform, I believe that the current set of programs and policies would benefit from a fresh, constitutionally based look.

So my judgments are not driven by a preference for any particular size and scope of government, though I am sympathetic with open, honest, principled efforts to reduce both. In general, I support markets as the basic means of deciding the allocation of resources and income. I support government policies that help markets work, such as property rights and the enforcement of contracts, and policies that solve collective action problems that markets do not solve.[1]

That said, I expect that the expenditure side of the federal government is larger than I would choose, and that it is riddled with efficiency-sapping

---

[1]   See Cooter and Siegel (2010) for an outstanding effort to link collective action problems to Article I, section 8.

provisions that are responsive to special interests and campaign contributions. Similarly, the internal revenue code is riddled with comparable provisions that reward votes or influence but have little justification in efficiency-oriented policy analysis. Still, it appears to me that there is genuine popular support for most of the expenditures of the federal government. Sometimes this is broad, as in support for Social Security and Medicare; sometimes it is narrow, as in support for agricultural policy.

Similarly, I am sure that the country would benefit enormously from a streamlining of the tax code, as in the Tax Reform Act of 1986. Many deductions are inefficient and go mainly to people who need them the least (see Mettler 2011). A thorough tax reform would raise considerable revenue without raising marginal rates.

Even though the structure and pattern of federal public expenditures and revenues are nowhere near what might be chosen by an efficiency- and growth-oriented benevolent dictator, they were all for the most part legitimately chosen through a democratic process. I find it unconscionable that our elected officials cannot agree on a program to match expenditures with revenues by lowering the former and raising the latter.

This book has investigated macroeconomic policy making in order to make inferences about the nature and consequences of democratic institutions, to get a grasp on problems that may be inherent in them, and to understand how alternative formulations of these institutions might affect performance. It has focused on recent experience in the United States. The concentration on macroeconomic issues has facilitated the evaluation of performance. The concentration on one nation has facilitated an understanding of the importance of process in democracy, and it has permitted an assessment of the consequences of institutional changes over time in that country.

However, economic performance is only one of the many values that may be facilitated or hindered by democratic institutions, and a focus on one country obscures an understanding of the ways in which alternative institutions that vary across countries can affect performance. In this final chapter, we consider some ways in which the single-country focus may be complemented by further investigation, though without speculating beyond macroeconomic issues. But first, a reflection on some of the implications of the methodological approach used in much of the analysis.

DEMOCRATIC POLITICS AND ECONOMIC METHOD

The book has used economic analysis in a sense that goes beyond the obvious character of the subject matter. A fundamental characteristic of economics is the method of constrained optimization. Economics is about how to identify the choices that will maximize welfare functions or minimize loss functions, subject to the constraint of possibility. Much of the traditional economic approach to policy analysis is, in effect, about how to give advice to benevolent dictators, who are presumed to wish to optimize some publicly oriented objective function. Modern political economics has made great strides by recognizing that those who decide public policy may have other, private motivations, such as the maximization of their prospects for reelection, of their incomes, or of some partial conception of what public policy ought to be. Models built on these features can predict the consequences of political motivations and compare them with what a benevolent dictator might do.

The optimizing methodology of economics has provided powerful leverage for understanding the nature of democratic politics. This book could not have been written without it. However, one central message of the book is that democracy cannot be adequately understood within the optimizing framework, which depends on externally defined goals for the objective functions. Chapter 6 argued that there is no authoritative or uncontestable welfare function that is not defined as part of the political process, and subject to revision in such a process. Optimizing analyses of democratic politics depend on arbitrarily defined objective functions that have no authority in the real world of democratic politics. Any theoretical comparison between the results of democratic politics and the choices of a benevolent dictator with respect to some welfare function presumes definitions of goals that, in fact, are defined only within the democratic political process.

Moreover, the diversity of views among leading macroeconomic theorists makes it clear that even if we wanted to delegate policy to a benevolent dictator, we might have to have a democratic election to decide whether he or she would be a new Keynesian or new classical. If that election were not to be a once-and-for-all choice, we might evaluate the performance of the theories that guide these benevolent dictatorships with the models of electoral accountability and choice presented in Chapters 3 and 4. Thus, even the economic method of analysis of democracy is embedded in a kind of political choice, rather than being logically antecedent. Even the imaginary alternative of a benevolent dictatorship does not escape some of the problems that must be understood as issues of democracy.

Conceptions of the preferences of voters can be used to define objective functions that can be incorporated into models of the democratic political process. Such models may suggest the ironic possibility that democratic institutions distort these same preferences into inferior policy, as in the Nordhaus (1975) model of the "political business cycle." In fact, democratic politics incorporates the selection of broad goals, the implementation of specific policies, and the evaluation of government performance in a fluid and continuous process that can be decomposed only analytically. Fiscal and monetary policy processes can produce results that are disappointing or inferior to other possible outcomes. These processes can be revised by reforms of the relevant formal institutions, but these reforms are themselves likely to have been watered down by the compromises that made them politically viable (see Primo 2007) or likely to have unanticipated consequences that lead to demands for further revision.

A leading source of undesired results is likely to be found in norms and patterns of behavior (i.e., informal institutions). Reforms of formal institutions are likely to fail if they do not take into account the incentives involved in these norms and patterns of behavior. A balanced budget amendment to the Constitution would be unlikely to have much more effect than the Gramm-Rudman-Hollings law unless people realized the magnitude of the combination of tax increases and spending cuts that would be necessary to bring revenues and expenditures in line.

Democracy is inevitably about process. Democracy can be analyzed and better understood with economic models, but the economic models hinge on some set of preferences or some objective function defined outside of the economic framework. Thus, there is a circularity to the understanding of democracy that economic models can help minimize, but from which they do not offer complete escape.

COSTS, RISKS, AND PATHOLOGIES

Still, our understanding of the costs, risks, and pathologies of democracy has depended very heavily on economic analysis. To repeat, costs are similar to prices and implicitly are to be compared to benefits. They are to be minimized, but some costs are likely to be the price of anything valuable. Risks are to be understood and minimized. A financial crisis or recession always has some nonzero risk. Prudent avoidance involves taking precautions to minimize these risks. Pathologies, on the other hand, are clearly undesirable and detrimental, associated with sickness or disease, and they need to be eliminated if at all possible.

Costs

Some costs of democracy are inevitable parts of the principal-agent character of representative government and the asymmetries of information between the electorate as principals and public officials as agents. One form of cost has to do with the backward-looking accountability issue. Just as in any principal-agent framework, there will be ways in which the government agents will try to make their performance look misleadingly good at the time that contracts are renewed, that is, at election time.

Another form of cost has to do with the forward-looking choice issue. Given the inevitable uncertainty about the consequences of choices that electorates make, there will always be ways in which the very possibility of choice carries with it costs that could be avoided only in some ideal world of perfect information. As William Bianco has observed, perfect control is impossible in all principal-agent situations in which there is asymmetric information: "The problem is not representative government; rather representative government is an example of a generic and intractable problem" (1994, p. 167).

I have discounted another candidate for a cost of democracy, one I should recognize as a possibility. This involves the failure of the public to appreciate the consequences of the actions it supports. In this view, the public supports or demands activity that makes it worse off than it might otherwise be. An example of an argument for such a cost is provided by Hibbs, who asserts that the "true" costs of inflation are not in the inflation itself, but in the recessions that are induced to curb inflation. In this view, the public is inflation averse in a way that cannot be explained by Hibbs's assessments of the objective and measurable costs: voters punish the politicians who create inflation, and they reward the politicians who create disinflationary recessions, which have more readily measurable costs (Hibbs 1987, pp. 118, 178).

I discount this view as one that depends heavily on Hibbs's own values, which are contestable in the framework I laid out in Chapter 6. His argument does not give the public enough credit for seeing real costs in inflation, even if we do not fall back on the argument that the public is the authoritative resolver of disputes of fundamental values. However, I do not mean to rule out the possibility of reasonable arguments that the public does not know the consequences of its preferences. Furthermore, when we consider preferences as endogenous, we do not need to consider observed behavior as a complete description of possible behavior. Just as individuals may change their preferences (say, for cigarettes) after learning the consequences of their preferences, so might the public change its preferences regarding something like inflation.

So, elections are the mechanism by which principals (the electorate) establish or renew contracts with their agents (elected officials). In this sense, elections are reflections of the well-known agency phenomenon.

But under asymmetric information, some costs are inevitable, and certainly bearable, especially when considered against the possibilities of no elections and no accountability or choice. Another generic cost of elections is the uncertainty that they introduce into policy making and governance, but the limitations on government feature of democracy constrain the amount of change any election can bring.

Risks and Pathologies

Democracy has been associated with patterns that some people do not like, such as redistribution of income or wealth through tax and transfer programs, a large public sector, inflation, and deficits. Opponents of these patterns may think of them as pathological tendencies of democracy, but democracy is neither necessary nor sufficient for the occurrence of such phenomena. As a general rule, such assessments are too contingent on the tastes and preferences of the observer or analyst, as distinguished from those of the electorate. The nature and extent of tax and transfer programs and the size of the public sector are matters of preference and judgment that are to be decided in a political process. Also, within certain ranges, nonzero values of inflation and government deficits may be legitimate and defensible products of democratic politics.

However, inflation and public indebtedness can go beyond tolerable ranges, though the definition of a boundary between the tolerable and intolerable is itself a matter of political judgment. Hyperinflation and unsustainably rising debt/GDP ratios are conditions that I have judged to be pathological, and democratic experience has included instances of both. For example, in the twentieth century, democratic regimes in Germany, Israel, and several Latin American countries experienced hyperinflations,[2] and Germany, Italy, Belgium, and Ireland experienced rapidly rising debt/ GDP ratios in peacetime.[3] The United States seems likely to join this group.

However, no connection necessarily exists between democracy and either hyperinflation or explosive public indebtedness. The greatest hyperinflations have occurred in countries devastated by wars (Cagan 1987), whether or not the countries were democratic. The institutional variable that is necessary (but obviously not sufficient) for hyperinflation is paper money, that is, fiat currency that is not backed by or not convertible into a commodity such as gold. Explosive growth of public debt is also associated with

[2] See Sargent (1986); Cagan (1987).
[3] See Alesina (1988b); Roubini and Sachs (1989a, 1989b).

wars. In the twentieth century, large debts have been experienced in third-world nations that have only intermittently been democratic.[4] Most democratic experiences in the United States and many other countries have not involved either hyperinflation or public debt crises. The aftermath of the global financial crisis of 2007–9 is challenging these generalizations, but there is little reason to believe that normal democratic processes have an inherent or systematic tendency to generate such pathological results.

However, among democratic institutions, evidence shows an asymmetry between the creation and elimination of problems. That is, there is reason to believe that democratic processes can systematically obstruct the resolution of pathological situations such as hyperinflation or debt crises – one of the main features of democracy is the capacity to protect one's self against the unwanted imposition of costs. Certain forms of democratic institutions do this more than others. Some democratic institutions facilitate majorities, whereas others enhance the prospect that minorities will be able to block change. The latter may better approximate popular preferences in general, although, at the same time, they may obstruct stabilization programs that would make everybody better off.

The recent financial crisis may have been enhanced by the simultaneous confluence of undesirable patterns that, by themselves, might not have had great adverse consequences. An aggressive effort to increase home ownership and lax regulation of the financial industry might not have created a national and global crisis. But the fact that these occurred at the same time as a bubble in house prices shows that poor practices may be more risky at some times than others.

INSTITUTIONAL ALTERNATIVES

The form of democracy in the United States is one of many alternatives. A useful way of classifying the alternatives was provided by Arend Lijphart (1999), who identified two pure types: majoritarian democracy and consensus democracy. Majoritarian democracy involves the concentration of executive power, cabinet dominance of a fused relationship between the cabinet and the legislature, a legislature dominated by the lower house, a two-party system organized along a single dimension, plurality elections, and centralized government. Great Britain is the classic case of this model, but Lijphart shows that New Zealand actually approximates it better. Whereas this "Westminster model" facilitates majority rule, consensus

---

[4] See Frieden (1991).

democracy restrains majorities in several ways (see also Persson and Tabellini 2003)

Consensus democracy involves the sharing of power through grand coalitions, separation of executive and legislative powers, balanced power in bicameral legislatures, multiparty systems organized along multiple dimensions, proportional representation, and federalism. Switzerland and Belgium are leading examples of this model. Lijphart described and classified thirty-six democracies according to the characteristics of these models.

The United States is obviously a hybrid, having features that facilitate and features that hinder majorities. In terms of partisan competition over the issues of inflation and unemployment rates, the United States is effectively modeled as a two-party majoritarian system, because the main differences in outcomes hinge on control of the presidency. However, for the purposes of understanding fiscal policy, the United States is more like the consensus model, because legislative changes demand agreement among dispersed powers.

Several studies have suggested that some relationships link such characteristics of the alternative democratic systems to macroeconomic performance. Roubini and Sachs have investigated the relationship between political conditions and budget deficits in OECD economies. They suggest that "when power is dispersed, either across branches of the government (as in the U.S.) or across many political parties in a coalition government (as is typical in Italy), or across parties through the alternation of political control over time, the likelihood of intertemporally inefficient budget policy is heightened" (1989a, p. 905).

Their argument is based on the experience of budget deficits in the industrial democracies. They contend that these nations were hit in the early 1970s by an exogenous shock that involved a growth slowdown and rising unemployment, and, in the late 1970s, rising interest rates. Their argument about political institutions is not that they caused the deficits that resulted from these shocks, but that they affected the efforts to reverse the deficits. This asymmetry is explained by the difficulty that coalition governments have in securing the cooperation of the several parties whose agreement is necessary for choosing and implementing a budget reduction package.

Grilli, Masciandaro, and Tabellini (1991) offer a related argument in which they find that governments with unsustainable debt growth tend to be countries with short-lived coalition governments. These authors distinguish possible sources of such patterns. One prediction is that public debts should be larger in unstable and polarized societies. This view is grounded in the theories of Alesina and Tabellini (1990) and Persson and Svensson (1989). The idea is that a government that expects to be replaced by a new government with very different preferences will actively use deficits to limit the choices of its successor in a conscious strategic move. A second prediction is more like the Roubini and Sachs view, in which unpopular but desirable policies can be blocked when the agreement of several decision makers is necessary in order to change policy. The first situation is characterized as instability, and the second as weakness.

The empirical analysis of Grilli and associates does not distinguish between the two views, but it does emphasize that government debts are highest in countries that they characterize as "representative democracies," countries that are closer to the consensus democracy pole of Lijphart's analysis. They have a high degree of "proportionality" of representation, which is indicated by the number of parliamentary seats per district: "All the countries that seem to have an unsustainable debt, except Ireland and Portugal, are governed by representational systems. Conversely, all representational democracies except Denmark have unsustainable fiscal policies" (Grilli et al. 1991, p. 351).

The studies by Roubini and Sachs and Grilli and associates recognize more than one source for the characteristics associated with undesirable debt policies. One source may be institutions that disperse power, as in the consensus model. Another may be the diversity or polarization of preferences within the system. There can be dispersed powers in a two-party system, as in the United States, but multiparty systems are likely to reflect a diversity and perhaps a polarization of preferences. Diversity of preferences and electoral systems that reflect rather than suppress diversity are unlikely to generate parties that win majorities on their own. Governments are likely to be either minority governments or coalitions of several parties.

George Tsebelis (1995, 2002) has brought both these elements into a single framework with the concept of the "veto player." He shows how either institutional actors (such as a president with a veto) or partisan actors (such as a party whose support is needed to create a parliamentary majority) can act as veto players and can have similar effects on the possibility that a political system will produce policy change. In a world in which unsustainable debts are imposed on governments by exogenous shocks, changes in policy are most likely to be obstructed in systems that enhance the power of the veto player, whether the source of veto power is institutional or partisan.[5]

---

[5]   Note echo of the McCubbins (1991) argument.

Whereas Tsebelis's argument hinges on the likelihood of a policy change away from an undefined status quo, Huber and Powell (1992) identify a different set of possible consequences of institutional alternatives. They distinguish between two "visions" of democratic processes in terms of how they may create congruence between citizen preferences and public policies. The alternatives are the "majority control" and "proportional influence" visions, and they parallel the differences between Lijphart's majoritarian and consensus models of democracy. However, Huber and Powell show how the political process in each might lead government policy to approximate popular preferences, after which they compare the cases empirically. From a test involving thirty-eight governments in twelve nations, they conclude that the proportionate influence vision of democratic processes does a better job of ensuring congruence of popular preferences and government policy.

The research reported in this section is provocative, though not conclusive. Even if we were to conclude that one set of institutional alternatives was inferior with respect to some indicator of macroeconomic performance, as two articles suggest, we would have to be prepared to consider that that set might have advantages with respect to other criteria of democratic values.[6]

REFLECTIONS

I have tried to minimize the degree to which my own values, beliefs, and preferences have influenced the message of this book, but there are limits to how successful such an effort can be. Recent experience has shaken the deep and fundamental faith in democratic institutions that I expressed in the first edition. This book is a revised attempt to confront honestly the worst that can be said about democracy in the context of macroeconomic performance, and to acknowledge the costs, risks, and pathologies of democratic practice in the real world.

Democratic institutions have produced plenty of policies and outcomes that I would not seek and do not approve of, but in many of those cases, the people were getting what they wanted. That is what democratic government is about. Occasionally, we find that people do not like the consequences of their choices, and the analyst trained in political economy may be able to suggest institutional changes that can improve the situation. But another message of this book is that institutional reforms often have unanticipated

---

[6]   See Shepsle (1988).

consequences, and that it is not easy to fix the undesired consequences of deeply held preferences with a new procedure or a new rule.

This book has emphasized the importance of informal institutions, or norms. The informal, unwritten norms regarding budget balance that prevailed before the 1960s were far more powerful in constraining deficits than were the written rules of the Gramm-Rudman-Hollings law, and I am convinced that they cannot be regenerated simply by putting a version of that deficit reduction rule into the Constitution. It would be best of all, perhaps, to recreate the old norms, but that task would be comparable to putting toothpaste back into a tube.

In many respects, this is a conservative book. I believe that there is always a risk of expecting too much from democratic government. I have recognized the foresight of the Republicans of the 1930s who opposed Social Security by entitlement. I have defended the instincts, if not the stated arguments, of those who insisted on watering down the full employment bill into the Employment Act of 1946. In hindsight, I believe that undermining the norm of balanced budgets in the 1960s was regrettable (though I did not think so at the time), because the ensuing lack of fiscal discipline is not, in my view, worth the extra stimulus. And I have defended the independence of the Federal Reserve as a monetary counterweight to the popularly based biases that now exist in fiscal institutions.

Though it is still a conservative book, and though the experience since the first edition is less about inevitable costs and more about risks and avoidable pathologies, it is still a defense of democratic institutions, in which an attempt has been made to step back from the preferences of observers and to recognize that many of the features of democratic politics involve people getting what they want. What they want is often different from what the observer or analyst wants, but in a framework of democratic values, it must be acknowledged if not respected. And what "the people" want is no easier to pin down that any other element of the fundamental equation relating preferences, institutions, and outcomes. People learn to want what they can get, but they can also change their minds if they see that they do not like what they wanted and got. In this way, changing patterns of preferences can lead to improvements or to deterioration in economic performance under democratic institutions.

The experience since the first edition of this book has highlighted the informal, unwritten practices and institutions that make the formal institutions of democracy work better. The previous version was sympathetic to rules, and this stance is intensified in this revised edition. Many of the policies that led us astray were efforts to give the people what they want.

Had there been stronger informal institutions of restraint, some of our problems, particularly in fiscal policy, might not have emerged.

There are no Archimedean points in democratic politics.[7] Even public preferences, which are fundamental, do not provide bedrock for analysis and evaluation. Rather, democratic politics is inherently about process. The process aggregates and filters preferences via institutions into outcomes, but the process also modifies the preferences in a public discourse.

In teaching the material in this book, I have occasionally found that I have either created or reinforced cynicism about democratic institutions. Although that has not been my intention, I can see how cynicism might emerge from a systematic review of the possibilities and consequences of selfishness and opportunism in democratic politics. A certain amount of cynicism is a healthy thing: it is surely better than naïveté. Yet, I still see in this material a far more positive and hopeful view of democratic institutions, even though opportunism does occur in democratic institutions, as it does in markets and bureaucracies.

Adam Smith pointed out, more than two centuries ago, that the market guides individual selfishness into social well-being, and modern microeconomic theory has developed Smith's insights into a coherent theory of competitive markets that is the crowning achievement of the social sciences.[8] There is no comparable theory that shows that competitive politics in a democracy has the same optimizing features as perfect markets under pure competition.[9] Indeed, Kenneth Arrow (1963), one of the theorists who demonstrated the optimizing qualities of markets, demonstrated the "impossibility" of similarly perfect democratic institutions. If perfection is impossible, or even undefinable, that suggests to me that tolerance of imperfections is in order. But we have found out that the political process in democratic institutions can lead us into situations that are inferior to realistic alternatives.

---

[7]　Grafstein said that "we have met the Archimedean point and it is us" (1990, p. 178).
[8]　See Arrow and Hahn (1971).
[9]　But see Wittman (1989).

References

Abrams, Burton A., and James L. Butkiewicz. 2012. The Political Business Cycle: New Evidence from the Nixon Tapes. *Journal of Money, Credit and Banking* 44: 385–99.

Achen, Christopher H. 2012. When Is Myopic Retrospection Rational? Prepared for delivery at the Annual Meeting of the American Political Science Association, New Orleans.

Achen, Christopher H., and Larry M. Bartels. 2004. Musical Chairs: Pocketbook Voting and the Limits of Democratic Accountability. Presented at the annual meeting of the American Political Science Association, Chicago.

Ahamed, Liaquat. 2009. *Lords of Finance: The Bankers Who Broke the World.* New York: Penguin Books.

Akerlof, George, and Robert Shiller. 2009. *Animal Spirits: How Human Psychology Drives the Economy and Why It Matters for Global Capitalism.* Princeton, NJ: Princeton University Press.

Aldrich, John H., and David W. Rohde. 2000. The Consequences of Party Organization in the House: The Role of the Majority and Minority Parties in Conditional Party Government. In Jon R. Bond and Richard Fleisher (eds.), *Polarized Politics: Congress and the President in a Partisan Era*, pp. 31–72. Washington, DC: CQ Press.

Alesina, Alberto. 1987. Macroeconomic Policy in a Two-Party System as a Repeated Game. *Quarterly Journal of Economics* 102: 651–78.

Alesina, Alberto. 1988a. Credibility and Policy Convergence in a Two-Party System with Rational Voters. *American Economic Review* 78: 796–805.

Alesina, Alberto. 1988b. The End of Large Public Debts. In Francesco Giavazzi and Luigi Spaventa (eds.), *High Public Debt: The Italian Experience*, pp. 34–89. New York: Cambridge University Press.

Alesina, Alberto. 1995. Elections, Party Structure and the Economy. In Jeff Banks and Eric Hanuschek (eds.), *Modern Political Economy: Old Topics, New Directions*, pp. 145–70. New York: Cambridge University Press.

Alesina, Alberto, Gerald D. Cohen, and Nouriel Roubini. 1992a. Macroeconomic Policy and Elections in OECD Democracies. In Alex Cukierman, Zvi Hercowitz, and Leonardo Leiderman (eds.), *Political Economy, Growth, and Business Cycles*, pp. 227–62. Cambridge, MA: MIT Press.

Alesina, Alberto, Gerald D. Cohen, and Nouriel Roubini. 1992b. Macroeconomic Policy and Elections in OECD Democracies. *Economics and Politics* 4: 1–30.

Alesina, Alberto, and Alex Cukierman. 1990. The Politics of Ambiguity. *Quarterly Journal of Economics* 105: 829–50.

Alesina, Alberto, and Allen Drazen. 1991. Why Are Stabilizations Delayed? *American Economic Review* 81: 1170–88.

Alesina, Alberto, John Londregan, and Howard Rosenthal. 1993. A Model of the Political Economy of the United States. *American Political Science Review* 87: 12–33.

Alesina, Alberto, and Howard Rosenthal. 1994. *Partisan Politics, Divided Government, and the Economy.* New York: Cambridge University Press.

Alesina, Alberto, and Jeffrey Sachs. 1988. Political Parties and the Business Cycle in the United States, 1948–1984. *Journal of Money, Credit, and Banking* 20: 63–82.

Alesina, Alberto, and Lawrence H. Summers. 1993. Central Bank Independence and Macroeconomic Performance. *Journal of Money, Credit, and Banking* 25: 151–62.

Alesina, Alberto, and Guido Tabellini. 1990. A Positive Theory of Budget Deficits and Government Debt. *Review of Economic Studies* 57: 403–14.

Alt, James E. 1979. *The Politics of Economic Decline: Economic Management and Political Behaviour in Britain since 1964.* New York: Cambridge University Press.

Alt, James E. 1985. Political Parties, World Demand, and Unemployment: Domestic and International Sources of Economic Activity. *American Political Science Review* 79: 1016–40.

Alt, James E. 1991. Leaning into the Wind or Ducking out of the Storm: U.S. Monetary Policy in the 1980s. In Alberto Alesina and Geoffrey Carliner (eds.), *Politics and Economics in the Eighties*, pp. 41–82. Chicago: University of Chicago Press.

Alt, James E., and K. Alex Chrystal. 1983. *Political Economics.* Berkeley: University of California Press.

Alt, James E., and Robert Lowry. 1994. Divided Government, Fiscal Institutions, and Budget Deficits: Evidence from the States. *American Political Science Review* 88: 759–74.

Alt, James E., and Charles Stewart III. 1990. *Parties and the Deficit: Some Historical Evidence.* Unpublished manuscript, Department of Government, Harvard University.

Alt, James E., and John T. Woolley. 1982. Reaction Functions, Optimization, and Politics: Modelling the Political Economy of Macroeconomic Policy. *American Journal of Political Science* 26: 709–40.

Aluise, Joseph. 1991. *The Microeconomic Foundations of the Natural Rate of Unemployment and the Leverage of Political Parties.* Unpublished manuscript, University of North Carolina at Chapel Hill.

Alvarez, R. Michael, Geoffrey Garrett, and Peter Lange. 1991. Government Partisanship, Labor Organization, and Macroeconomic Performance. *American Political Science Review* 85: 539–56.

Andrabi, Tahir. 1993. *Seignorage, Taxation, and Weak Government.* Unpublished manuscript, Department of Economics, Pomona College.

Ariely, Dan. 2008. *Predictably Irrational: The Hidden Forces That Shape Our Decisions.* New York: HarperCollins Publishers.

Arndt, H. W. 1978. *The Rise and Fall of Economic Growth: A Study in Contemporary Thought.* Chicago: University of Chicago Press.

Arrow, Kenneth J. 1963. *Social Choice and Individual Values,* 2nd ed. New York: Wiley.

Arrow, Kenneth J., and F. H. Hahn. 1971. *General Competitive Analysis.* San Francisco: Holden-Day.

Asher, Martin A., Robert H. DeFina, and Kishor Thanawala. 1993. The Misery Index: Only Part of the Story. *Challenge* 36(2): 58–62.

Auerbach, Alan J. 2008. Federal Budget Rules: The U.S. Experience. *Swedish Economic Policy Review* 15(1): 57–82.

Auerbach, Alan J., William G. Gale, and Benjamin H. Harris. 2010. Activist Fiscal Policy. *Journal of Economic Perspectives* 24(4, Fall): 141–64.

Bagehot, Walter. 1873/2012. *Lombard Street: A Description of the Money Market*. Seattle: Amazon.com.

Bailey, Stephen K. 1950. *Congress Makes a Law: The Story Behind the Employment Act of 1946*. New York: Columbia University Press.

Balke, Nathan S. 1991. Partisanship Theory, Macroeconomic Outcomes, and Endogenous Elections. *Southern Economic Journal* 57: 920–34.

Baron, David P. 1991. Majoritarian Incentives, Pork Barrel Programs, and Procedural Control. *American Journal of Political Science* 35: 57–90.

Barro, Robert J. 1973. The Control of Politicians: An Economic Model. *Public Choice* 14: 19–42.

Barro, Robert J. 1979. On the Determination of the Public Debt. *Journal of Political Economy* 87: 940–71.

Barro, Robert J. 1986. U.S. Deficits since World War I. *Scandinavian Journal of Economics* 88: 195–222.

Barro, Robert J., and David Gordon. 1983. Rules, Discretion, and Reputation in a Model of Monetary Policy. *Journal of Monetary Economics* 12: 101–22.

Bartels, Larry M. 2008. *Unequal Democracy: The Political Economy of the New Gilded Age*. Princeton, NJ: Princeton University Press.

Bartlett, Bruce. 2009. *The New American Economy: The Failure of Reaganomics and a New Way Forward*. New York: Palgrave Macmillan.

Baumgartner, Frank, and Bryan D. Jones. 2009. *Agendas and Instability in American Politics*. Chicago: University of Chicago Press.

Beck, Nathaniel. 1982. Parties, Administrations, and American Macroeconomic Outcomes. *American Political Science Review* 76: 83–93.

Beck, Thorsten, George Clarke, Alberto Groff, Philip Keefer, and Patrick Walsh. 2001. New Tools in Comparative Political Economy: The Database of Political Institutions. *World Bank Economic Review*. 15: 165–76.

Berdejó, Carlos and Daniel Chen. 2010. Priming Ideology: Electoral Cycles among Unelected Judges. Working paper, Duke University Law School.

Bernhard, William, J. Lawrence Broz, and William Roberts Clark. 2003. *The Political Economy of Monetary Institutions*. Cambridge, MA: MIT Press.

Bernholz, Peter. 2003. *Monetary Regimes and Inflation: History, Economics and Political Relationships*. Northampton, MA: Edward Elgar Publishing, Inc.

Besley, Timothy. 2006. *Principled Agents: The Political Economy of Good Government*. New York: Oxford University Press.

Bianco, William T. 1994. *A Proper Responsibility: Representatives, Constituents, and Decisions about Trust*. Ann Arbor: University of Michigan Press.

Blais, Andre, Donald Blake, and Stephane Dion. 1993. Do Parties Make a Difference? Parties and the Size of Government in Liberal Democracies. *American Journal of Political Science* 37: 40–62.

Blanchard, Olivier. 2009. The State of Macro. *Annual Review of Economics* 1:209–28. Accessible online at econ.annualreviews.org. NBER Working Paper 14259.

Blanchard, Olivier, and Stanley Fischer. 1989. *Lectures on Macroeconomics*. Cambridge, MA: MIT Press.

Blanchard, Olivier, and John Simon. 2001. The Long and Large Decline in U.S. Output Volatility. *Brookings Papers on Economic Activity*, 135–74.

Blinder, Alan S. 1987. *Hard Heads, Soft Hearts: Tough Minded Economics for a Just Society*. Reading, MA: Addison-Wesley.

Blinder, Alan S. 2006. The Case against the Case against Fiscal Policy. Chapter 2 in Richard W. Kopke, Geoffrey M. B. Tootell, and Robert K. Triest (eds.), *The Macroeconomics of Fiscal Policy*. Cambridge, MA: MIT Press.

Blinder, Alan S. 2013. *After the Music Stopped: The Financial Crisis, the Response, and the Work Ahead*. New York: The Penguin Press.

Blinder, Alan S., and Douglas Holtz-Eakin. 1984. Public Opinion and the Balanced Budget. *American Economic Review, Papers and Proceedings* 74: 144–49.

Blinder, Alan S., and Robert M. Solow. 1974. Analytical Foundations of Fiscal Policy. In Alan S. Blinder et al. (eds.), *The Economics of Public Finance*, pp. 3–115. Washington, DC: Brookings Institution.

Bordo, Michael D. 1990. The Lender of Last Resort: Alternative Views and Historical Experience. *Federal Reserve Bank of Richmond Economic Review* January/February.

Bordo, Michael D., and David C. Wheelock. 2011. The Promise and Performance of the Federal Reserve as Lender of Last Resort 1914–1933. Cambridge, MA: National Bureau of Economic Research. Working Paper 16763. (Originally prepared for the Federal Reserve Bank of Atlanta Conference Commemorating the 100th Anniversary of the Jekyll Island Conference, Jekyll Island, GA, November 5–6, 2010.)

Brady, David, and Mark A. Morgan. 1987. Reforming the Structure of the House Appropriations Process: The effects of the 1885 and 1919–20 Reforms on Money Decisions. In Mathew McCubbins and Terry Sullivan (eds.), *Congress: Structure and Policy*, pp. 207–34. New York: Cambridge University Press.

Bratton, Kathleen A. 1994. Retrospective Voting and Future Expectations: The Case of the Budget Deficit in the 1988 Election. *American Politics Quarterly* 22: 277–96.

Brender, Adi, and Allan Drazen. 2005. Political Budget Cycles in New versus Established Democracies. *Journal of Monetary Economics* 52: 1271–95.

Brown, E. Cary. 1956. Fiscal Policy in the "Thirties": A Reappraisal. *American Economic Review* 46: 857–79.

Brown, E. Cary. 1990. Episodes in the Public Debt History of the United States. In Rudiger Dornbusch and Mario Draghi (eds.), *Public Debt Management: Theory and History*, pp. 229–62. New York: Cambridge University Press.

Broz, J. Lawrence. 1993. *Wresting the Scepter from London: The International Political Economy of the Founding of the Federal Reserve*. Doctoral dissertation, University of California at Los Angeles.

Broz, J. Lawrence. 1997. *The International Origins of the Federal Reserve System*. Ithaca, NY: Cornell University Press.

Bryant, Ralph C. 1980. *Money and Monetary Policy in Interdependent Nations*. Washington, DC: Brookings Institution.

Buchanan, James M. 1969. *Cost and Choice: An Inquiry in Economic Theory*. Chicago: Markham Publishing Company.

Buchanan, James M., Charles K. Rowley, and Robert D. Tollison (eds.). 1986. *Deficits.* Oxford, UK: Basil Blackwell.

Buchanan, James M., and Richard E. Wagner. 1977. *Democracy in Deficit: The Political Legacy of Lord Keynes.* New York: Academic Press.

Budge, Ian, and Richard I. Hofferbert. 1990. Mandates and Policy Outputs: U.S. Party Platforms and Federal Expenditures. *American Political Science Review* 84: 111–32.

Cagan, Phillip. 1987. Hyperinflation. In John Eatwell, Murray Milgate, and Peter Newman (eds.), *The New Palgrave: A Dictionary of Economics,* vol. 2, pp. 704–6. London: Macmillan.

Campbell, James E. 2011. The Economic Records of the Presidents: Party Differences and Inherited Economic Conditions. *Forum* 9: 1–29.

Canes-Wrone, Brandice. 2006. *Who Leads Whom? Presidents, Policy, and the Public.* Chicago: University of Chicago Press.

Canes-Wrone, Brandice, and Jee-Kwang Park. 2012. Electoral Business Cycles in OECD Countries. *American Political Science Review* 106: 103–22.

Caplan, Bryan. 2007. *The Myth of the Rational Voter: Why Democracies Choose Bad Policies.* Princeton, NJ: Princeton University Press.

Carpenter, Daniel. 2010. Institutional Strangulation: Bureaucratic Politics and Financial Reform in the Obama Administration. *Perspectives on Politics* 8(3): 825–46.

Cassidy, John. 2009. *How Markets Fail: The Logic of Economic Calamities.* New York: Farrar, Straus and Giroux.

Chappell, Henry W., Jr., Thomas M. Havrilesky, and Rob Roy MacGregor. 1993. Partisan Monetary Policies: Presidential Influence through the Power of Appointment. *Quarterly Journal of Economics* 108: 185–219.

Chappell, Henry W., Jr., and William R. Keech. 1985a. A New View of Accountability for Economic Performance. *American Political Science Review* 79: 10–27.

Chappell, Henry W., Jr., and William R. Keech. 1985b. The Political Viability of Rule-based Monetary Policy. *Public Choice* 46: 125–40.

Chappell, Henry W., Jr., and William R. Keech. 1986a. Party Differences in Macroeconomic Policies and Outcomes. *American Economic Review, Papers and Proceedings* 76: 71–4.

Chappell, Henry W., Jr., and William R. Keech. 1986b. Policy Motivations and Party Differences in a Dynamic Spatial Model of Party Competition. *American Political Science Review* 80: 881–99.

Chappell, Henry W., Jr., and William R. Keech. 1988a. The Unemployment Consequences of Partisan Monetary Policy. *Southern Economic Journal* 55: 107–22.

Chappell, Henry W., Jr., and William R. Keech. 1988b. Choice and Circumstance: The Consequences of Partisan Macroeconomic Policies. Paper presented at the annual meeting of the American Political Science Association, Washington, DC.

Chappell, Henry W., Jr., Rob Roy McGregor, and Todd A. Vermilyea. 2005. *Committee Decisions on Monetary Policy: Evidence from Historical Records of the Federal Open Market Committee.* Cambridge, MA: MIT Press.

Cheibub, José Antonio, Jennifer Gandhi, and James Raymond Vreeland. 2010. Democracy and Dictatorship Revisited. *Public Choice* 143: 67–101.

Clarida, Richard, Jordi Galí, and Mark Gertler. 2000. Monetary Policy Rules and Macroeconomic Stability: Evidence and Some Theory. *Quarterly Journal of Economics* 115: 147–80.

Clark, William Roberts, Sona Golder, and Paul Poast. 2012. Monetary Institutions and the Political Survival of Democratic Leaders. *International Studies Quarterly* (first published online in November).

Clark, William Roberts, and Vincent Arel-Bundock. 2013. Independent but not Indifferent: Partisan Bias in Monetary Policy at the Fed. *Economics and Politics* 25: 1–25.

Cole, Harold L., and Lee E. Ohanian. 2004. Great Depression: A Neoclassical Analysis. *Journal of Political Economy* 112: 779–816.

Collender, Stanley E. 1992. *A Guide to the Federal Budget, Fiscal 1993*. Washington, DC: Urban Institute Press.

Comiskey, Michael, and Lawrence C. Marsh. 2012. Presidents, Parties, and the Business Cycle, 1949–2009. *Presidential Studies Quarterly* 42: 59.

Conley, Patricia Heidotting. 2001. *Presidential Mandates: How Elections Shape the National Agenda*. Chicago: University of Chicago Press.

Cooter, Robert D., and Neil Siegel. 2010. Collective Action Federalism: A General Theory of Article I, Section 8. *Stanford Law Review* 63: 115–85.

Cukierman, Alex. 1992. *Central Bank Strategy, Credibility, and Independence*. Cambridge, MA: MIT Press.

Cukierman, Alex, and Allan Meltzer. 1986. A Positive Theory of Discretionary Policy, the Costs of Democratic Government, and the Benefits of a Constitution. *Economic Inquiry* 24: 367–88.

Cukierman, Alex, and Allan Meltzer. 1989. A Political Theory of Government Debt and Deficits in a Neo-Ricardian Framework. *American Economic Review* 79: 69–95.

Cukierman, Alex, and Mariano Tommasi. 1998. When Does It Take a Nixon to Go to China? *American Economic Review* 88: 180–97.

Dahl, Robert A. 1971. *Polyarchy: Participation and Opposition*. New Haven, CT: Yale University Press.

Dahl, Robert A. 1989. *Democracy and Its Critics*. New Haven, CT: Yale University Press.

Dahl, Robert A. 2002. *How Democratic Is the American Constitution?* New Haven, CT: Yale University Press.

Dam, Kenneth. 1982. *The Rules of the Game*. Chicago: University of Chicago Press.

DeVroey, Michel, and Pedro Garcia Duarte. 2012. In Search of Lost Time: The Neoclassical Synthesis. Sao Paolo, Brazil: USP Department of Economics. Working Paper #2012-07. http://ssrn.com/abstract=2199668

Downs, Anthony. 1957. *An Economic Theory of Democracy*. New York: Harper.

Drazen, Allan. 2000. *Political Economy in Macroeconomics*. Princeton, NJ: Princeton University Press.

Dryzek, John S. 1990. *Discursive Democracy: Politics, Policy, and Political Science*. New York: Cambridge University Press.

Duch, Raymond M., and Randolph T. Stevenson. 2008. *The Economic Vote: How Political and Economic Institutions Condition Election Results*. New York: Cambridge University Press.

Dynan, Karen E., Douglas W. Elmendorf, and Daniel E. Sichel. 2006. Can Financial Innovation Help to Explain the Reduced Volatility of Economic Activity? *Journal of Monetary Economics* 53: 123–50.

Economic Report of the President. Washington, DC: U.S. Government Printing Office. Various years.

Edwards, George C, III. 1990. *Presidential Approval: A Sourcebook*. Baltimore: Johns Hopkins University Press.

Eichengreen, Barry (ed.). 1985. *The Gold Standard in Theory and History*. New York: Methuen.

Eichengreen, Barry. 1992a. *Golden Fetters: The Gold Standard and the Great Depression*. New York: Oxford University Press.

Eichengreen, Barry. 1992b. Designing a Central Bank for Europe: A Cautionary Tale from the Early Years of the Federal Reserve System. In Matthew B. Canzoneri, Vittorio Grilli, and Paul R. Masson (eds.), *Establishing a Central Bank: Issues in Europe and Lessons from the U.S.*, pp. 13–48. Cambridge, UK: Cambridge University Press.

Eisner, Robert. 1986. *How Real Is the Federal Deficit?* New York: Free Press.

Elmendorf, Douglas W., and N. Gregory Mankiw. 1999. Government Debt. In John B. Taylor and Michael Woodford (eds.), *Handbook of Macroeconomics*, pp. 1615–69. Amsterdam: Elsevier.

Erikson, Robert S. 1989. Economic Conditions and the Presidential Vote. *American Political Science Review* 83: 567–73.

Erikson, Robert S. 1990. Economic Conditions and the Congressional Vote: A Review of the Macrolevel Evidence. *American Journal of Political Science* 34: 373–399.

Erikson, Robert S., Michael B. MacKuen, and James A. Stimson. 2000. Bankers or Peasants Revisited: Economic Expectations and Presidential Approval. *Electoral Studies* 19: 295–312.

Fair, Ray C. 1978. The Effect of Economic Events on Votes for President. *Review of Economics and Statistics* 60: 159–73.

Fair, Ray C. 1984. *Specification, Estimation, and Analysis of Macroeconomic Models*. Cambridge, MA: Harvard University Press.

Fair, Ray C. 1988. The Effect of Economic Events on Votes for President: 1984 Update. *Political Behavior* 10: 168–79.

Fair, Ray C. 1990. *The Effect of Economic Events on Votes for President: 1988 Update*. Unpublished manuscript, Department of Economics, Yale University.

Fair, Ray C. 2009. Presidential and Congressional Vote-Share Equations. *American Journal of Political Science* 53(1): 55–72.

Farmer, Roger E. A. 2008. Animal Spirits. In L. Blume and S. Durlauf (eds.), *The New Palgrave Dictionary of Economics*, vol. 1, pp. 157–63. London: Palgrave Macmillan.

Farmer, Roger E. A. 2009. Review. *Economic Record*. 85: 357–8.

Farmer, Roger E. A. 2010a. *Expectations, Employment and Prices*. New York: Oxford University Press.

Farmer, Roger E. A. 2010b. *How the Economy Works and How to Fix It When It Doesn't: Confidence, Crashes and Self-Fulfilling Prophecies*. New York: Oxford University Press.

Fearon, James D. 1999. Electoral Accountability and the Control of Politicians: Selecting Good Types versus Sanctioning Poor Performance. In Adam Przeworski, Susan C. Stokes, and Bernard Manin (eds.), *Democracy, Accountability, and Representation*, pp. 55–97. New York: Cambridge University Press.

Feldstein, Martin. 2010. Preventing a National Debt Explosion. Cambridge, MA: NBER Working Paper 16451.

Fenno, Richard F. 1966. *The Power of the Purse: Appropriations Politics in Congress.* Boston: Little, Brown.

Ferejohn, John. 1986. Incumbent Performance and Electoral Control. *Public Choice* 50: 5–25.

Financial Crisis Inquiry Commission. 2011. *Financial Crisis Inquiry Report.* New York: Public Affairs. Available at http://www.fcic.gov/report.

Fiorina, Morris. 1981. *Retrospective Voting in American National Elections.* New Haven, CT: Yale University Press.

Fiorina, Morris. 1992. *Divided Government.* New York: Macmillan.

Fiorina, Morris. 2009. *Disconnect: The Breakdown of Representation in American Politics.* Norman: University of Oklahoma Press.

Fischer, Stanley. 1986. *Indexing, Inflation, and Economic Policy.* Cambridge MA: MIT Press.

Fischer, Stanley, and John Huizinga. 1982. Inflation, Unemployment, and Public Opinion Polls. *Journal of Money, Credit, and Banking* 14: 1–19.

Fischer, Stanley, Ratna Sahay, and Carlos A. Végh. 2002. Modern Hyper- and High Inflations. *Journal of Economic Literature* 40: 837–80.

Fishback, Price V. 2010. US Monetary and Fiscal Policy in the 1930s. *Oxford Review of Economic Policy* 26: 385–413.

Fisher, Louis. 1975. *Presidential Spending Power.* Princeton, NJ: Princeton University Press.

Fisher, Louis. 1985. Ten Years of the Budget Act: Still Searching for Controls. *Public Budgeting and Finance* 5: 3–28.

Forgette, Richard. 1993. Budget Balance and Government Party Control: Does Divided Government Matter? Paper presented at the annual meeting of the American Political Science Association, Washington, DC.

Fox, Justin. 2009. *The Myth of the Rational Market: A History of Risk, Reward, and Delusion on Wall Street.* New York: HarperCollins Publishers.

French, Kenneth R., et al. 2010. *The Squam Lake Report: Fixing the Financial System.* Princeton, NJ: Princeton University Press.

Frey, Bruno S. 1983. *Democratic Economic Policy: A Theoretical Introduction.* New York: St. Martin's Press.

Frey, Bruno S., and Friedrich Schneider. 1978. An Empirical Study of Politico-Economic Interaction in the U.S. *Review of Economics and Statistics* 60: 174–83.

Frieden, Jeffry A. 1991. *Debt, Development and Democracy: Modern Political Economy and Latin America, 1965–1985.* Princeton, NJ: Princeton University Press.

Friedman, Milton. 1953a. A Monetary and Fiscal Framework for Economic Stability. In Milton Friedman (ed.), *Essays in Positive Economics*, pp. 133–56. Chicago: University of Chicago Press. Reprinted from *American Economic Review* 38: 245–64 (1948).

Friedman, Milton. 1953b. *Essays in Positive Economics.* Chicago: University of Chicago Press.

Friedman, Milton. 1960. *A Program for Monetary Stability.* New York: Fordham University Press.

Friedman, Milton. 1962. Should There Be an Independent Monetary Authority? In Leland B. Yeager (ed.), *In Search of a Monetary Constitution*, pp. 219–43. Cambridge, MA: Harvard University Press.

Friedman, Milton. 1968. The Role of Monetary Policy. *American Economic Review* 58: 1–17.

Friedman, Milton. 1977. Nobel Lecture: Inflation and Unemployment. *Journal of Political Economy* 85: 451–72.

Friedman, Milton, and Anna Jacobson Schwartz. 1963. *A Monetary History of the United States, 1867–1960*. Princeton, NJ: Princeton University Press.

Froyen, Richard T. 2009. *Macroeconomics: Theories and Policies*, 9th ed. Upper Saddle River, NJ: Pearson Prentice Hall.

Gali, Jordi, and Luca Gambetti. 2009. On the Sources of the Great Moderation. *American Economic Journal: Macroeconomics* 1: 26–57.

Garrett, Geoffrey, and Peter Lange. 1991. Political Responses to Interdependence: What's "Left" for the Left? *International Organization* 45: 539–64.

Gelinas, Nicole. 2009. *After the Fall: Saving Capitalism from Wall Street – and Washington*. New York: Encounter Books.

Gerber, Elisabeth R., and Arthur Lupia. 1995. Campaign Competition and Policy Responsiveness in Direct Legislation Elections. *Political Behavior*, 17: 287–306.

Gilmour, John B. 1990. *Reconcilable Differences? Congress, the Budget Process and the Deficit*. Berkeley: University of California Press.

Golden, David G., and James M. Poterba. 1980. The Price of Popularity: The Political Business Cycle Reexamined. *American Journal of Political Science* 24: 696–714.

Goodfriend, Marvin. 2002. Monetary Policy in the New Neoclassical Synthesis: A Primer. *International Finance* 5: 165–91.

Goodfriend, Marvin. 2007. How the World Achieved Consensus on Monetary Policy. *Journal of Economic Perspectives*. Fall, 47–68.

Goodhart, Charles A. E. 2011. The Squam Lake Report: Commentary. *Journal of Economic Literature* 49: 114–19.

Gorton, Gary. 2010. *Slapped by the Invisible Hand: The Panic of 2007*. New York: Oxford University Press.

Grabell, Michael. 2012. *Money Well Spent? The Truth behind the Trillion-Dollar Stimulus, the Biggest Economic Recovery Plan in History*. New York: Public Affairs.

Grafstein, Robert. 1990. Missing the Archimedean Point: Liberalism's Institutional Presuppositions. *American Political Science Review* 84: 177–94.

Gramlich, Edward M. 1983. Models of Inflation Expectations Formation: A Comparison of Household and Economist Forecasts. *Journal of Money, Credit, and Banking* 15: 155–73.

Gramlich, Edward M. 1991. U.S. Budget Deficits: Views, Burdens, and New Developments. In James M. Rock (ed.), *Debt and the Twin Deficits Debate*, pp. 173–87. Mountain View, CA: Mayfield Publishing.

Gramlich, Edward M. 2007. *Subprime Mortgages: America's Latest Boom and Bust*. Washington, DC: The Urban Institute.

Granato, Jim, and M. C. Sunny Wong. 2005. Using Monetary Policy to Coordinate Price Information: Implications for Economic Stability and Development. *The Whitehead Journal of Diplomacy and International Relations* 6(2): 49–60.

Granato, Jim, and M. C. Sunny Wong. 2006. *The Role of Policymakers in Business Cycle Fluctuations*. New York: Cambridge University Press.

Greene, Jay P. 1993. Forewarned Before Forecast: Presidential Election Forecasting Models and the 1992 Election. *PS: Political Science and Politics* 26: 17–21.

Greider, William. 1987. *Secrets of the Temple: How the Federal Reserve Runs the Country.* New York: Simon & Schuster.

Grier, Kevin D. 1989. On the Existence of a Political Monetary Cycle. *American Journal of Political Science* 33: 376–89.

Grier, Kevin. 1993. *On the Existence and (Constrained) Optimality of the Political Business Cycle.* Unpublished manuscript, Department of Economics, George Mason University.

Grilli, Vittorio, Donato Masciandaro, and Guido Tabellini. 1991. Institutions and Policies. *Economic Policy* 13: 341–92.

Grunwald, Michael. *The New New Deal: The Hidden Story of Change in the Obama Era.* New York: Simon & Shuster.

Hahm, Sung Deuk, Mark S. Kamlet, and David C. Mowery. 1993. The Political Economy of Deficit Spending in Parliamentary Democracies: The Role of Fiscal Institutions. Paper presented at the annual meeting of the American Political Science Association, Washington, DC.

Hall, Robert E. 2010. Why Does the Economy Fall to Pieces after a Financial Crisis? *Journal of Economic Perspectives* 24(4): 3–20.

Hallerberg, Mark, Rolf Rainer Strauch, and Jürgen von Hagen. 2009. *Fiscal Governance in Europe.* New York: Cambridge University Press.

Hamilton, Alexander, James Madison, and John Jay. 1961. *The Federalist Papers.* New York: The New American Library of World Literature.

Hanke, Steve H., and Alex K. F. Kwok. 2009. On the Measurement of Zimbabwe's Hyperinflation. *Cato Journal* 29: 353–64.

Hargrove, Erwin C., and Samuel A. Morley (eds.). 1984. *The President and the Council of Economic Advisors.* Boulder, CO: Westview Press.

Harrington, Joseph E., Jr. 1993. Economic Policy, Economic Performance, and Elections. *American Economic Review* 83: 27–43.

Havrilesky, Thomas. 1987. A Partisanship Theory of Fiscal and Monetary Policy. *Journal of Money, Credit, and Banking* 19: 308–25.

Havrilesky, Thomas. 1993. *The Pressures on American Monetary Policy.* Boston: Kluwer.

Havrilesky, Thomas, Henry Chapped, John Gildea, and Rob McGregor. 1993. Congress Threatens the Fed. *Challenge* 36(2): 50–7.

Hayek, Friedrich A. 1967. *Studies in Philosophy, Politics and Economics,* Chapter 6. Chicago: University of Chicago Press.

Haynes, Stephen E., and Joe A. Stone. 1989a. Political Models of the Business Cycle Should Be Revived. *Economic Inquiry* 28: 442–65.

Haynes, Stephen E., and Joe A. Stone. 1989b. Political Parties and the Variable Duration of Business Cycles. *Southern Economic Journal* 60: 869–85.

Heller, Walter. 1966. *New Dimensions of Political Economy.* Cambridge, MA: Harvard University Press.

Henisz, Witold J. 2000. The institutional environment for economic growth. *Economics and Politics* 12(1): 1–31.

Henisz, Witold J. 2002. The Institutional Environment for Infrastructure Investment. *Industrial and Corporate Change,* 11(2): 355–89.

Henisz, Witold J. 2004. Political Institutions and Policy Volatility. *Economics and Politics,* 16: 1–27.

Henisz, Witold J. 2012. Polcon_2011 Codebook (with data to 2007). http://www-management.wharton.upenn.edu/henisz/ (accessed December 3, 2012).

Henisz, Witold J., and Edward D. Mansfield. 2006. Votes and Vetoes: The Political Determinants of Commercial Openness. *International Studies Quarterly, Wiley Online Library* 50: 189–212.

Henisz, Witold J., and Bennet A. Zelner. 2001. The Institutional Environment for Telecommunications Investment. *Journal of Economics and Management Strategy* 10: 123–47.

Hibbs, Douglas A., Jr. 1977. Political Parties and Macroeconomic Policy. *American Political Science Review* 71: 1467–87.

Hibbs, Douglas A., Jr. 1982. President Reagan's Mandate from the 1980 Elections: A Shift to the Right? *American Politics Quarterly* 10: 387–420.

Hibbs, Douglas A., Jr. 1987. *The American Political Economy*. Cambridge, MA: Harvard University Press.

Hibbs, Douglas A., Jr. 1992. Partisan Theory after Fifteen Years. *European Journal of Political Economy* 8: 361–73.

Hibbs, Douglas A., Jr. 1994. The Partisan Model of Macroeconomic Cycles: More Theory and Evidence for the United States. *Economics and Politics* 6: 1–24.

Hibbs, Douglas A., Jr. 2006. Voting and the Macroeconomy. In Barry R. Weingast and Donald A. Wittman (eds.), *Oxford Handbook of Political Economy*, pp. 565–86. New York: Oxford University Press.

Hibbs, Douglas A., Jr. 2012a. "Bread and Peace" and "Bread and Incumbency" Models for the 2012 US Presidential and House Elections. Powerpoint slides prepared for the World Congress of the Public Choice Society, Miami.

Hibbs, Douglas A., Jr. 2012b. Obama's Reelection Prospects under "Bread and Peace" Voting in the 2012 US Presidential Election. *PS: Political Science and Politics* 46: 635–9.

Hibbs, Douglas A., Jr., and Christopher Dennis. 1988. Income Distribution in the United States. *American Political Science Review* 87: 467–90.

Hirschman, Albert O. 1991. *The Rhetoric of Reaction*. Cambridge, MA: Harvard University Press.

Hoover, Kevin D. 1988. *The New Classical Macroeconomics: A Skeptical Inquiry*. London: Basil Blackwell.

Hoover, Kevin D. 2001. *Causality in Macroeconomics*. New York: Cambridge University Press.

Hoover, Kevin D. 2012. *Applied Intermediate Macroeconomics*. New York: Cambridge University Press.

Hoover, Kevin D., and Michael Sheffrin. 1992. Causation, Spending and Taxes: Sand in the Sandbox or Tax Collector for the Welfare State. *American Economic Review* 82: 225–48.

Hoover, Kevin D., and Mark V. Siegler. 2000. Taxing and Spending in the Long View: The Causal Structure of US Fiscal Policy, 1791–1913. *Oxford Economic Papers* 52: 745–73.

Hoshi, Takeo. 2011. Financial Regulation: Lessons from the Recent Financial Crises. *Journal of Economic Literature* 49: 120–8.

Huber, John D., and G. Bingham Powell Jr. 1992. Congruence between Citizens and Policymakers in Two Views of Liberal Democracy. Paper presented at the annual meeting of the Midwest Political Science Association, Chicago.

Huntington, Samuel P. 1968. *Political Order in Changing Societies*. New Haven, CT: Yale University Press.

Igan, Deniz, Prachi Mishra, and Thierry Tressel. 2009. A Fistful of Dollars: Lobbying and the Financial Crisis. IMF Working Paper WP/09/287.

Ilzetzki, Ethan, Enrique G. Mendoza, and Carlos A. Végh. 2010. How Big or Small Are Fiscal Multipliers? NBER Working Paper 16479.

Ingrassia, Paul. 2010. *Crash Course: The American Automobile Industry's Road from Glory to Disaster*. New York: Random House.

Ippolito, Dennis S. 2012. *Deficits, Debt, and the New Politics of Tax Policy*. New York: Cambridge University Press.

Iversen, Torben, and David Soskice. 2006. New Macroeconomics and Political Science. *Annual Reviews of Political Science* 9: 425–53.

Jacobson, Gary C. 1990. Does the Economy Matter in Midterm Elections? *American Journal of Political Science* 34: 400–404.

Jamieson, Kathleen Hall. 1992. *Dirty Politics: Deception, Distraction, and Democracy*. New York: Oxford University Press.

Johnson, James. 1993. Is Talk Really Cheap? Prompting Conversation between Critical Theory and Rational Choice. *American Political Science Review* 87: 74–86.

Johnson, Simon, and James Kwak. 2010. *13 Bankers: The Wall Street Takeover and the Next Financial Meltdown*. New York: Pantheon Books.

Johnson, Simon, and James Kwak. 2012. *White House Burning: The Founding Fathers, Our National Debt, and Why It Matters to You*. New York: Pantheon Books.

Kahn, R. F. 1931. The Relation of Home Investment to Unemployment. *Economic Journal* 41: 173–98.

Kahneman, Daniel. 2011. *Thinking Fast and Slow*. New York: Farrar, Straus and Giroux.

Kamlet, Mark S., David C. Mowery, and Tsai-Tsu Su. 1988. Upsetting National Priorities: The Reagan Administration's Budgetary Strategy. *American Political Science Review* 82: 1293–308.

Kane, Edward J. 1990. Bureaucratic Self-interest as an Obstacle to Monetary Reform. In Thomas Mayer (ed.), *The Political Economy of American Monetary Policy*, pp. 283–98. New York: Cambridge University Press.

Keech, William R. 1992. Rules, Discretion, and Accountability in Macroeconomic Policymaking. *Governance* 5: 259–78.

Keech, William R. 1999. Policy Innovations and Policy Reversals. In Nelson W. Polsby and Raymond E. Wolfinger (eds.), *On Parties: Essays Honoring Austin Ranney*, pp. 203–18. Berkeley: Institute of Governmental Studies Press.

Keech, William R. 2009. A Scientifically Superior Conception of Democracy. Paper presented at the Midwest Political Science Association Meetings, Chicago.

Keech, William R., and G. Patrick Lynch. 1992. Business Cycles and Presidential Elections in the United States: Another Look at Key and Downs on Retrospective Voting. Paper presented at the annual meeting of the American Political Science Association, Chicago.

Keech, William R., and Irwin L. Morris. 1997. Appointments, Presidential Power, and the Federal Reserve. *Journal of Macroeconomics* 19: 253–67.

Keech, William R., and Kyoungsan Pak. 1989. Electoral Cycles and Budgetary Growth in Veterans' Benefit Programs. *American Journal of Political Science* 33: 901–11.

Keech, William R., and Carl P. Simon. 1985. Electoral and Welfare Consequences of Political Manipulation of the Economy. *Journal of Economic Behavior and Organization* 6: 177–202.

Kehoe, Timothy J., and Edward C. Prescott (eds.). 2007. *Great Depressions of the Twentieth Century*. Minneapolis: Federal Reserve Bank of Minneapolis.

Kelley, Stanley, Jr. 1983. *Interpreting Elections*. Princeton, NJ: Princeton University Press.

Kettl, Donald F. 1986. *Leadership at the Fed*. New Haven, CT: Yale University Press.

Key, V. O., Jr. 1966. *The Responsible Electorate: Rationality in Presidential Voting 1936–1960*. Cambridge, MA: Harvard University Press.

Keynes, John Maynard. 1936. *The General Theory of Employment, Interest, and Money*. London: Macmillan. Reissued in 1964 by Harcourt Brace Jovanovich.

Keyssar, Alexander. 2000. *The Right to Vote: The Contested History of Democracy in the United States*. New York: Basic Books.

Kiewiet, D. Roderick. 1981. Policy-oriented Voting in Response to Economic Issues. *American Political Science Review* 75: 448–59.

Kiewiet, D. Roderick. 1983. *Macroeconomics and Micropolitics*. Chicago: University of Chicago Press.

Kiewiet, D. Roderick, and Mathew D. McCubbins. 1991. *The Logic of Delegation: Congressional Parties and the Appropriations Process*. Chicago: University of Chicago Press.

Kingdon, John W. 1984. *Agendas, Alternatives, and Public Policies*. Boston: Little, Brown.

Klamer, Arjo. 1984. *Conversations with Economists: New Classical Economists and Opponents Speak Out on the Current Controversy in Macroeconomics*. Totowa, NJ: Rowman & Allanheld.

Klein, Martin, and Manfred J. M. Neumann. 1990. Seignorage: What Is It and Who Gets It. *Weltwirtschafiiches Archiv* 126: 205–21.

Knight, Jack. 1992. *Institutions and Social Conflict*. New York: Cambridge University Press.

Kotlikoff, Laurence J. 1992. *Generational Accounting: Knowing Who Pays, and When, for What We Spend*. New York: Free Press.

Kramer, Gerald H. 1971. Short-Term Fluctuations in U.S. Voting Behavior, 1896–1964. *American Political Science Review* 65: 131–43.

Kramer, Gerald H. 1983. The Ecological Fallacy Revisited: Aggregate- versus Individual-Level Findings on Economics and Elections and Sociotropic Voting. *American Political Science Review* 77: 92–111.

Kreps, David M. 1990. *A Course in Microeconomic Theory*. Princeton, NJ: Princeton University Press.

Krugman, Paul. 1992. *The Age of Diminished Expectations: U.S. Economic Policy in the 1990s*. Cambridge, MA: MIT Press.

Krugman, Paul. 2009. How Did Economists Get It So Wrong? *New York Times Magazine*. September 2.

Kuklinski, James H., and Darrell M. West. 1981. Economic Expectations and Voting Behavior in United States House and Senate Elections. *American Political Science Review* 75: 436–47.

Kydland, Finn, and Edward C. Prescott. 1977. Rules Rather than Discretion: The Inconsistency of Optimal Plans. *Journal of Political Economy* 83: 473–91.

Kydland, Finn, and Edward C. Prescott. 1982. Time to Build and Aggregate Fluctuations. *Econometrica* 50: 1345–70.

Leeper, Erik M. 2010. Monetary Science, Fiscal Alchemy. Presented at Jackson Hole, WY, conference sponsored by the Kansas City Fed.

Lewis-Beck, Michael S. 1988. *Economics and Elections: The Major Western Democracies*. Ann Arbor: University of Michigan Press.

Lewis-Beck, Michael S., and Richard Nadeau. 2011. Economic Voting Theory: Testing New Dimensions. *Electoral Studies* 30: 288–94.

Lijphart, Arend. 1999. *Patterns of Democracy: Government Forms and Performance in Thirty-Six Countries*. New Haven, CT: Yale University Press.

Lindblom, Charles E. 1977. *Politics and Markets: The World's Political-Economic Systems*. New York: Basic Books.

Loewenstein, Roger. 2010. *The End of Wall Street*. New York: Penguin Press.

Lohmann, Susanne. 1992. Optimal Commitment in Monetary Policy: Credibility vs. Flexibility. *American Economic Review* 82: 273–86.

Lowi, Theodore J. 1979. *The End of Liberalism: The Second Republic of the United States*, 2nd ed. New York: Norton.

Lucas, Robert E., Jr. 1981. *Studies in Business Cycle Theory*. Cambridge, MA: MIT Press.

Lucas, Robert E., Jr. 2009. In Defence of the Dismal Science. *The Economist*, August 6, p. 67.

MacKuen, Michael B., Robert S. Erikson, and James A. Stimson. 1992. Peasants or Bankers: The American Electorate and the U.S. Economy. *American Political Science Review* 86: 597–611.

Majone, Giandomenico. 1989. *Evidence, Argument, and Persuasion in the Policy Process*. New Haven, CT: Yale University Press.

Mankiw, N. Gregory. 1990. A Quick Refresher Course in Macroeconomics. *Journal of Economic Literature* 28: 1645–60.

Mankiw, N. Gregory, and David Romer (eds.). 1991. *New Keynesian Economics*, 2 vols. Cambridge, MA: MIT Press.

Mankiw, N. Gregory, and Matthew Weinzierl. 2011. An Exploration of Optimal Stabilization Policy. *Brookings Papers on Economic Activity* Spring: 209–49.

Mann, Thomas E., and Norman J. Ornstein. 2012. *It's Even Worse Than It Looks: How the American Constitutional System Collided with the New Politics of Extremism*. New York: Basic Books.

Mashaw, Jerry L. 1989. The Economics of Politics and the Understanding of Public Law. *Chicago-Kent Law Review* 65: 123–61.

May, Kenneth O. 1952. A Set of Independent, Necessary, and Sufficient Conditions for Simple Majority Decision. *Econometrica* 20: 680–4.

Mayhew, David R. 1991. *Divided We Govern: Party Control, Lawmaking, and Investigations 1946–1990*. New Haven, CT: Yale University Press.

McCallum, Bennett. 1978. The Political Business Cycle: An Empirical Test. *Southern Economic Journal* 45: 504–15.

McCallum, Bennett T. 1988. Robustness Properties of a Rule for Monetary Policy. *Carnegie-Rochester Conference Series on Public Policy* 29: 173–204.

McCarty, Nolan, Keith Poole, and Howard Rosenthal. 2006. *Polarized America: The Dance of Ideology and Unequal Riches*. Cambridge, MA: MIT Press.

McCubbins, Mathew D. 1991. Party Governance and U.S. Budget Deficits: Divided Government and Fiscal Stalemate. In Alberto Alesina and Geoffrey Carliner (eds.), *Economics and Politics in the 1980s*, pp. 83–122. Chicago: University of Chicago Press.

McConnell, Perez-Quiros. 2000. Output Fluctuations in the United States: What Has Changed since the Early 1980s? *AER*: 90: 1464–76.

McKinley, Vern. 2011. *Financing Failure: A Century of Bailouts*. Oakland, CA: The Independent Institute.

McLean, Bethany, and Joe Nocera. 2010. *All the Devils Are Here: The Hidden History of the Financial Crisis*. New York: The Penguin Group.

Meltzer, Allan H. 1986. Financial Failures and Financial Policies. In G. G. Kaufman and R. C. Kormendi (eds.), *Deregulating Financial Service: Public Policy in Flux*, pp. 79–96 Cambridge, MA: Ballinger.

Meltzer, Allan H. 1987. Limits of Short-Run Stabilization Policy: Presidential Address to the Western Economic Association. *Economic Inquiry* 25: 1–11.

Meltzer, Allan H. 1988. *Keynes's Monetary Theory: A Different Interpretation*. New York: Cambridge University Press.

Meltzer, Allan H. 2003. *A History of the Federal Reserve. Volume 1: 1913–1951*. Chicago: University of Chicago Press.

Meltzer, Allan H. 2009. *A History of the Federal Reserve. Volume 2: 1951–1986*. Chicago: University of Chicago Press.

Merton, Robert K. 1936. The Unanticipated Consequences of Purposive Social Action. *American Sociological Review* 1: 894–904.

Mettler, Suzanne. 2011. *The Submerged State: How Invisible Government Policies Undermine American Democracy*. Chicago: University of Chicago Press.

Mian, Atif, Amir Sufi, and Francesco Trebbi. 2010a. The Political Economy of the Subprime Mortgage Credit Expansion. Cambridge, MA: NBER Working paper 16107.

Mian, Atif, Amir Sufi, and Francesco Trebbi. 2010b. The Political Economy of the US Mortgage Default Crisis. *American Economic Review* 100: 1967–98.

Miller, Arthur H., and Martin P. Wattenberg. 1985. Throwing the Rascals Out: Policy and Performance Evaluations of Presidential Candidates, 1952–1980. *American Political Science Review* 79: 359–73.

Miller, Marcus, Paul Weller, and Lei Zhang. 2002. Moral Hazard and the US Stock Market: Analyzing the "Greenspan Put." *Economic Journal* 112: 171–86.

Modigliani, Andre, and Franco Modigliani. 1987. The Growth of the Federal Deficit and the Role of Public Attitudes. *Public Opinion Quarterly* 51: 459–80.

Morgenson, Gretchen, and Joshua Rosner. 2011. *Reckless Endangerment: How Outsized Ambition, Greed, and Corruption Led to Economic Armageddon*. New York: Times Books.

Morris, Irwin L. 1994. *Congress, the President, and the Federal Reserve: The Politics of American Monetary Policy*. Doctoral dissertation, University of North Carolina at Chapel Hill.

Morris, Irwin L. 2000. *Congress, the President, and the Federal Reserve: The Politics of American Monetary Policy-Making*. Ann Arbor: University of Michigan Press.

Mosley, Paul. 1984. *The Making of Economic Policy: Theory and Evidence from Britain and the United States since 1945*. New York: St. Martin's Press.

Mueller, Dennis. 2003. *Public Choice III*. New York: Cambridge University Press.

National Commission on Fiscal Responsibility and Reform. 2010. *The Moment of Truth*. http://www.fiscalcommission.gov/sites/fiscalcommission.gov/files/documents/TheMomentofTruth12_1_2010.pdf

Ng, Ging Cee, and Andrea Tambalotti. 2012. The Great Moderation, Forecast Uncertainty, and the Great Recession. http://libertystreeteconomics.newyorkfed.org/2012/05/the-great-moderation-forecast-uncertainty-and-the-great-recession.html (accessed June 12, 2012).

Niskanen, William A. 2008. *Reflections of a Political Economist*. Washington, DC: The Cato Institute.

Nordhaus, William. 1975. The Political Business Cycle. *Review of Economic Studies* 42: 169–90.

Nordhaus, William. 1989. Alternative Approaches to the Political Business Cycle. *Brookings Papers on Economic Activity* 2: 1–68.

Okun, Arthur. 1973. Comment on Stigler's Paper. *American Economic Review, Papers and Proceedings* 63: 172–80.

Okun, Arthur. 1975. *Equality and Efficiency: The Big Tradeoff*. Washington, DC: Brookings Institution.

Olson, Mancur, Jr. 1982. *The Rise and Decline of Nations*. New Haven, CT: Yale University Press.

Olson, Mancur, Jr. 1984. Beyond Keynesianism and Monetarism. *Economic Inquiry* 22: 297–322.

Olson, Mancur, Jr. 1993. Dictatorship, Democracy, and Development. *American Political Science Review* 87: 567–76.

"The Other-Worldly Philosophers." 2009. *The Economist*, July 18, p. 65.

Paldam, Martin. 1991. How Robust Is the Vote Function: A Study of Seventeen Nations over Four Decades. In Helmut Norpoth, Michael S. Lewis-Beck, and Jean Dominique Lafay (eds.), *Economics and Politics: The Calculus of Support*, pp. 9–31. Ann Arbor: University of Michigan Press.

Paul, Ron. 2009. *End the Fed*. New York: Grand Central Publishing.

Peltzman, Sam. 1991. Voters as Fiscal Conservatives. *Quarterly Journal of Economics* 107: 327–61.

Persson, Torsten, and Lars E. O. Svensson. 1989. Why a Stubborn Conservative Would Run a Deficit: Policy with Time-Inconsistent Preferences. *Quarterly Journal of Economics* 105: 325–45.

Persson, Torsten, and Guido Tabellini. 1990. *Macroeconomic Policy, Credibility and Politics*. Chur, Switzerland, and New York: Harwood Academic Publishers.

Persson, Torsten and Guido Tabellini. 2003. *The Economic Effects of Constitutions*. Cambridge, MA: MIT Press.

Peterson, Paul. 1985. The New Politics of Deficits. In John Chubb and Paul Peterson (eds.), *New Directions in American Politics*, pp. 365–97. Washington, DC: Brookings Institution.

Peterson, Peter. 1993. *Facing Up: How to Rescue the Economy from Crushing Debt and Restore the American Dream*. New York: Simon & Schuster.

Petrocik, John R. 1996. Issue Ownership in Presidential Elections with a 1980 Case Study. *American Journal of Political Science* 40: 825–50.

Phelps, Edmund S. 1990. *Seven Schools of Macroeconomic Thought*. Oxford, UK: Clarendon Press.

Phillips, A. W. 1958. The Relation between Unemployment and the Rate of Change of Money Wage Rates in the United Kingdom, 1861–1957. *Economica* (NS) 25: 283–99.

Plott, Charles R. 1991. Will Economics Become an Experimental Science? *Southern Economic Journal* 57: 901–20.

Portney, Paul R. 1976. Congressional Delays in U.S. Fiscal Policymaking: Simulating the Effects. *Journal of Public Economics* 5: 237–47.

Poterba, James M. 1994. State Responses to Fiscal Crises: The Effects of Budgetary Institutions and Politics. *Journal of Political Economy* 102: 799–821.

Prescott, Edward C. 2006. Nobel Lecture: The Transformation of Macroeconomic Policy and Research. *Journal of Political Economy* 114: 203–35.

Primo, David M. 2007. *Rules and Restraint: Government Spending and the Design of Institutions*. Chicago: University of Chicago Press.

Quattrone, George, and Amos Tversky. 1988. Contrasting Rational and Psychological Analyses of Political Choice. *American Political Science Review* 82: 719–36.

Quinn, Dennis P., and Robert Y. Shapiro. 1991. Economic Growth Strategies: The Effects of Ideological Partisanship on Interest Rates and Business Taxation. *American Journal of Political Science* 35: 656–85.

Rajan, Raghuram. 2010. *Fault Lines: How Hidden Fractures Still Threaten the World Economy*. Princeton, NJ: Princeton University Press.

Rawls, John. 1971. *A Theory of Justice*. Cambridge, MA: Harvard University Press.

Reinhart, Carmen M., and Vincent Reinhart. 2010. After the Fall. Presented at Jackson Hole, WY, conference sponsored by the Kansas City Fed.

Reinhart, Carmen M., and Kenneth S. Rogoff. 2009. *This Time Is Different: Eight Centuries of Financial Folly*. Princeton, NJ: Princeton University Press.

Reischauer, Robert D. 1990. Taxes and Spending under Gramm-Rudman-Hollings. *National Tax Journal* 44: 223–32.

Remmer, Karen E. 1993. The Political Economy of Elections in Latin America, 1980–1991. *American Political Science Review* 87: 393–407.

Richards, Daniel J. 1986. Unanticipated Money and the Political Business Cycle. *Journal of Money, Credit, and Banking* 18: 447–57.

Riker, William H. 1982. *Liberalism against Populism: A Confrontation between the Theory of Democracy and the Theory of Social Choice*. Prospect Heights, IL: Waveland Press.

Rivers, Douglas. 1988. Heterogeneity in Models of Electoral Choice. *American Journal of Political Science* 32: 737–57.

Rock, James M. (ed.). 1991. *Debt and the Twin Deficits Debate*. Mountain View, CA: Mayfield Publishing Co.

Rogoff, Kenneth. 1985. The Optimal Degree of Commitment to an Intermediate Monetary Target. *Quarterly Journal of Economics* 100: 1169–90.

Rogoff, Kenneth. 1990. Equilibrium Political Budget Cycles. *American Economic Review* 80: 21–36.

Rogoff, Kenneth, and Anne Sibert. 1988. Elections and Macroeconomic Policy Cycles. *Review of Economic Studies* 55: 1–16.

Romer, Christina D., and David H. Romer. 2007. Do Tax Cuts Starve the Beast? The Effect of Tax Changes on Government Spending. National Bureau of Economic Research Working Paper 13548. http://www.nber.org/papers/w13548

Roubini, Nouriel, and Stephen Mihm. 2010. *Crisis Economics: A Crash Course on the Future of Finance*. New York: The Penguin Press.

Roubini, Nouriel, and Jeffrey D. Sachs. 1989a. Political and Economic Determinants of Budget Deficits in the Industrial Democracies. *European Economic Review* 33: 903–38.

Roubini, Nouriel, and Jeffrey D. Sachs. 1989b. Government Spending and Budget Deficits in the Industrialized Countries. *Economic Policy* 4: 100–32.

Sachs, Jeffrey D., and Felipe Larraín 1993. *Macroeconomics in the Global Economy*. Englewood Cliffs, NJ: Prentice Hall.

Salsman, Richard Michael. 2012. *The Political Economy of Public Credit*. PhD dissertation, Duke University.

Samuelson, Paul A., and Robert M. Solow. 1960. Analytical Aspects of Anti-Inflation Policy. *American Economic Review, Papers and Proceedings* 50: 177–94.

Sargent, Thomas. 1986. *Rational Expectations and Inflation*. New York: Harper & Row.

Sargent, Thomas, and Neil Wallace. 1976. Rational Expectations and the Theory of Economic Policy. *Journal of Monetary Economics* 2: 169–83.

Savage, James D. 1988. *Balanced Budgets and American Politics*. Ithaca, NY: Cornell University Press.

Schick, Allen. 1993. Governments versus Budget Deficits. In R. Kent Weaver and Bert A. Rockman (eds.), *Do Institutions Matter? Government Capabilities in the United States and Abroad*, pp. 187–236. Washington, DC: Brookings Institution.

Schlozman, Kay L., and Sidney Verba. 1979. *Injury to Insult: Unemployment, Class, and Political Response*. Cambridge MA: Harvard University Press.

Schneider, Friedrich, and Bruno S. Frey. 1988. Politico-Economic Models of Macroeconomic Policy: A Review of the Empirical Evidence. In Thomas D. Willett (ed.), *Political Business Cycles: The Political Economy of Money, Inflation, and Unemployment*, pp. 239–75. Durham, NC: Duke University Press.

Scitovsky, Tibor. 1992. *The Joyless Economy*, rev. ed. New York: Oxford University Press.

Seater, John J. 1993. Ricardian Equivalence. *Journal of Economic Literature*. 31: 142–90.

Sen, Amartya K. 1993. The Economics of Life and Death. *Scientific American* 268: 40–7.

Shepsle, Kenneth A. 1988. Representation and Governance: The Great Legislative Trade-off. *Political Science Quarterly* 103: 461–84.

Shepsle, Kenneth A. 1991. Discretion, Institutions, and the Problem of Government Commitment. In Pierre Bourdieu and James S. Coleman (eds.), *Social Theory for a Changing Society*, pp. 245–65. Boulder, CO: Westview Press.

Shepsle, Kenneth A. 1992. Congress Is a "They," not an "It": Legislative Intent as Oxymoron. *International Review of Law and Economics* 12: 239–56.

Shepsle, Kenneth A., and Barry R. Weingast. 1981. Political Preferences for the Pork Barrel: A Generalization. *American Journal of Political Science* 25: 96–112.

Shepsle, Kenneth A., and Barry R. Weingast. 1984. Political Solutions to Market Problems. *American Political Science Review* 78: 417–34.

Simon, Herbert. 1978. Rationality as Process and as Product of Thought. *American Economic Review, Papers and Proceedings* 68: 1–16.

Simon, Herbert. 1983. *Reason in Human Affairs*. Stanford, CA: Stanford University Press.

Sleeman, A. G. 2011. Retrospectives: The Phillips Curve: A Rushed Job? *Journal of Economic Perspectives* 25(1): 223–37.

Smith, Adam. 1976/1776). *An Inquiry into the Nature and Causes of the Wealth of Nations*. Chicago: University of Chicago Press.

Sniderman, Paul M., Richard A. Brody, and Philip E. Tetlock. 1991. *Reasoning and Choice: Explorations in Political Psychology*. New York: Cambridge University Press.

Soneji, Samir, and Gary King. 2012. Statistical Security for Social Security. *Demography* 49: 1037–60.

Sowell, Thomas. 2010. *The Housing Boom and Bust* (rev. ed.). New York: Basic Books.

Sowell, Thomas. 2012. *"Trickle Down" Theory and "Tax Cuts for the Rich."* Stanford, CA: Hoover Institution Press Publication No. 635.

Stein, Herbert. 1969. *The Fiscal Revolution in America*. Chicago: University of Chicago Press.

Stein, Herbert. 1978. The Decline of the Budget-Balancing Doctrine or How the Good Guys Finally Lost. In James M. Buchanan and Richard E. Wagner (eds.), *Fiscal Responsibility in Constitutional Democracy*, pp. 35–58. Boston: Martinus Nijhoff.

Stein, Herbert. 1989. *Governing the $5 Trillion Economy*. New York: Oxford University Press.

Stein, Herbert. 1994. *Presidential Economics: The Making of Economic Policy from Roosevelt to Clinton*. Washington, DC: American Enterprise Institute.

Stein, Herbert. 1996. *The Fiscal Revolution in America: Policy in Pursuit of Reality* (2nd rev. ed.). Washington, DC: The AEI Press.

Stern, Gary H., and Ron J. Feldman. 2004/2009. *Too Big to Fail: The Hazards of Bank Bailouts*. Washington, DC: The Brookings Institution Press.

Stewart, Charles. 1989. *Budget Reform Politics: The Design of the Appropriations Process in the House of Representatives 1865–1921*. New York: Cambridge University Press.

Stigler, George J. 1973. General Economic Conditions and National Elections. *American Economic Review, Papers and Proceedings* 63: 160–7.

Stiglitz, Joseph E., and Linda J. Bilmes. 2008. *The Three Trillion Dollar War: The True Cost of the Iran Conflict*. New York: W. W. Norton.

Stiglitz, Joseph E., Amartya K. Sen, and Jean-Paul Fitoussi. 2009. *Report by the Commission on the Measurement of Economic Performance and Social Progress*. www.stiglitz-sen-fitoussi.fr

Stock, James H., and Mark W. Watson. 2002. Has the Business Cycle Changed and Why? In National Bureau of Economic Research, *Macroeconomics Annual* 17: 159–218.

Stockman, David. 1986. *The Triumph of Politics: Why the Reagan Revolution Failed*. New York: Harper & Row.

Stokes, Susan C. 2001. *Mandates and Democracy; Neoliberalism by Surprise*. New York: Cambridge University Press.

Su, Tsai-Tsu, Mark S. Kamlet, and David C. Mowery. 1993. Modeling U.S. Budgetary and Fiscal Outcomes: A Disaggregated, Systemwide Perspective. *American Journal of Political Science* 37: 213–45.

Subramanian, Arvind. 2011. *Eclipse: Living in the Shadow of China's Economic Dominance*. Washington, DC: Peterson Institute of International Economics.

Summers, Lawrence H. 1990. *Understanding Unemployment*. Cambridge, MA: MIT Press.

Sundquist, James L. 1983. *Dynamics of the Party System*, rev. ed. Washington, DC: Brookings Institution.

Sundquist, James L. 1992. *Constitutional Reform and Effective Government*, rev. ed. Washington: Brookings Institution.

Suskind, Ron. 2004. *The Price of Loyalty: George W. Bush, the White House, and the Education of Paul O'Neill*. New York: Simon & Shuster.

Suskind, Ron. 2011. *Confidence Men: Wall Street, Washington, and the Education of a President*. New York: HarperCollins Publishers.

Suzuki, Motoshi. 1991. The Rationality of Economic Voting and the Macro-economic Regime. *American Journal of Political Science* 35: 624–42.

Suzuki, Motoshi. 1994. Evolutionary Voter Sophistication and Political Business Cycles. *Public Choice* 81: 241–61.

Tabellini, Guido, and Alberto Alesina. 1990. Voting on the Budget Deficit. *American Economic Review* 80: 37–49.

Tax Foundation. 2012 Putting a Face on America's tax Returns: A Chart Book http://taxfoundation.org/slideshow/putting-face-americas-tax-returns accessed May 20, 2013.

Taylor, John B. 1993. Discretion versus Policy Rules in Practice. *Carnegie-Rochester Conference Series on Public Policy* 39: 195–214.

Taylor, John B. 1999. A Historical Analysis of Monetary Policy Rules. In John B. Taylor (ed.), *Monetary Policy Rules*, pp. 319–41. Chicago: University of Chicago Press.

Taylor, John B. 2009. *Getting Off Track: How Government Actions and Interventions Caused, Prolonged, and Worsened the Financial Crisis*. Stanford, CA: Hoover Institution Press.

Taylor, John B. 2010. Better Living through Monetary Economics In John Siegfried (ed.), *Better Living through Economics*, pp. 146–63. Cambridge, MA: Harvard University Press.

Taylor, John B. 2011. The Cycle of Rules and Discretion in Economic Policy. *National Affairs* 7(Spring): 55–65.

Temin, Peter. 1989. *Lessons from the Great Depression*. Cambridge, MA: MIT Press.

Thaler, Richard H., and Cass R. Sunstein. 2009. *Nudge: Improving Decisions about Health, Wealth, and Happiness*. New York: Penguin Books.

Therriault, Sean. 2008. *Party Polarization in Congress*. New York: Cambridge University Press.

Timberlake, Richard H. 1978. *The Origins of Central Banking in the United States*. Cambridge, MA: Harvard University Press.

Timberlake, Richard H. 1993. *Monetary Policy in the United States: An Intellectual and Institutional History*. Chicago: University of Chicago Press.

Tinbergen, Jan. 1952. *On the Theory of Economic Policy*. Amsterdam: North Holland.

Tobin, James, and Murray Weidenbaum (eds.). 1988. *Two Revolutions in Economic Policy*. Cambridge, MA: MIT Press.

Tsebelis, George. 1990. *Nested Games: Rational Choice in Comparative Politics*. Berkeley: University of California Press.

Tsebelis, George. 1995. Decision Making in Political Systems: Veto Players in Presidentialism, Parliamentarism, Multicameralism, and Multipartism. *British Journal of Political Science* 25: 289–325.

Tsebelis, George. 2002. *Veto Players: How Political Institutions Work.* Princeton, NJ: Princeton University Press.

Tufte, Edward R. 1978. *Political Control of the Economy.* Princeton, NJ: Princeton University Press.

Vanhanen, Tatu. 2000. A New Dataset for Measuring Democracy, 1810–1998. *Journal of Peace Research* 37: 251–65.

Wagner, Richard E. 2012. *Deficits, Debt, and Democracy: Wrestling with Tragedy on the Fiscal Commons.* Cheltenham, UK: Edward Elgar.

Walker, David M. 2008. U.S. Financial Conditions and Fiscal Future Briefing. Government Accountability Office. GAO-08-395CG. www.gao.gov/cghome.htm. Power Point slides presented at the 2008 Economic Forecast Forum, Research Triangle Park, NC, January 2.

Weatherford, M. Stephen. 1983. Economic Voting and the "Symbolic Politics" Argument: A Reinterpretation and a Synthesis. *American Political Science Review* 77: 92–111.

Weatherford, M. Stephen. 1987. The Interplay of Ideology and Advice in Economic Policy-Making: The Case of Political Business Cycles. *Journal of Politics* 49: 925–52.

Weatherford, M. Stephen. 1988. An Agenda Paper: Political Business Cycles and the Process of Economic Policymaking. *American Politics Quarterly* 16: 99–136.

Weaver, R. Kent. 1988. *Automatic Government: The Politics of Indexation.* Washington, DC: Brookings Institution.

Weaver, R. Kent, and Bert A. Rockman (eds.). 1993. *Do Institutions Matter? Government Capabilities in the United States and Abroad.* Washington, DC: Brookings Institution.

Weingast, Barry R., and William J. Marshall. 1988. The Industrial Organization of Congress; or, Why Legislatures, Like Firms, Are Not Organized as Markets. *Journal of Political Economy* 96: 132–63.

Weise, Charles L. 2012. Political Pressures on Monetary Policy during the US Great Inflation. *American Economic Journal: Macroeconomics* 4(2): 33–64.

Wessel, David. 2009. *In Fed We Trust: Ben Bernanke's War on the Great Panic.* New York: Crown Business.

Wessel, David. 2012. *Red Ink: Inside the High-Stakes Politics of the Federal Budget.* New York: Crown Business.

White, Joseph, and Aaron Wildavsky. 1989. *The Deficit and the Public Interest.* Berkeley: University of California Press.

Whitely, Paul. 1986. *Political Control of the Macroeconomy: The Political Economy of Public Policy Making.* Beverly Hills, CA: Sage.

Wildavsky, Aaron. 1964. *The Politics of the Budgetary Process.* Boston: Little, Brown.

Williams, John T. 1990. The Political Manipulation of Macroeconomic Policy. *American Political Science Review* 84: 767–96.

Wintrobe, Ronald. 1990. The Tinpot and the Totalitarian: An Economic Theory of Dictatorship. *American Political Science Review* 84: 849–72.

Wittman, Donald. 1983. Candidate Motivation: A Synthesis of Alternative Theories. *American Political Science Review* 77: 142–57.

Wittman, Donald. 1989. Why Democracies Produce Efficient Results. *Journal of Political Economy* 97: 1395–424.

Woodford, Michael. 2009. Convergence in Macroeconomics: Elements of the New Synthesis. *American Economic Journal: Macroeconomics* 1: 267–79.

Woon, Jonathan. 2012. Democratic Accountability and Retrospective Voting: A Laboratory Experiment. *American Journal of Political Science* 56: 773–1069.

Woolley, John T. 1984. *Monetary Politics: The Federal Reserve and the Politics of Monetary Policy.* New York: Cambridge University Press.

Wright, John R. 2012. Unemployment and the Democratic Electoral Advantage. *American Political Science Review* 106: 685–702.

Index